GENDER AND
INTERNATIONAL MIGRATION

19-38
121-176

GENDER AND INTERNATIONAL MIGRATION

FROM THE SLAVERY ERA TO THE GLOBAL AGE

KATHARINE M. DONATO
AND DONNA GABACCIA

Russell Sage Foundation · New York

The Russell Sage Foundation

The Russell Sage Foundation, one of the oldest of America's general purpose foundations, was established in 1907 by Mrs. Margaret Olivia Sage for "the improvement of social and living conditions in the United States." The Foundation seeks to fulfill this mandate by fostering the development and dissemination of knowledge about the country's political, social, and economic problems. While the Foundation endeavors to assure the accuracy and objectivity of each book it publishes, the conclusions and interpretations in Russell Sage Foundation publications are those of the authors and not of the Foundation, its Trustees, or its staff. Publication by Russell Sage, therefore, does not imply Foundation endorsement.

Library of Congress Cataloging-in-Publication Data

Donato, Katharine M.
 Gender and international migration : from the slavery era to the global age / Katharine M. Donato and Donna Gabaccia.
  pages cm
 Includes bibliographical references and index.
 ISBN 978-0-87154-546-6 (pbk. : alk. paper) — ISBN 978-1-61044-847-5 (ebook) 1. Women immigrants—History. 2. Emigration and immigration—Social aspects—History. I. Gabaccia, Donna R., 1949– II. Title.
 JV6347.D66 2016
 305.48—dc23

2014040895

Text design by Suzanne Nichols

RUSSELL SAGE FOUNDATION
112 East 64th Street, New York, New York 10065
10 9 8 7 6 5 4 3 2 1

Dedicated to the Memory of Patricia Pessar (1949–2012):
Friend, Colleague, Inspiration

Contents

═══ List of Figures and Tables ═══

= About the Authors =

Katharine M. Donato is professor and chair of sociology at Vanderbilt University.

Donna Gabaccia is professor of history in the Department of Historical and Cultural Studies at the University of Toronto-Scarborough.

═ Acknowledgments ═

This book had a very long genesis—far longer than Suzanne Nichols, our editor at the Russell Sage Foundation, might have wished. We appreciate the careful comments by our reviewers and did our best to incorporate them into a manuscript that is much improved as a result. We began to work together and to share our quite specific—and at the time highly idiosyncratic but consciously interdisciplinary—interests in sex ratios even before scholars began to talk about the feminization of migration in the 1990s. In 1990, historian Donna Gabaccia had just completed an extensive annotated bibliography on immigrant women in North America; as she began planning for an edited collection to focus on the multidisciplinarity of the scholarly literature she had just surveyed, she approached Katharine Donato, a recent sociology Ph.D. from Stony Brook, for a contribution. Katharine's article, "Understanding U.S. Immigration: Why Some Countries Send Women and Others Send Men," appeared in Donna's *Seeking Common Ground: Multidisciplinary Perspectives on Immigrant Women* (1992). Inspired by Katharine's question, Donna then dug into the historical flow data on U.S. immigration and published an essay on the history of the gender composition of U.S. immigrants in "Women of the Mass Migrations: From Minority to Majority" (1996).

Engaged in its own interdisciplinary field-building in the mid-1990s, the Social Science Research Council (SSRC)—largely on the urging of Donna Gabaccia and Patricia Pessar—eventually funded a working group on gender and migration. At that point, Donna—who was neither numerophobic nor innumerate but whose methodological range after 1980 had shifted decidedly toward the historical humanities—invited Katharine to join the group's multidisciplinary planning committee and to represent within the group the more quantitatively oriented of the empirical social sciences. The SSRC working group eventually also included the anthropologists Patricia Pessar and Martin Manalansan and the political scientist Jennifer Holdaway. Together the group solicited contributions from experts in many disciplines and edited for publication a special issue on "Gender and Migration" for *International Migration Review* (2006). Throughout, Katharine's expertise in demography and quantitative methods proved invaluable but also challenging to a group of scholars largely schooled in the qualitative methodologies more commonly used in gender, women, and sexuality studies. While the special issue identified how new work on gender and migration typically rested on a foundation of mixed methodologies, it also highlighted the difficulties that scholars using quantitative methodologies had experienced in responding to feminist theory. Private conversations among the planning team often hinted at resistance from gender and women's studies scholars to all forms of quantitative analysis. Similarly, as organizers of our special issue, we had experienced some resistance from empirical social scientists and were unable at that time to recruit an economist to write a review essay. (Since then, the journal *Feminist Economics* published a special issue in 2012 on gender and international migration.) As a result, resistance and collaboration across methodological lines became a major focus for the book we then decided to write.

This book would not have been written without the support and inspiration of the SSRC Working group. We have dedicated our book to Patricia Pessar, our friend and colleague who died—far too early in her productive life as scholar and teacher—while we were writing it. We intensely miss Patricia and wish she had been here to provide her own critique—as we know it would have been a trenchant one! This collaboration would not have been possible without the many insights we learned from her throughout our work together. We also wish to thank both Josh DeWind and Jennifer Holdaway at the SSRC and our stalwart and ever-energetic colleague Martin Manalansan for unflagging support and the considerable pleasure of their company over the years. As we planned our special issue, we also learned a great deal from Saskia Sassen, Mary Powers, Kitty Calavita, Sara Curran, Sarah Mahler, Nicola Piper, Desiree Qin, Suzanne Sinke, Carola Suárez-Orozco, and Rachel Silvey.

In 2006, Donna again asked Katharine to join her in a new research project that, following the results of the SSRC project, would focus specifically on the issue of gender ratios in migrant populations. The research team had its home base at the University of Minnesota and drew on the expertise of a shifting group of scholars. In addition to Donna and Katharine, these included J. Trent Alexander (a demographer then at the Minnesota Population Center, now at the Census Bureau), Bianet Castellanos (Anthropology and American Studies, University of Minnesota), Johanna Leinonen (a Ph.D. student in history at the University of Minnesota, and now at the University of Turku in Finland), Annemarie Steidl (a demographic and economic historian at the University of Vienna), and Elizabeth Zanoni (a Ph.D. student in history at the University of Minnesota, now at Old Dominion University). With funding from the University of Minnesota's Immigration History Research Center, Minnesota Population Center, Office of International Programs, from the College of Arts and Science at Vanderbilt University, and from the Russell Sage Foundation, the group held a number of workshops (in 2006, 2007, and 2009) in Minneapolis and in New York City. We extend special thanks to the Russell Sage Foundation, to Eric Wanner, its former director, and to Suzanne Nichols and Aixa Cintrón-Vélez, for encouraging us to think about the intersection of research on gender with the policy-oriented social sciences about the feminization of migration. We also want to thank several of participants in these workshops for their insights and feedback, notably Marcela Cerrutti, Belinda Dodson, Nancy Foner, Adam McKeown, Nana Oishi, and Joel Perlmann.

We are grateful also to Adam McKeown for sharing data on departures and arrivals of Chinese migrants at various Pacific ports, and we also extend thanks to Elizabeth Sinn for compiling this data. Historians of modern migration have not yet filled the many holes in published flow data as effectively as have the slave trade scholars, whose work (and major scholarly product, the Atlantic Slave Trade Database) both inspired us and provided us with rich data. We are also indebted to Hania Zlotnick, Steven Ruggles, and Robert McCaa for sharing their own thoughts on the evolution of data collection and analysis. We start our book with a quote from Hania, whose work offers many insights about gender and international migration. Katharine's interview with her helped clarify the shifts in statistical practices that eventually revealed women's presence in international migration to social scientists and other scholars. We also thank Steven Ruggles and Robert McCaa, historians and demographers who developed the IPUMS-USA and IPUMS-International. Both were very generous with their time in interviews that helped establish that a key foundation for IPUMS-International originated in Chile in the 1960s—well before U.S. and other scholars began undertaking efforts to harmonize census data over time.

Over the years, the Gender Ratios and International Migration research group organized scholarly panels for the Population Association of America, the Berkshire Conference on the History of Women, and the Social Science History Association, and prepared a series of publications for International Migration Review and Social Science History. We thank those who commented on our ideas while they were still in formation, especially Jose Moya, Pierrette Hondagneu-Sotelo, and Evan Roberts. We now also owe special thanks also to those who read some or all of the draft chapters of the book: Nancy Green, Dirk Hoerder, Johanna Leinonen, Leslie Moch, Jeffrey Pilcher, Marlou Schrover, Annemarie Steidl, and Liz Zanoni. We also received important leads to the female demographers of Europe from Sylvia Hahn and Alexander Pinwinkler. Such generosity from colleagues both internationally and across disciplines remains an inspiration and a model for us and for all scholars who hope to do interdisciplinary work.

Along the way, Donna and Katharine used every possible venue to continue to educate graduate students interested in gender and migration about the importance of finding the right mix of quantitative and qualitative methods for their own research questions. Katharine's former graduate student and research assistant Blake Sisk attended the 2010

Transatlantic Summer Institute on gender and migration at the University of Minnesota, taught by Donna and sociologist Mirjana Morokvasic (the editor of an earlier, 1984, special issue of *International Migration Review* that had focused on "Women and Migration").

Donna also thanks all the graduate students—Johanna Leinonen, Elizabeth Zanoni, Erika Busse, and Nate Holdren—who helped compile data and bibliography for a writing project as wide-ranging as this one, and she offers a special thanks to University of Minnesota graduate student Bryan Pekel for his detailed knowledge of the gender relations that shaped migration to the British Antipodes. Katharine thanks Blake Sisk, who as a graduate student began analyzing the IPUMs data in ways that helped us think about consequences, and Bhumika Piya, whose M.A. thesis also used IPUMs data to examine migrant gender composition. Other Vanderbilt graduate students involved were Anna Jacobs, whose careful yet intrepid analytic skills updated IPUMs data you see in chapters 6 and 7, and Gabriela León-Pérez, who provided assistance in finalizing some figures in the early chapters and in formatting references. In addition, we both want to thank Katie Gilliam for her careful reading and editing of the entire manuscript and its references.

In 2011 and 2012, Katharine and Donna were privileged to co-teach an SSRC Dissertation Proposal Development Fellowship seminar for fourteen extremely talented graduate students working on gender and migration in every corner of the world; the group was able to meet a third time to focus directly on mixed methodologies in the fall of 2012 with support from SSRC and Vanderbilt University. We especially thank the team of students—Erin Collins, Annabel Ipsen, Sarah DeMott, and Laura Enriquez—who planned the third workshop and convinced the SSRC to provide critically important seed funding for it. The inspiration, persistence, and energy of this new generation of scholars kept us continually motivated to keep working on our book during some very difficult times.

Donna offers personal thanks to Katharine Fennelly and to M. J. Maynes for methodological and epistemological challenges, often offered while she was working with them on projects only tangentially related to migration or gender ratios. Jeffrey Pilcher had the strength and courage to live through many long discussions of matters far from his own scholarly interests. Katharine wants to thank Andrea Tyree who first introduced her to this topic in their collaborations long ago. Katharine also offers personal thanks to Audrey Singer whose incisive comments toward the end of the writing of the first draft were very helpful, and to her two daughters, Marlo and Stella, for being the catalysts they are and for spurring their mother to finally get this written.

Introduction

"Clearly, statistics are not what they used to be. The challenge is to understand their language so as to decipher the story that they are trying to tell."
—Hania Zlotnik, former director, UN Department
of Economic and Social Affairs, Population Division[1]

In 1984, demographers at the U.S. Department of Labor published data showing more women than men among U.S. immigrants. Appearing in the first special issue devoted to research on immigrant women in the flagship journal, *International Migration Review*, the authors documented a female majority of 52.3 percent among recent immigrants to the United States. In the same issue, scholars also examined migrant women's work, lives, and experience in other parts of the world. For example, Saskia Sassen-Koob pointed to the feminization of the workforce in small-scale agricultural production in sending areas characterized by male out-migration, in global assembly plants in Asia and in wealthy nations that increasingly sought for foreign women as domestic laborers.[2] Less than a year later, the *New York Times* reported on its front page that men made up just one-third of U.S. immigrants,[3] suggesting a decline of immigrants entering the labor market as the proportion of women rose. Then, approximately a decade later, social scientists Stephen Castles and Mark Miller further spread the news about migration's feminization in their widely read book, *The Age of Migration*.[4]

The discovery of migration's feminization sparked intense scholarly attention to gender and migration.[5] Today, documentation of the feminization of migration continues as part of the broader study about how gender shapes every dimension of migration, not just into the United States but internationally.[6] Frequent calls for policy interventions have accompanied the development of scholarship on gender and migration.[7] References to the feminization of migration often frame studies of the trafficking of women or girls and exploitation of largely female domestic servants and care workers.[8] Even Wikipedia has an entry on the feminization of migration; it begins, "The feminization of migration is a recent trend in which gendered patterns are changing and a higher rate of women are migrating for labor or marriage."[9] But in fact, as we show, feminization is not a recent development and the migration of women and girls has a long history.

This book documents that women have been part of migration flows for more than four centuries. We show that balanced and even predominantly female migrations are not particularly new. Instead, it is the discovery and naming of feminization that are new. We offer a historical analysis of how and why the composition of migrant populations has shifted over time, sometimes quite dramatically, and we ask readers to think about why these changes occur and why they have remained invisible for so long. All existing data point toward great variability in the balance of men and women and boys and girls among migrants, and it is this variability—in both coerced and free migrations in the centuries between 1600 and 2000 across the globe—that is our focus. Underlying these variations are patterns and shifts in gender relations and gender ideologies in sending and receiving societies; these shifts reflect gender dynamics—not biological sex—in a larger political and economic context that has become more global over time. Our analysis also reveals the paucity of evidence for any widespread or negative consequences of sizeable contingents of women among migrants, past or present. Together, these findings suggest that the shift toward more women among international migrants has produced a global period of gender balance among migrants in the early twenty-first century.

Gender balance characterizes most human populations and imbalance—most often a preponderance of men in national populations—has been a recent concern of scholars and policymakers studying population dynamics mainly in China and India, where national policies (such as China's One-Child Policy) and popular practices (that may result in high rates of death among female infants and small children) produce male-predominant populations. Our book documents a long-term trend toward gender balance in migration occurring across the entire twentieth century. The main consequence of such balance has been a pronounced convergence in the composition of mobile international populations and sedentary national ones, and thus between natives and foreigners in many countries. Demographically, natives and foreigners have become more alike—for example, in their fertility and rates of wage-earning—with the feminization of migration. Although it is not possible to know whether this long-term trend will reverse in the future or whether it is a permanent transition comparable to well-documented fertility and mortality transitions,[10] gender balance is one indicator that international migrations have become normalized and predictable.

The Feminization of Migration Goes Global

By the first decade of the twenty-first century, the feminization of migration was no longer unique to the United States and northern Europe. Especially influential in extending the discussion of feminization of migration to the global level was a 2006 United Nations (UN) report on

Figure I.1   Trends in Female Migration, 1960–2005

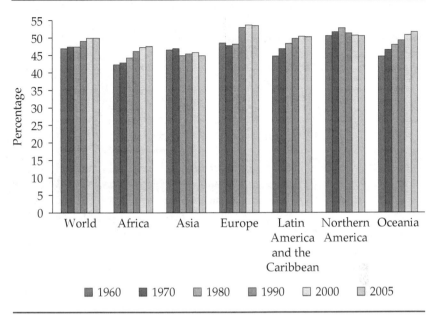

Source: Alcalá 2006.

the status of world populations.[11] Figure I.1, from that report, describes the percentage of women and girls in migrant populations worldwide. Using census data that represent a sequence of demographic snapshots across ten-year periods, the empirical data presented in the chart document a worldwide increase of the proportion female among resident foreigners, from 46.7 to 49.6 percent between 1960 and 2005. Yet the increase itself, only 2.9 percentage points in forty-five years, was modest. Some scholars, such as Hania Zlotnik at the United Nations, openly acknowledge that the increased share of women among migrants was modest.

The main revelation of the new set of global estimates by sex is that women and girls have accounted for a very high proportion of all international migrants for a long time. In 1960, female migrants already accounted for nearly forty-seven of every one hundred migrants living outside their countries of birth. Since then, the share of female migrants among all international migrants has been rising steadily, to 48 percent in 1990 and nearly 49 percent in 2000. Although this trend is consistent with an increasing feminization of international migration, the increase recorded is small compared with the high level in 1960.

One of the most important changes occurring in the fifty years between 1960 and 2010 was not in the relative numbers of males and females among migrants, but in the overall growth of migrants and refugees of both sexes. But even that seemed less cataclysmic on closer examination. By 2005, persons living outside the country of their birth constituted 3 percent of the world's population. True, the numbers of women and girl migrants had more than doubled between 1960 and 2005—from roughly thirty-five to seventy-eight million—but so had the numbers of migrant men and boys. World populations more than doubled from three billion to more than six billion between 1960 and 2005.[12] So if doubling the numbers of women and girls does not, as Hania Zlotnik notes, constitute feminization, what does feminization after 1960 mean? And why had scholars not noticed it before 1960?

Ultimately, this UN report emphasizes that the world's recent migrant population includes large numbers of mobile women and men, and that the shares of women have shifted modestly upward, but more so in some regions than in others, creating a story that is largely one of gender balance by the end of the twentieth century. What has not been discussed is why such small upward shifts attracted great attention from scholars and policymakers yet feminization before 1960 was ignored. Our book offers some answers to these questions.

Defining a Migrant: Inclusion and the Limits of Existing Data

How nation-states define migrants and thus how they measure migration flows mattered far more in the twentieth century than it had before 1920. Before World War I, borders were relatively open, but gave way—gradually, after 1880—to restrictions on the basis of race, ethnicity, national origins, and class. In the absence of strong national commitments to restrict migration, nations in the nineteenth century (and often before) did not create complex categories that differentiated among migrants of differing motivations or intentions. For example, there was no need to assess whether they sought work or refuge or whether they intended to remain permanently.[13] Adam McKeown has shown how proliferating restrictions on migration created a new "melancholy order" as nation-states around the world—notably in Australia, Canada, the United States, and Europe—chose to restrict the numbers of migrants and to exclude those deemed racially or ethnically undesirable. In this new twentieth-century world, categories became mechanisms of governance.[14] Thus some social scientists refer to the creation of migration regimes aimed at governing international mobility in the interests of selective nation-building, national development, or security.[15]

Restrictions on migration required the creation of categories that differentiated among more and less desirable forms of migrants as each individual nation understood them. Restriction both required complex typologies of mobility (see, for example, the one created by the International Labour Organization in 1927) and created enormous obstacles to standardizing those categories cross-nationally for purposes of international or global analysis.[16] From the 1920s until the 1960s, growing numbers of new nations in Africa and Asia faced the task of deciding how to restrict and how to distinguish among proliferating categories of migrants. Over time, restrictions based on race and ethnicity were replaced by other categories such as labor migrants, skilled or professional workers, visiting intellectuals and artists, expatriates, refugees, displaced persons, internally displaced persons, tourists, travelers, permanent and temporary migrants, asylum seekers, international students, trafficking victims, adopted children, trailing spouses, and many, many others. As a consequence, migrants often try to fit themselves into these new categories to gain admission from nation-states.[17]

We begin by stating that our definition of a migrant is necessarily very broad: he or she is any migrant who crosses an international border (or, in the past, an ocean) and is found in one of the four series of data that we analyze in this book. These data series include flow data (counts of individuals, generally made at borders) for most of the historical analysis before 1970 and census, or stock, data collected from households after 1970. Together, the data permit us to be as inclusive as possible about who is a migrant, but they complicate any effort to place migrants within contemporary categories. Using a broad definition enables us to extend our analysis beyond existing studies based on either flow or stock data, but not both, and to link analyses of migrant gender composition from the past to the present. We describe each of the four data sets to provide a better understanding of the migrants our analysis covers.

The first and earliest data series derives from the Trans-Atlantic Slave Trade Database and is analyzed in chapter 3.[18] These data are drawn from ship captains' handwritten records of their human freight. Under the leadership of historian David Eltis, thousands of ship, port, and customs records have been integrated into a single digital database that describes more than thirty-four thousand slave ship voyages. Estimates suggest that the data set includes at least two-thirds of all voyages that transported slaves from Africa to the Americas between 1500 and 1867.[19] The database establishes the general dynamics of the slave trade and identifies points of embarkation or exit from Africa and points of disembarkation or entry into the Americas. Yet the data are not perfect because some records contain more information than others,[20] and information by sex is available for only a subset of voyages (4,699—approximately 13 percent of all voyages). We therefore analyze these data cautiously, following in the footsteps of others who have done so.[21] Despite these limitations, the data set contains information on sex for almost a million persons, though fewer for years before 1650 when migrations were still small, and more for the period after 1650 as slave transports grew. The data define migrants by their embarkations, for example, emigration, from the significant regions of slave capture in Africa, and disembarkations, for example, immigration, to almost every significant destination or receiving region in the Americas.

The second data series we use originates from international flow data compiled by the International Labour Organization (ILO) and published in 1929 by Walter Willcox and Imre Ferenczi, who understood that state bureaucracies in different countries routinely create data about individual migrants in diverse ways. In this data set, one person may be recorded as two or even more migrants. An individual emigrant who leaves one country may or may not be counted a second time as an immigrant by the destination country; similarly, an immigrant may not have been counted as an emigrant upon departure. Transportation infrastructure and migrants' decisions also meant that some individuals born or living in one country and counted on departure may travel to a second country to depart for a third, and thus be counted three times. In addition, someone who circulated repeatedly over the years may be counted many times, each time he or she exited or entered a country. Further complicating these data is variability in nations' practices collecting emigrant-immigrant sex, nationality, culture, religion or citizenship, and place of birth. Countries receiving large numbers of immigrants often failed to count emigrants or, if they did count them, failed to distinguish between departing immigrant foreigners returning to their homelands and citizens going abroad temporarily or permanently. The reverse was also true: nations that worried about emigration of citizens may not have bothered to enumerate them when they returned or to distinguish them from foreign immigrants. In still other countries, foreigners' registration with the police (as residents) or their applications for work permits substituted for counts of border-crossers.

Like Willcox and Ferenczi, we are very aware of the limits of these data. Although those authors worried that the numbers of emigrants leaving one country for another rarely matched the (usually larger) number of immigrants counted as arriving in a host country from a particular origin, we worry less about this issue because our analysis is about the relative numbers of male and female migrants. In addition, the data describe a substantial portion—we estimate one-half to three-quarters—of all nineteenth-century long-distance international migrations: the number of emigrants from forty-two sending areas and the number of immigrants to thirty-nine receiving areas total more than seventy-five million emigrants and more than seventy-seven million immigrants.

The third data series we use was first generated by the ILO in collaboration with the League of Nations and subsequently with the United Nations. In 1953, the UN Population Division published a compilation of multi-year data in a volume titled "Sex and Age of International Migrants" that summarized flow data between 1918 and 1947. Beginning in 1948, the UN's *Demographic Yearbook* published annual flow data that also included breakdowns by sex for many—but not all—countries. Overall, about one-third of the data in the 1953 compilation came from Europe and another third from North America, the Caribbean, and South America. Representation of Africa and Asia was better than in the Willcox and Ferenczi volume, including at least some data for a number of nations in these regions, but the annual numbers of departures and arrivals still differed. Many countries did not differentiate aliens or foreigners from citizens or nationals in arrival and departure data. In both Africa and Asia, colonies reported data separately for racial and religion or European-origin and non-European-origin migrants; among the former, Europeans were almost always enumerated more systematically or more often. Some countries distinguished permanent from temporary migrants or transcontinental from intercontinental migrants; others did not. As in the past, some counted only arrivals or only departures. Yet, once again, the coverage of these data is impressive. We estimate that the data available by sex from this volume constitute slightly more than half of global migrants—that is to say, emigrants and immigrants—during this time.

The final data series differs from the first three—an issue we discuss in greater detail in chapters 2 and 5. In the final section of this book, we use stock data that define international migrants as persons born outside their country of birth. These data are individual-level data drawn from national censuses that have been harmonized and made available by the Minnesota Population Center as part of the Integrated Public Use Microdata Series (IPUMS-International and IPUMS-USA). Although these data are from the largest global population data source, include information that extends well beyond nativity and gender, and offer the ability to control for sex-differences in longevity, they too do not cover the entire world. For the analysis found in chapters 6 and 7, we use data from sixty-six nations and a total of 176 censuses that contain information about nativity and describe more than five hundred million people after 1960.

Stock data derived from censuses are different from flow data sources: rather than providing specific counts of individuals leaving and entering, stock data count people living in households at the time of each census. In the United States, the foreign-born population is any household member who was not a U.S. citizen at birth and includes those who have become U.S. citizens through naturalization. Although most nations define nativity in a similar way, there is still some variation. For example, the Israeli census includes in its foreign-born population only foreign-born Jews residing in the country. All noncitizen foreign-born workers who are not Jewish are not counted in the census. Although we note such differences in our subsequent discussion of these data, we rely on stock data about migrants to include as many migrants as possible. We prefer inclusivity given that our key objective is to examine the extent of migrant gender composition over time and across space; this objective would be severely compromised if we focused only on one or two specific types of migration, such as that related to marriage or labor.

Therefore, we analyze both flow and stock data and many types of international migrants, such as regular immigrants, temporary workers, refugees, slave laborers, and unauthorized migrants. To be sure, these data have limits but, for the sake of our research question about variations in gender composition, we argue that the benefits exceed the limits. One key advantage is that the available data do roughly distinguish between two types migrations. First are those motivated by the recruitment of individual labor (a group that included Atlantic slaves and indentured servants before 1800 and various kinds of contract workers and free labor migrants after 1800). Second are those through which both migrants and receiving societies expected cultural and biological reproduction to occur in a new setting that includes old world slave migrations, refugees, and settler colonizers as well as twentieth-century marriage or family migrants. Although it becomes muddy as we explore specific times and places, this broad distinction does allow us to consider how reproductive and productive labor figured in shaping the gender composition of migrant populations.

Defining Feminization: A Typology of Migrant Gender Composition

We believe it both possible and important to document and analyze the numbers of male and female migrants over time and space. To do this, we develop a typology of gender composition that distinguishes between routine and predictable variations in gender composition and the increases or decreases in the percentage female that are more likely caused by diversity in gender relations and in gender ideology. Recognizing that scholars, journalists, and students have defined feminization in very different ways, we decided to use our measure of migrant gender composition in a very narrow way. Some use it to refer to rising numbers of women migrants between two individual years or across multiple years or periods. Others use it to refer to increasing shares of women among all migrants, again to assess change between two or more years or periods. Still others use it only to describe recent upward shifts in women's presence. How feminization is measured also varies by discipline. For example, demographers often assume that even small variations in age or gender composition may have significant consequences, especially in large populations. They prefer to measure feminization, or the gender composition of a population, with a sex ratio that some assume captures small variations better than percentages. Historians, in contrast, often use the percentage female to assess the gender composition of migrant populations over long periods.[22] Adding to this complexity are the disciplinary differences in assessing variability: historians typically emphasize continuities or similarities whereas sociologists portray the present as a sharp rupture from the past.[23]

Because no generally accepted typology for migrant gender composition exists, we develop one here and use it throughout this book. It is based on the idea that predictable variations in gender composition are a product of the changing age composition of populations. Our typology discusses and compares migrations with male and female majorities as male predominant and female predominant. We do not—as do some studies of feminization—distinguish between male and female dominant because we do not assume that greater numbers automatically deliver more power.[24] Instead, we use the word *predominant* because its meaning is more numeric.[25] Although we recognize that gender relations involve power, we are not sure whether and how the relative numbers of male and female migrants empower either group. Thus, we use predominant in its numeric sense to create a typology of migrant gender composition.

Prior studies have used a simple typology composed of two categories: historical male-predominant and contemporary balanced or female-predominant migrations. Feminization is typically defined as a shift from the first to the second category and masculinization—which is almost never discussed—a shift from the second to the first category. We make three significant additions to this overly simple typology. First, we create a third category of gender-balanced migration, which has been used in the past but never applied to studies about the feminization of migration. Second, because it is pointless to insist that gender balance exists only when the numbers or shares of males and female are exactly equal, we define a range—between 47 and 53 percent—as constituting gender balance. We also define male-predominant migrations as less than 47 percent female and female-predominant migrations as greater than 53 percent female. Third, rather than insist on using one broad category for either male- or female-predominant migrant populations, we define heavily male-predominant populations as less than 25 percent female and heavily female-predominant populations as more than 75 percent female.

Thus, although our typology may need revision in the future, it is clearly defined. In too many prior studies terms such as *overwhelmingly male* appear without any definition.[26] Eventually, we hope that studies documenting the consequences of male-predominant migrations will make it possible to identify a sensible upper limit based on the analysis of the consequences of gender imbalance. Until then, we choose to define heavily male-predominant rather broadly. As the chapters ahead demonstrate, evidence exists for heavily male-predominant, male-predominant, gender-balanced, and female-predominant migrations for almost every period, every spatial scale, and every part of the world. Some chapters in this volume focus particular attention on heavily male and on the gender-balanced or female-predominant migrant populations, using them as case studies of the diverse gender relations that produce variation. Prior studies influenced our choice of case studies that then permit us to situate heavily male and gender-balanced and female-predominant migrations in a particular social or historical context, and to identify the types of gender relations and gender ideologies in sending or host societies associated with each category.

By creating a typology of migrant gender composition, we also aim to more concisely establish a foundation for defining feminization. In this book, we suggest and use three definitions of feminization. Our most generous definition defines it simply as any multiyear rise in the percentage female among migrants. In the chapters ahead, we show that many periods of short-term and temporary feminization of migrant populations were followed by years of masculinization. Our second definition is based more narrowly on the typology of gender composition: feminization is any shift from one category to another (from heavily male to male-predominant, or from male-predominant to gender-balanced) just as masculinization is a shift from female-predominant to gender-balanced, or from male-predominant to heavily male-predominant. Finally, a third definition defines feminization as any increase in the proportion female that has demonstrable consequences for migrants, for their homelands, or for the new societies they enter.

Emphasis on Gender

Throughout this book, we emphasize the gender of migrants and focus on gender relations and ideology rather than on biological sex or on women migrants alone. We adopt a long-term historical perspective that reveals gender and migration as processes occurring over time and across spatial scales, from the local to the global. In the book, we remain poignantly aware of how inequality, including that based on sex and gender, affects migration and its consequences. Scholars have pointed to the inequality associated with too many women or too many men in a population.[27] Considerable scholarship on contemporary societies also addresses the negative social consequences for women when young men outnumber them, as they do, for example, in contemporary China or India.[28] The same may be true of migrant populations with too many women.

Our choice to focus on gender does not delegitimize the dichotomous and bivariate male and female categories that make quantitative study of empirical data possible. Many theorists insist—and we agree—that gender and sex are not fixed categories or the product of biology but instead malleable, fluid social constructions shaped by relationships of power.[29]

We also agree, however, with the feminist demographers of the United Nations who—for decades—insisted that the reporting of empirical data about the sex of migrants, labeling migrants as male or female was an important political demand to change international record-keeping practices that had historically ignored sex. Without that data, gender analysis of quantitative data is impossible. In a review of scholarship on gender and migration, Katharine Donato and her colleagues insist that distinguishing male from female is a necessary foundation for gender analysis in the quantitative social sciences.[30] Collecting bivariate data on sex makes it possible to measure the composition of populations but it does not preclude gender analysis. As Hania Zlotnik suggests in the quotation with which we open this book, statistics too are a language that can be analyzed with the methods of gender studies. In fact, by documenting gender variation in migrant populations, we can assert that it is not biological sex driving migrant gender composition. If it were, the sex of migrants would vary very little, as it does, for example, among babies at the time of birth.[31] Variations in the relative numbers of male and female migrants are the product of complex culturally diverse gender relations in sending and receiving societies.

Understanding how we can know sex and gender is related to methodological concerns that have at times divided scholars into two camps: those who reject and those who support quantitative social scientific quantitative methodologies. Many feminists of the 1970s and 1980s rejected quantitative methods as hierarchical, female-unfriendly, and malestream tools, and instead cited African American poet Audre Lorde's trenchant observation that "the master's tools will never dismantle the master's house."[32] These scholars preferred qualitative over quantitative methodologies that essentialized male and female as sex or biological difference. For their part, quantitative social scientists in the 1980s and 1990s have too often characterized qualitative analyses as uniformly tainted by the radical relativity of postmodernist philosophers.[33] To begin to bridge this divide, chapter 1 explains in some detail why gender has been a key constituting factor in only a small set of social scientific migration studies.[34]

Recently, the methodological chasm separating qualitative gender studies from quantitative social science has narrowed somewhat. By using an eclectic array of methods from diverse disciplines—especially from history (with its penchant for temporal interpretations), demography (with its preference for quantitative methods and empirical evidence), and anthropology (with its focus on theory about sex and gender and about linkages among local, national, and global studies),[35] we aim to show that empirical evidence and systematic quantitative analysis of bivariate data about sex reveals the fluidity and relationality of gender as constructed in both sending and receiving societies. In our use of quantitative methods, we follow Mary Fonow and Judith Cook, who emphasize how feminist quantitative research represents "the ways in which key concepts were operationalized, the careful matching of statistical techniques to research questions, the transparency with which the researchers presented their data and analysis, and the focus of the analysis on disenfranchised groups."[36]

Outline of Book

This book analyzes the composition of migrant populations over the long term and across a variety of spatial scales, from the global and macroregional to the national and subnational. Given Zlotnik's observations about feminization in 1960, some historical perspective seems essential. We decided to push beyond the usual and often narrow social science understanding of the past (for example, as a period that may begin with 1986 or 1996 and ends with the present) by adopting the large temporal scale of global historians. Unlike social scientists who often portray recent migrations as unprecedented, world and global historians examining long-term migration patterns instead describe mobility not as a problem or the norm but rather as a common and not-unexpected dimension of human existence.[37]

Scholarly attention to the relative numbers of males and females among migrants began long before recent interest in the feminization of migration. For readers interested in the sociology of knowledge production about gender and migration, chapter 1 provides an overview of the two scholarly fields that have most shaped inquiry about gender and migration and describes the divergence of gender studies and quantitative social sciences in the last quarter of the twentieth century and some recent efforts to reconnect the two fields. The focus is on how scholars have understood sex and gender in the migration process and on how scholarship itself has often been associated with masculinity or femininity. Chapter 2 also takes a long-term perspective on the study of migration by examining the creation of several types of data—notably flow and stock data—collected by states and international organizations to document human mobility. It traces the development of scholarly measures—from sex ratios to percentages female—that facilitate analysis of the two types of data. In both chapters, we focus on the ways concepts were operationalized.[38]

Readers interested in historical and contemporary shifts in the gender composition of immigrants, and the factors and consequences associated with such shifts, may wish to turn immediately to chapter 3. Chapters 3, 4, and 5 use historical flow data to trace the gender composition of a number of large-scale migrations over four centuries and three significant eras of global integration and human mobility. They seek to explain variations in gender composition and identify possible consequences. Why were some migrations heavily male and others gender-balanced or even female-predominant? How have scholars described the social, economic, or cultural consequences of variations in migrant gender composition? Chapter 3 analyzes settler, coerced, and slave migrations in and around the early modern Atlantic between 1600 and 1860 and points to gender imbalance among labor migrants and gender balance among settler colonizers and refugees. Chapter 4 then explores and contrasts settler and labor migrations of the nineteenth century, identifying the masculinization of global migrations and presenting evidence of a beginning convergence toward gender balance shortly after 1900. Chapter 5 documents the persistence of this convergence as volumes of migration first fell and then rose again across the twentieth century and attributes it both to increased restriction and management of human mobility and to a gendered shift in demand for migrant labor. It describes and explains the belated scholarly discovery of the feminization of migration by grounding that discovery in a shift—initiated at the United Nations—from the analysis of flow to stock data, which were widely available but also exaggerated female representation in international migrations.

Chapters 6 and 7 analyze IPUMS micro-level stock data for the years after 1970. Chapter 6 uses the data to correct a methodological flaw of the influential 2006 UN report, explores contemporary variations in migrant gender composition, and reveals that the feminization of migration—or, as we prefer to call it, the convergence toward gender balance—is both more modest than the UN suggested, yet also real and replicable. Chapter 7 tackles a question that has generally remained unstated and unexamined in recent quantitative analyses of the feminization of migration. Few scholars have presented evidence that the relatively modest increase in female representation over the past fifty years has had any demographic, social, or political consequences, whether in rates of marriage, female or male wage-earning, female emancipation, or the building or collapse of feminist movements. Why should we care about how many women or men move about, leave one region, or work or settle in another? Focusing on the United States, chapter 7 analyzes effects of variations in the gender composition among U.S. immigrants and suggests limited and temporary consequences of modestly unbalanced migrations, whether male- or female-predominant. It reveals convergence of native and immigrant marriage and work patterns over time, and suggests that the convergence is sometimes the product of shifts in the native population and sometimes a consequence of shifts that have accompanied the changing volumes and composition of the immigrant population. Finally, the conclusion summarizes key findings and considers their policy implications. Although we do not use data that permit us to directly assess these effects, our goal is to begin a dialogue about possible links between migrant gender composition and several specific policies and practices in nations that receive and send immigrants.

Twentieth-Century Global Convergence Toward Gender Balance

This book uses methods from the disciplines of history, gender studies, and the social sciences and reveals that what others have described as feminization is a gradual, intermittent, and ongoing twentieth-century global convergence toward gender balance in migrant populations. Our historical analysis demonstrates that migrant gender composition has always varied and that feminization and masculinization are two important forms of variation. We document cases of short-term feminizations and shorter- and longer-term masculinizations of migrant populations. During every important era of migration, from the early modern period to the present, we also show cases of female and heavily female-predominant migration. Migrant populations in Europe seem particularly noteworthy because they have been gender balanced for more than a century, whereas the United States, Canada, and Australia have been roughly gender balanced for at least ninety years. In fact, the achievement of gender balance is probably of less significance—in terms of its social and cultural consequences—than the eighteenth- to nineteenth-century masculinization that preceded it. More recently, we see that women's migration has been on the rise in some other nations worldwide. In some Asian countries, women's rising productivity, in part reflected by growing numbers of migrant women and the remittances they send back to origin households, has helped fuel an export boom that in turn propels more women to migrate in search of work.[39] In other nations, immigrant populations are more gender balanced because of refugee flows and the reunification of reproducing family groups.[40]

Yet the consequences of the shift from male-predominant to gender-balanced immigrant populations in the United States offer limited evidence of dramatic consequences. Immigrant women were more likely to be married and less likely to work for wages during periods of heavily male-predominant migration, and over time, as immigrant populations have become more gender balanced, migrants have become more similar to natives in their demographic attributes and behavior. The evidence for significant consequences is therefore fairly modest; it includes small changes in rates of intermarriage and convergence in the employment patterns of natives and migrants as the shift toward gender balance among U.S. immigrants has occurred.

We hope the analysis and findings in this book will be the foundation for future scholarship about gender and international migration. What we know is that some factors more than others encouraged unbalanced migrant populations. Coercive and heavily regulated systems of labor recruitment, including the slave systems and contract- and indenture-based labor systems of the nineteenth century and guest-worker migrations of our own times, are most likely to result in unbalanced migrations. Although many times they have been almost exclusively male, coercive systems of recruitment of labor have included and do include women, especially as domestic and service workers, including nurses and slaves. Other factors, such as government interventions in the form of restricted or supported policies and programs, migrant autonomy and independence, and the desire to marry or to settle, encourage the migration of gender-balanced populations or produce female-predominant migrations that offset those that were heavily male in the past. Almost all these factors are directly or indirectly related to human reproduction and reproductive labor, whether paid or unpaid. These patterns are unlikely to change as long as reproductive work is assigned—as it is, and has been historically—to women and girls across national and cultural borders.

PART I

UNDERSTANDING SEX, GENDER, AND MIGRATION STUDIES

= Chapter 1 =

Data and Discipline:
Discovering the Feminization
of Migration

S cholars who discussed the feminization of migration at the end of the twentieth century suggested that it was a recent development even as they presented findings pointing toward much earlier change. In this book, we present considerable evidence of earlier periods of feminization and offer an explanation for a shift toward gender balance that stretched across the entire twentieth century. Before we present that historical evidence, however, it seems important to answer the question implicit in Hania Zlotnik's acknowledgment that most feminization occurred before 1960. If migrations had begun to feminize already in the 1910s and 1920s (as we show they did), why did discussions of feminization begin only seventy to eighty years later? And why was the discussion not led by scholars in the new and rapidly expanding scholarly field of gender and women's studies?

Answering those questions becomes even more important when we realize that scholarly interest in the sex of migrants is not new. On the contrary, foundational scholarship in the multidisciplinary field of migration studies addressed the topic beginning in the nineteenth century. Furthermore, women scholars interested in sex and gender have been studying migration for more than a century. Explaining why the feminization of migration was labeled only in the final years of the twentieth century thus reveals much about the origins, development, and practices of the scholarly field—interdisciplinary migration studies—to which this book contributes.

More than a literature review of the most recent research findings on sex, gender, and migration, this chapter (and the next) offers what German-speakers might call a Begriffsgeschichte[1] or what English-speakers describe as an historical sociology of knowledge[2] of the three analytical categories—gender, sex, and migration—that define the intersection of gender and migration studies. Begriffsgeschichte and the sociology of knowledge share a profound respect for the ways in which *knowledge production*—a term more commonly used in gender studies—intersects with and depends on social structures, relations, and processes of scholarly inquiry. In this chapter, we argue that migration studies scholars' understanding of sex, gender, and migration always reflect the influence of gender ideology and gender relations on scholarship itself.[3] Changing societal assumptions and prescriptions about sex difference (sometimes called gender ideology) structure gender relations society-wide, and in scholarly institutions, training, research, and professional employment. For a very long time, gender ideology and relations, not biological sex, closed off scholarly knowledge production to women, along with many other activities, limiting them to familial, domestic, and reproductive life. Gender relations and ideology also subsequently made knowledge production in some scholarly disciplines seem more appropriate for female or male scholars. As a result, disciplines and even methods could be gendered male or female. Tracing how gender affects disciplines, data, and research methods over time, this chapter suggests why few scholars in migration studies looked for or recognized the feminization of migration as it began in the early twentieth century, and why it was demographers and statisticians—rather than scholars in gender studies—who first labeled feminization in the 1980s.

The State Sciences and the Study of Population, Sex, and Migration

Scholarly study of migration began with states' efforts to govern people residing in their territories and to differentiate resident insiders from potentially ungovernable outsiders or foreigners.[4] Almost all contemporary scholars in gender studies trace such insights about the governmentality of humans by states to Michel Foucault's critique of the modern state.[5] But state efforts to describe and register people in order to govern them are, in fact, very old. The so-called state sciences (Staatswissenschaften)—the scholarship and disciplines that produce knowledge useful to states[6]—and the development of demography and population studies of mobile populations—are more recent developments.[7] From its origins in the seventeenth century, the discipline now called demography made biological sex a fundamental category of analysis that gave states important information about the strength, decline, or increase of populations through reproduction, birth and aging. The earliest scholarly studies described migrant populations, too, as structured by sex difference. Almost all these early studies of populations—whether sedentary or mobile—were the work of male scholars and researchers.

Both world historians and social scientists have recently described how a sedentary bias has profoundly affected scholarly knowledge of human life.[8] Since the invention of the written word, humans have differentiated sedentary from mobile people. The first agrarian states, which emerged with the spread of agriculture and the Neolithic revolutions in east, west, and south Asia, typically distinguished themselves from foragers, hunters, and nomadic herders—groups whose lives and cultures remained defined by constant patterned movement.[9] The differentiation was not neutral: whether in China or the classical Mediterranean, imperial states associated civilization with sedentarism and mobility with their enemies, the "barbarians." Although the civilized (who alone left written documents for historians to study) had every reason to exaggerate barbarian mobility,[10] world historians have instead pointed to the many forms of mobility that made civilization possible, including military mobilizations, imperial expansion, labor migrations to build Egypt's pyramids or China's Great Wall, and long-distance trade.[11]

Despite ancient cultural suspicions of mobile people, the scholarly study of migration began only with the development of the state sciences within emerging, expanding, and often imperially motivated nation-states. In the seventeenth century, rulers of Europe's states first began to see the persons they governed as constituting a population. In England, Francis Bacon suggested that rulers must understand and provide for their populations if they expected to govern them.[12] Counting a population and evaluating its size and attributes soon became key empirical foundations for enlightened or scientific governance. Thus the first English population researcher, the hatter John Graunt, along with his better-educated collaborator, William Petty, called their recordings and enumerations of births and deaths political arithmetic. Graunt was the first of many demographers to note that male babies outnumbered girl babies at birth, setting into motion population scientists' long-term interest in tracking age and sex in human populations. By the 1800s, population statisticians even called themselves statists.[13] Across the nineteenth century, statists demonstrated the interaction of age and mortality through what they called population sex ratios. Because mortality differed by sex across the life course, male predominance among newborns gradually shifted toward female majorities among the elderly. The early modern scientific revolution that Bacon pioneered had challenged theocratic explanations for state power by making sex and biological population reproduction, not God's grace, key measures of a state's strength.

By the eighteenth century, Thomas Malthus's (1766–1834) more pessimistic predictions, including that a growing population inevitably outstripped the agricultural production and livestock required to feed it,[14] deeply disturbed a British society in the midst of rapid industrialization, urbanization, and population growth and ultimately motivated greater attention by statists to human mobility.[15] It is striking that the earliest mobility statistics in France and England focused less on foreigners' arrivals than on internal movements as mobile citizens and subjects relocated from the countryside (where they raised food) to cities and industrial jobs (where they consumed food). Scholars today debate whether any transition from lower to higher rates of mobility accompanied these changes; the issue remains unresolved.[16] The political elites at the time certainly believed both that mobility was increasing and that it was potentially threatening. Statisticians' long-standing interest in the relationship of sex, reproduction, and population growth assured that the earliest studies of mobility, too, paid some attention to sex and thus to male and female migration patterns.[17]

The oft-cited work of British statistician and geographer E. G. Ravenstein (1834–1913) and his laws of migration—which appeared in publications of 1876, 1885, and 1889—illustrate how one founder of modern migration studies understood the relationship between sex and migration. Born into a family of German cartographers, Ravenstein migrated as a young man to England and became a naturalized citizen.[18] He developed his ideas about sex and migration as he analyzed the 1871 and 1881 population censuses of Great Britain. In addition to listing individuals' current places of residence, sex, and age, census-takers had asked about both the place of birth and sex of all natives of the British Isles (including colonial Ireland). They had distinguished natives from aliens but had not noted aliens' places of birth or nationality. On this basis, Ravenstein claimed to have discovered what he called laws of migration in 1885. In a second article, Ravenstein claimed universality for his laws by providing evidence from other European countries—Germany, France, Austria, Hungary—and from Canada and the United States.[19]

In one of his most influential laws, Ravenstein argued that sex determined the distance migrants journeyed, asserting that "Woman is a greater migrant than man." In a clear nod toward Victorian ideology of separate (public and domestic) spheres for male and female activity,[20] he acknowledged that "This may surprise those who associate women with domestic life, but the figures of the census clearly prove it."[21] However, Ravenstein mainly documented that women were more migratory than men within the kingdom (for example, England, Scotland, or Wales) of their birth. In his typology of local, short- and long-journey stage migration and temporary (short-term) migration (a schema that did not distinguish migrations within the British Isles from those with foreign origins), short-journey migrations were by far the most common, making women the greater migrant. Men, by contrast, predominated among migrants venturing beyond the kingdom of their birth, whether internally (within Great Britain) or internationally (into Great Britain from foreign states). Ravenstein also noted and commented on an important exception to this law linking masculinity and long-distance migration: he found more women than men among migrants born in Ireland but living in England, Scotland, and Wales.

Ravenstein's conclusions about sex and migration were empirically grounded but also mirrored late-Victorian understandings of proper sex roles. In explaining migrations, for example, Ravenstein largely ignored familial or marital motivations for moving about. Thus, he did not consider the possibility[22] that marriage customs (especially women's moves to their husbands' village or farm) explained women's greater propensity to move short distances.[23] When Ravenstein did note the influence of private or domestic concerns, furthermore, he linked them exclusively to female migrants and female morality. He suggested, for example, that counties with spa towns had attracted grass widows, who were women whose husbands had deserted them, forcing them to work as prostitutes, or were away in the military, thus releasing them from household responsibilities and allowing them to enjoy indolent lives as hotel boarders.

Ravenstein—and much subsequent scholarship—focused on migrations motivated by labor demand in receiving or host societies. Ravenstein especially emphasized how sex-specific demand for waged workers in urban labor markets drove migration, such that towns with large military garrisons drew predominantly male migrants. He also described male migrants outnumbering female migrants in mining and metal-working towns, but acknowledged that women, too, sought work as migrants. He described women as migrating "quite as frequently into certain manufacturing districts" and concluded that "the workshop is a formidable rival of the kitchen and scullery" (in urban middle-class households) in demanding female labor.[24] Presumably, the manufacturing districts described as attracting female migrants included England's many urban centers of textile production.[25] Thus, while Victorian gender ideology prescribed domestic roles for women, Ravenstein acknowledged that both sexes responded to labor market demand as they traveled to different destinations.

Despite his argument that "woman was the greater migrant," Ravenstein also became the first in a long line of researchers who imagined men as the primary migration decision-makers. As Ravenstein sought to explain the Irish anomaly of female majorities among long-distance movers, he also noted that "Whilst emigrants from England or Scotland depart in most instances without 'incumbrances' it appears to be a common practice for entire families to leave Ireland in search of new homes."[26] Ravenstein wrote several decades after the end of the Irish potato famine—an event that might have provided him with an explanation for Irish distinctiveness and the international migration of more women than men. Instead, he imagined male decision-makers traveling with or without family dependents (a group that presumably included both women and children), but he never explained why male migrations encumbered with families would result in female majorities. Nor did he consider the possibility that more Irish women than men migrated because demand for female labor in textiles and domestic service may have surpassed demand for male labor in mining and industry.

Over time, the study of internal or domestic migrations and the study of international movements developed as separate scholarly fields of study. The male majorities that characterized long-distance movers became a persistent focus in research on international migration. Some critics have even claimed that the unencumbered or individual labor migrant who traveled in pursuit of economic advantage became the archetypical figure in migration research.[27] This also made the long-distance male migrant most deserving of study; female migrants seemed interesting only when they outnumbered males or when they—like males—sought wage-earning work as unencumbered persons without families. A century later, feminist scholars continued to complain that scholarship treated female and children migrants as uninteresting dependents of men.[28]

Historians have described how the ideas of Ravenstein and others circulated widely, influencing governance and record-keeping around the Atlantic.[29] In the Americas, however, it was international migration—what Americans increasingly called immigration[30]—and not urbanization that garnered the greatest attention from the founders of migration studies. In America, where Christiane Harzig and Dirk Hoerder locate a second birthplace of modern migration studies, sex and migration remained objects of inquiry but were researched within a scholarly world that included more female scholars.[31] Complex scholarly gender relations help draw disciplinary boundaries around the production of knowledge about sex and migration in important ways.

Sex, Gender, and American Immigration Studies

Like Ravenstein, male American statists were interested in sex and migration. For example, they repeatedly demonstrated that years of massive immigration had raised the proportion of men in the U.S. population beyond normal levels.[32] Over time, however, statists' conclusions about sex and migration became marginalized in U.S. immigration studies. In part, this reflected declining levels of international migration after 1920 and a shift in the immigration research disciplines that bifurcated scholarship into separate groups focused on internal and international moves. U.S. scholars have long celebrated the Chicago School of Sociology and the immigrant-origin Harvard historian most influenced by the Chicago sociologists' work, Oscar Handlin, as founders of U.S. immigration studies.[33] By contrast, scholars in statistics and demography and the state sciences—rather than in history, anthropology, and sociology—produced the most research on sex, gender, and migration, whether internal or international.

Although some sociologists now question whether the early sociologists at the University of Chicago constituted an intellectually coherent school,[34] few in the United States question the importance of Chicago sociologists such as Robert Park (1864–1944), W. I. Thomas (1863–1947), Ernest Burgess (Canada, 1886–1966), and Louis Wirth (Germany, 1897–1952). These men were intensely interested in foreign-born immigrants, but more as social than as sexual or reproducing mobile people.[35] Rather than study migrants' mobility, the Chicago sociologists analyzed immigrants' social, cultural, and socio-psychological adjustments to modern American society. The Chicago School was not disinterested in mobility but treated it mainly as the initiator of the social and cultural changes that Chicago scholars found most interesting.[36] The Chicago sociologists used an eclectic but decidedly qualitative mix of methods that emphasized careful, direct, ethnographic, or biographical observations of urban life. From these micro-studies emerged ecological models of urban development as well as theories of immigrant disorganization, alienation, and marginality and of assimilation and a race relations cycle.[37] Oscar Handlin later brought these themes to a broader audience with his influential history of immigrant alienation and assimilation.[38]

Historians have recently identified other intellectual fonts of U.S. immigration studies, all with significant input from women researchers, few of whom could obtain positions in American universities. Dirk Hoerder labels Jane Addams (1860–1935) and the Progressive social reformers who created the American settlement house movement as founders of a women's Chicago School.[39] As reformers, political activists, and researchers, they documented and analyzed immigrant women's and men's lives at work, in neighborhoods, and at home. Mary Jo Deegan argues that departments of sociology excluded the Chicago women researchers as politically biased naïve reformers or mere social workers.[40] A multiracial, multiethnic, and interdisciplinary network of both male and female students trained at Columbia under immigrant anthropologist Franz Boas (Germany, 1858–1942), also produced new research on immigrants. Donna Gabaccia and Jon Gjerde identify sons and daughters of immigrants working at Midwestern state universities as the earliest historians of immigration.[41] However, Kate Asaphine Everest Levi—who wrote the first history dissertation on immigration at the University of Wisconsin—found work as director of a social settlement house, not in a university history department.[42] Only the students of Boas found significant academic employment.

Still invisible in these newer genealogies were the women researchers—many with interests in sex and migration—who became population scientists in the 1920s and 1930s. Even as specialized academic training, research and teaching in other fields became progressively more masculine professional arenas after 1920, women trained as statisticians found work and even exercised leadership inside universities and as state scientists.

This association between women researchers and quantitative methodologies and statistical population research was quite powerful in the twentieth-century United States. The social settlement movement (an integrated but female-predominant arena of scholarship) and the Women's Chicago School had together helped pioneer the development of social surveys. Designed explicitly to influence public policy, surveys were collaborative projects to collect and then analyze massive amounts of data about urban and industrial life. Early surveys facilitated intimate, detailed, but often statistical analyses of immigrants' jobs, families, budgets, homes, and neighborhoods. Whether in Chicago,[43] as part of the 1907 Pittsburgh Survey team,[44] or with funding from the initially woman-initiated and -controlled Russell Sage Foundation,[45] women researchers published important surveys of immigrant life; some even wrote explicitly about the lives, jobs, and consumer habits of immigrant women.[46]

Separate from the Chicago School of Sociology was the School of Civics and Philanthropy (later renamed the University of Chicago's School of Social Administration). Many graduates were women and found employment in municipal and state governments as researchers and administrators of social welfare and public health agencies or in the federal Women's Bureau. Edith Abbott (1876–1957), an early dean of the Chicago School of Civics and Philanthropy, was an expert on immigration and one of the drafters of the American Social Security Act. Known today mainly as a founder of social work, she authored so many quantitative analyses of immigrants, female employment, and criminality that she was initially known as "the passionate statistician."[47]

Passionate statisticians of both sexes ensured that migration and mobility remained central themes in demography and increasingly in economics. In the 1920s, statisticians' senior academic representative, Cornell University Professor Walter F. Willcox, supported several projects about international migration from his position at the National Bureau of Economic Research (NBER), including a collaboration with Hungarian Imre Ferenczi (1884–1945) at the International Labour Organization (ILO). Their work confirmed—on a far more international scale than earlier studies—the overall male predominance among nineteenth-century transcontinental migrants and the anomalous female majorities among Irish migrants in many places, not just Great Britain.[48]

University-trained U.S. women demographers with expertise on migration quickly assumed leadership in the discipline of demography and in the Population Association of America (PAA). Because international migrations declined after 1920, however, most of these women studied internal migration, using methods and sources that Ravenstein would have recognized.[49] During the 1950s, Irene B. Taeuber (1906–1974), Dorothy Swaine Thomas (1899–1977), and Margaret Jarman Hagood (1907–1963) served as back-to-back presidents of the PAA. Thomas also served as first female president (in 1952) of the American Sociological Society (later Association). Her election reflected the degree to which quantitative methodologies had—by that date—moved closer to the mainstream of U.S. sociology and, by the time of her death, had come to define it generally[50]—although not American immigration studies. Thomas and other female demographers distinguished themselves and their empirical research from earlier sociologists, but they also differentiated themselves from the Chicago women and survey methods that Harriett Bartlett (herself a Chicago-trained social worker) characterized in 1928 as a form of fact-finding aimed at social control and thus different from real research that "deals with general data divorced from time and place" and "seeks to test a general hypothesis."[51] These demographers did not, in other words, embrace research as a form of political arithmetic; they considered themselves social scientists, not state scientists.

E. G. Ravenstein's foundational laws of migration echoed through the work of Dorothy Thomas, Irene Taeuber, and a third woman demographer, Hope Tisdale Eldridge (1904–1991). Thomas pioneered in applying quantitative methodologies to the study of internal migrations in both Sweden and the United States.[52] Although she began as a student of internal migration,[53] Eldridge later edited the UN *Demographic Yearbook,* a publication that continued Willcox's and Ferenczi's documentation of international migrations after World War II. Eldridge also worked with Thomas on the third volume of the monumental *Population Redistribution and Economic Growth, United States, 1870–1950,* a work that sought to understand the economic causes and consequences of internal migrations.[54] Conrad and Irene Taeuber too initially researched internal migrations in the United States, but Irene Taeuber then turned to international work on development, demography, and migration issues in Europe, Japan, and China.[55]

Attentive to how sex structured both migration and fertility, Irene Taeuber and Hope Eldridge pondered the demographic foundations of what feminist scholars in the 1970s would call sex or gender roles.[56] Eldridge's work went well beyond Ravenstein in noting how shifts in sex composition were understood by nonspecialists.[57] She argued that popular alarm over the new (and very small) female majorities emerging in the U.S. population (largely as a consequence of immigration restriction and declining fertility) was not warranted. Although less attentive to sex in her co-authored publications, Taeuber repeatedly called attention to how the usefulness of population records diminished when record keepers failed to differentiate individuals by sex.[58]

Although it would clearly be an exaggeration to claim that population statistics was understood as scholarly work especially appropriate for women, it had become a field of significant achievement and leadership by women. Taeuber was remembered after her death not only for making international studies more central to the field of U.S. demography but also as a "feminist and a humanist" who strove at the same time for scientific objectivity.[59] Taeuber's desire to combine feminist humanism with scientific objectivity is worth emphasizing because within a decade of her death a newer generation of female scholars, seeking to shift the analytical focus of migration studies from sex to gender, sometimes offered harsh critiques of both science and scientific objectivity. As the new women's studies of the 1970s gave way in the mid-1980s to gender analysis, many completely rejected the epistemological foundation of the women's statisticians' research on sex and migration, making it as impossible for them to see the feminization of migration as it had been for the Chicago School sociologists fifty years earlier.

The Gender Challenge

The challenge of gender analysis to the long trajectory of studies of sex and migration within the state sciences and population studies developed slowly but ultimately produced a dramatic reversal of the positive association of quantitative methodologies with female scholars. Initially, a new feminist movement in the 1960s, accompanied by growing numbers of women gaining specialized training in history, anthropology, demography, and sociology, promised a bright future of new insights about the relationship of sex and migration. Feminist scholars first studied what had been ignored in the past, notably the lives and experiences of women migrants. New research on migrant women and families—much of it drawing on population and survey data created by the Women's Chicago School—flew off the presses of American universities and journals in the 1970s and 1980s.[60] Even in work focused exclusively on migrant women, however, a new generation of women studies researchers increasingly distinguished gender from sex and sought to explain sex differences through attention to gender relations and to the exercise of power in private and public spheres. After 1985, the rise of postmodernist philosophy in the humanities and (to a lesser extent) the social sciences changed the meaning of gender analysis, initiating debates among feminist scholars and further complicating communication between migration scholars in humanities and the social sciences.

Etymologically, the concept of gender originates in classificatory grammars typical of Indo-European languages, which distinguish among masculine, feminine, and neuter nouns and pronouns. The word *moon*, for example, is masculine in some languages and feminine or neuter in others. Because linguistic gender is completely unrelated to biology, it provided a powerful example of how human behaviors completely unrelated to biological sex were wrongly understood as determined by sex difference.

Already in the 1960s, scholars across many disciplines began to substitute the term *gender* for *sex* to bring more sharply into focus and to question and criticize this type of unexamined attribution of malleable and diverse social and cultural practices to biological sex differences. Thus, the analysis of gender accompanied a general, contemporary intellectual shift away from biological, sexual, and racial modes of explanation and toward social and cultural theories of causation. The popularity of social constructionist theory contributed greatly to this early adoption of gender as an analytical category in the social sciences and in history.[61] For scholars in feminist and women's studies, the difference of sex and gender was not merely semantic. Such scholars wanted to know how and why humans transformed socially constructed notions of gender into certainties about biological difference because they wanted to change such assumptions. Anthropologists' studies showed that gender ideologies differed cross-culturally, but that many cultures understood human life to be organized around separate masculine or public realms and feminine or private realms. Many furthermore associated human culture with the public realm and the private sphere as ruled by nature and biological reproduction.[62] Their work influenced new research on immigrant women, as did other studies about how boys and girls were socialized into appropriate gender roles and employment.[63]

Such social constructionist understandings of gender did not deny the biological reality of sex difference but did reject explanations of social and cultural behavior as originating in biology. Focused mainly on internal movements, demographers of the previous generation had done little to disrupt Ravenstein's laws because the laws were applied to long-distance migrants only.[64] One result was that social scientists studying female international migrants in the 1970s confronted persistent questions about the value of their work, given the normalcy of male majorities and male decision-makers among international migrants. Anthony Leeds offered a particularly dismissive critique of new studies of female migrants as reductionist and unnecessary.[65] Forced to document the presence and significance of women migrants, feminist scholars continued to turn to statistical evidence. Still, their growing skepticism of the most abstract claims of scientific objectivity that accompanied quantitative methodologies was already palpable.[66] Feminist scholars proved particularly skeptical of what Harriet Bartlett in 1928 called "data divorced from time and place."[67] They generally preferred grounded theory and data, which often meant analysis of data either created by women or in which women's voices and agency could be heard or recognized.[68] Many feminist scholars of the 1970s also hoped to produce knowledge that would be more useful to the powerless than to the powerful.[69]

Even those women studies scholars who rejected the intellectual traditions of the state sciences did not always jettison quantitative analysis of statistical data on sex. The special issue "Women in Migration," edited in 1984 by Mirjana Morokasic for *International Migration Review* (*IMR*), the flagship journal of migration studies, included the first report of the labor statisticians on female predominance in U.S. immigration and devoted an entire section to "Census-Based Quantitative Analyses of Female Immigrants and their Labor Market Characteristics: An International Comparison." A subsequent series of interdisciplinary monographs and essay collections on immigrant women also included or referred to quantitative research.[70]

Although not focused exclusively on migrant populations, the posthumously published 1983 book *Too Many Women? The Sex Ratio Question*, by social psychologists Marcia Guttentag (1932–1977) and Paul Secord illustrated how social constructionist notions of gender changed analysis of sex composition while rejecting the expectations of policy relevance typical of the state sciences. The two authors may have been unaware of the work of Ravenstein and the female demographers studying internal migration, but they had absorbed the conventions of demography, with its interest in tracking and counting the relative numbers of men and women in human populations. At the same time, they made the feminist movement's concern with personal power central to their analysis and clearly wanted to assist feminists in understanding the origins of feminist mobilization and the demographic challenges inherent in overcoming patriarchy.[71]

Guttentag and Secord explored the impact of changing shares of male and female on the interaction of what they called dyadic or personal relationship power—which routinely favors the underrepresented sex, especially in the negotiation of marriage—with structural or societal power that is, or was, almost universally monopolized by men. When men seriously outnumber women, Guttentag and Secord argued, women use their increased dyadic power to gain marital advantages and men use structural power to control and restrict female sexuality. The result is highly traditional gender relations, which includes male-headed households, high rates of female nuptiality, high rates of marital fertility, and low rates of female labor force participation. When women outnumber men, by contrast, a sexually more permissive society, with higher rates of female employment, emerges but men so undervalue women as sexual and marital partners that their misogyny sparks female resentment and encourages feminist mobilization.

Guttentag and Secord illustrated these ideas with a series of historical and sociological case studies, some more plausible than others.[72] Several case studies posited migration as a cause of unbalanced sex composition. For example, they treated Chinese immigrants in the United States as an example of a heavily male population in which almost all women were prostitutes,[73] and contrasted the migrations of medieval France and Spain[74] to explain the development of courtly love. Their study of the migrations of European colonizers and settlers of North America[75] initiated a lively discussion of the politics of marriage formation in early America.[76] The authors also identified sharp differences in the composition of African American and Jewish American populations (both female predominant)[77] and Hispanics (male predominant, largely as a result of migration). They encouraged scholars to explore the social, demographic, and cultural consequences of such variations, including changing "sexual behaviors and sexual mores . . . patterns of marriage and divorce, childrearing conditions and practices, family stability, and certain structural aspects of society itself."[78] In addition, they focused special attention on how the fall in U.S. fertility in the 1930s and its swift rise again after the end of World War II created a marriage squeeze for baby-boom females and they traced to this "marriage squeeze" the rebirth of American feminism in the 1960s. Guttentag and Secord, in other words, suggested that changing sex ratios had consequences as well as causes.

Guttentag and Secord's work did not gain broad recognition or acceptance from feminist scholars, perhaps because the shift away from women's toward gender studies had already begun by the time it was published.[79] By the mid-1980s, feminist scholars' uncomfortable awareness about how women-centered inquiry had contributed to marginalization within the academy preceded but was strongly reinforced by the turn toward studies of culture and discourse, based on the foundation of postmodernist philosophy and radically relativist scholarly epistemologies.[80] Even those who did not accept postmodernists' assumptions came to appreciate that gender was not so much a measureable thing but a relationship between culturally constructed notions of masculine and feminine such that any change in ideas about masculinity required changes in ideas about femininity. Gender, unlike sex, was relational but also changeable and fluid. Pushing further, queer theorists soon also challenged the biological foundations of sex difference, too, denying that sex was fixed, invariable, dichotomous or even measureable.[81] Indeed, many gender scholars challenged all binaries, or dichotomies, seeing in them the origins of unequal power, hierarchy, and patriarchy. In this view, only a challenge to the binary of male and female sex can challenge male power itself.

Scholars in migration studies did not ignore these developments,[82] but they had little impact on scholars working with quantitative methodologies. Without binary, dichotomous, or bivariate categories of data—notably of male and female sex—quantitative and statistical study of migration seemed impossible. Indeed, feminist scholars since Taeuber generally insisted that the creation of data on sex was necessary if scholars are to study the lives of women as well as men. In a review of scholarship on gender and migration, Katharine Donato and her colleagues also see data distinguishing male from female as the foundation for gender analysis using quantitative methods.[83]

Exacerbating this epistemological divergence were other closely related methodological concerns. Beginning in the 1970s and 1980s, increasing numbers of feminist scholars began to reject quantitative methods as hierarchical, female-unfriendly, or even malestream tools of analysis, approvingly citing African American poet Audre Lorde's trenchant observation that "The master's tools will never dismantle the master's house."[84] In this formulation, quantitative methods and the state sciences are the master's tools; the master's house is patriarchy. This kind of thinking suggests but rarely states outright that quantitative work—so long an arena of female accomplishment—is instead a masculine methodology. By the 1990s, feminist scholars in gender studies increasingly privileged qualitative methodologies while, for their part, some quantitative social scientists characterized gender analysis as tainted by the radical relativity of postmodernist philosophers.[85] As a result, according to Sara Curran and her colleagues, gender is a key constituting factor in only a minority of recent sociological migration studies; other scholars agree.[86]

Despite the so-called linguistic turn, the methods of postmodernist literary scholars have never completely dominated newer studies of gender and migration. While they certainly devote greater attention to subjectivity, to gender relations, and to masculinity and femininity, and certainly employ a wider range and mixture of methodologies, newer studies rarely question the material reality of a human body—that of the migrants—that move from one place to another. In very few studies of gender do scholars treat the migrant—as was sometimes the case in the humanities—as a disembodied "text" to be interpreted independent of social or historical context. Attention to the fluidity of gender certainly empower Patricia Pessar and Sherri Grasmuck to challenge scholarship organized around the male migrant and to suggest that complex gender dynamics within families, kin groups, and households are as important in shaping migration decisions and trajectories as the more frequently studied search of male employment in global labor markets.[87] Divisions of labor within families determine which persons migrated without jeopardizing the functions and needs of the household. Both in Europe and in the United States, new studies seek to demonstrate how gender mattered in migration theory, decisions to move, work, or reproduce, and in citizenship, welfare, and politics.[88] Depending on social and economic resources, young men may have more or fewer incentives to migrate than young women; access to and rates of naturalization may also differ by gender, as well as the forms of political activity open to or undertaken by male or female migrants.

For their part, demographers, population scientists, and economists interested in migration sometimes wrestle with and sometimes try to ignore the linguistic turn. Russell Menard concludes simply that "the notion of a postmodern demography is an oxymoron."[89] Despite such pessimism, feminist demographers sometimes seek to bring into their social science discipline some insights from postmodernist understandings of gender more common in the humanities, when studying the relationship of cultural understandings to fertility.[90] Some social science journals publish occasional quantitative studies of migrant women,[91] but quantitative studies in history have almost completely disappeared.[92]

As gender theorists mounted their challenge to studies of dichotomous sex, feminist demographers working outside universities in governmental and international organizations continued to follow the paths of their own discipline and to build on the example of earlier feminist demographers. At the United Nations, feminist demographers called for better recording of migrant sex and more analysis of women migrants. As they increasingly sought—and found—new data, they also created the foundation for the discovery of the feminization of migration by scholars who still used quantitative methods and statistical data, even as fewer and fewer scholars in gender studies did so.

Naming the Feminization of Migration

Among the newer generation of feminist demographers, none did as much as Hania Zlotnik to facilitate the discussion of the feminization of migration. By the time she retired as the first woman director of the UN Population Division in 2012, the feminization of migration had become a buzz word in scholarly discussions. The United Nations, along with many other international and nongovernmental organizations (NGOs), were also being asked to solve problems that seemed to snap into focus after scholars had identified the feminization of migration and acknowledged—statistically and demographically—the presence of women. Still, as Eldridge noticed in 1947, that awareness could also spark popular alarm. In this case, concern focused on the victimization of women migrants as exploited domestic workers and as trafficked victims of a global sex industry.

Zlotnik studied mathematics in Mexico before completing a 1977 Ph.D. in demography at Princeton. In a recent interview,[93] she expresses her early frustrations that the ILO (the international agency that had initiated the collection of data on migration in the 1920s) collected data in which women migrants remained largely invisible. At the time, the ILO was concerned mainly with the problems of male labor migrants in Europe. Many of Zlotnik's generation shared that perception: Mirjana Morokvasic expressed her own frustration in titling her important early publication, "Birds of Passage [that is, labor migrants] are also Women."[94] A few years later, with more knowledge acquired as a UN insider, Zlotnik acknowledged that both the ILO and the UN had been working hard to correct problems in the collection of migration data. Still, she summed up her reading of decades of such work with the conclusion that "the crusade to achieve greater homogeneity in the concepts underlying flow statistics on international migration was started at least 55 years ago, but despite some encouraging developments, it is unlikely that homogeneity will be achieved during the rest of this century."[95]

As an employee of the UN Population Division after 1982, Zlotnik and like-minded demographers spearheaded a movement to analyze sex and migration based not on ILO data but on stock or census data that the UN had begun to compile in the 1950s. By using new data, the demographers hoped, the world could gain a clearer understanding of sex and migration because almost all censuses differentiated by sex and noted place of birth, allowing researchers to identify "persons living outside their country of birth" as migrants. In rapid succession, the UN Statistical Office issued new recommendations on how national censuses should collect data on the sex of persons born abroad, and specialists in both Europe and Asia tackled the data collection problems specific to migrations in their regions.[96]

By 1986, the UN Department of International Economic and Social Affairs (through its Population Division) had surveyed the availability of national data sources (again, mainly census reports but also population registration systems) and proposed methods to estimate international migration. The UN Population Division was itself busily engaged in analysis of this data.[97] At the start of the next decade, Zlotnik wrote that "women constituted 48 percent of all persons enumerated outside their country of birth at some point during 1970–1987," but added (undoubtedly after reading Houstoun) that "in terms of flows, until the early 1980s women had predominated over men among permanent immigrants admitted by the United States."[98] In 1990, the UN Secretariat sponsored an Expert Group meeting on International Policies and the Status of Female Migrants in which Zlotnik was a prominent participant, well positioned to spread the word about the importance of women among international migrants counted in census data.[99]

Then, in 1993, as indicated in the introduction to this volume, Stephen Castles and Mark Miller published the first edition of their influential and widely read *Age of Migration*. Well aware of the UN initiatives, they made the feminization of migration, along with the ubiquity and rising rates of migration in every region of the world, a signal characteristic of the new global age they proclaim. Their book introduced the feminization of migration to a readership well beyond university graduate seminars, sparking discussions that have continued to the present. The book also inevitably suggests that feminization is a recent development, closely linked to new forms of global integration.

What is most striking about the spreading attention to feminization is that it occurred only after the UN demographers chose to estimate, model, and begin to publish migrant population characteristics using census data. Only then could social scientists, accustomed to working with such data, see and name the feminization of migration. Yet as we discovered in the course of our research, and as we show in the chapters that follow, other data had long existed and pointed toward the rising presence of women among international migrants. For example, a 1953 compilation of ILO data that had thoroughly documented feminization had been almost totally ignored, even after being advertised in sociology, statistics, and demography journals in 1954 and 1955. Social scientists did not use it, and its first scholarly citation did not appear for forty years, in a study of modern slavery written by an historian.[100] That statisticians had been using census data to study sex and migration since the days of Ravenstein, and that most studies of internal migration by feminist demographers in the interwar years were also based on census data, were powerful influences on Zlotnik and colleagues. The use of new data made feminization itself seem a new development.

Discussion of the feminization of migration has had mixed consequences. On the positive side, it has helped make gender dynamics of migration, understood as shaped by gender relations and ideology rather than by sex, a somewhat more central concern of migration scholars working with quantitative methods. At the same time, it meets feminist theorists' call for extending gender analysis beyond the study of local, family, or household movements to all spatial scales, including the global, an approach that Pessar and Mahler call gendered geographies of power.[101] In small ways, it also encourages scholars of migration to rethink the causes of male and female migration and the composition of different types of migrations.

The discovery of the feminization of migration also encourages greater attention to women as autonomous labor migrants, especially as workers doing paid, reproductive work as nannies, caregivers, and domestic servants.[102] Such research has begun to call into question the still-powerful association of individual labor migration with masculinity.[103] Scholars now also emphasize the high proportions of women and children in refugee migrations.[104]

Positively, too, scholars have begun to explain the causes of feminization by examining both emigration and immigration. In 1984, U.S. labor statisticians suggested that feminization was a consequence of U.S. immigration restriction, reduced volumes of immigration, and economic crisis.[105] Using the same evidence, Gabaccia finds that early U.S. restrictions— imposed, for example, on the Chinese and Japanese—resulted in significantly higher proportions female among Japanese than Chinese migrants (discussed further in chapter 4).[106] Working with Immigration and Naturalization Service (INS) data, Donato finds that heavily female recent migrations to the United States are from countries with major U.S. military bases, suggesting that family formation and family unification—once privileged by U.S. rules for allotting scarce visas—offer a powerful explanation for feminization.[107] Comparing Zambia and the Philippines, Maria Floro and Kendall Schaefer follow Sassen-Koob in attributing the feminization of migration to increasing demand for care and service workers, as does Kofman.[108] In addition, Erin Hofmann and Cynthia Buckley suggest that the rising prevalence of divorce, lack of local economic opportunities, and the importance of human capital were the initial motivators for women's outmigration from postsocialist Georgia.[109]

Recent scholarship on female migrants focuses considerably more attention on the most exploited and vulnerable of female migrants rather than on the majority of women who are well educated, high- and low-skilled workers, or traveling to unify families. This focus is evident in the 2006 UN report; its analysis of migrant gender compositions worldwide provided a springboard to two chapters titled "Trafficking in Women and the Exploitation of Domestic Servants" and "Refugee Women and Asylum Seekers." In addition, although domestic violence, HIV/AIDS, genital cutting, honor crimes, and violence against women are not limited to migrant populations, these themes also receive ample coverage. References to the feminization of migration often frame studies of women and girl trafficking.[110] Indeed, although no one has ever suggested that more than a small minority of migrant women are trafficked, about one-third of scholarly articles appearing after 1983 and addressing the feminization of migration focus exclusively on the sexual trafficking of migrants or on women working in the sex industry. In addition, studies of labor exploitation of largely female domestic servants and health-care workers often reference the feminization of migration.[111] Rarely do authors present data on how common or uncommon such labor exploitation is. Intentionally or not, and without recourse to data, such studies suggest that the feminization of migration has been largely driven by or resulted in the exploitation of women migrants. One important exception is Rhacel Parreñas, who challenges this perspective by describing how Filipina hostesses in Japan are working women who migrate by choice and are not coerced into prostitution, though they remain vulnerable due to the imposition of regulation by nation-states.[112]

Scholars have now begun to describe how more popular and journalistic writings about female migration also encourage a discourse of popular alarm over rising levels of female migration.[113] Focusing largely on Europe, Marlou Schrover concludes that in popular discourse, "migrant men are seen as causing problems and migrant women as having them."[114] Such negative attention to women's problems during periods of massive

migrants as 'problems'

migration are by no means new; neither is the tendency to understand migration as threatening women morally. In the nineteenth century, awareness of male majorities among migrants raised questions about women's moral behavior when they were left behind in sending societies,[115] and evidence of even relatively small shares of women among migrants fueled concerns about a white slave trade operated by exploitative migrant male procurers.[116]

Advocates for migrant women and scholars in gender studies sometimes also build their arguments for policy interventions around the vulnerability of contemporary female migrants. Thus Glenda Labadie-Johnson notes, "Until recently governments and international fora have done very little to address . . . the issues raised" by the feminization of migration.[117] In the course of our own research, we repeatedly encountered evidence that awareness of the feminization of migration was provoking popular alarm. In March 2010, we received an e-mail invitation to participate in a virtual briefing (by telephone) on "Gender, Race, and Migration," organized by representatives of advocacy groups such as Women Watch Africa, Domestic Workers United, Global Fund for Women, and Priority Africa Network. The invitation began by citing the 2006 UN report but then asserted, "What is particularly alarming is the increase in the number of women who are now leaving their homes in higher numbers than ever before. Traditionally," the invitation continued, "men had left home and sent remittances back home to women, children and the elderly who stayed put on the land carrying on traditions, farming lands, and caring for communities. Women are now almost equal to men in leaving their homes seeking employment in largely service industries." It concluded, "the sex industry and trafficking of women are also contributing to increased migration"—an argument never made in the 2006 UN report.[118] Most recently, a professor of European immigration law responded to a scholarly presentation of our finding (that gender balance and not feminization was the most important trend in the present moment) with a blunt request for an assessment of whether feminization of migration was good or bad for women. He was quite clear in enunciating his fear that exploitation of trafficked women and of domestic and sex workers had produced what we instead describe as gender balance and a kind of demographic normalcy in migrant populations. One goal of this book is to extricate the study of gender and migration from such popular discourses of alarm.

Conclusion

By focusing on how migrations became relatively more female and relatively less male, new scholarship on the feminization of migration has begun to reverse the sharp divergence of quantitative studies of migration and gender studies that emerged in the 1980s. Numbers, too, can reveal and help scholars understand the fluidity of gender ideology and gender relations, and even those in history and the humanities seem more willing to learn the language of statistics. In 1994, a high-profile historian proclaimed the arrival in migration studies of a post-structuralist structuralism that incorporates the insights of both structuralism and its critics.[119] The past decade has seen both rising enthusiasm for mixed methodologies and a growing awareness of how qualitative and quantitative research produce perspectival but useful and sometimes complementary knowledge about gender.[120] Our book appears then as the methodological chasm separating gender studies and quantitative social science has narrowed somewhat.

Using an eclectic array of methods from diverse disciplines, we seek to demonstrate that empirical evidence and systematic quantitative analysis of bivariate data on sex reveals the fluidity and relationality of gender as it is constructed in both sending and receiving societies, assisting scholars to move beyond the idea that the feminization of migration is new or unprecedented. In the next chapter, we focus specifically on key concepts such as the difference between sex ratios and gender composition, and the origins, creation, and uses of flow and stock data. We use these data to present a four-century survey of how gender ideologies and gender relations created differing kinds of migrations with significantly different balances of male and female migrants. For readers in both the social sciences and humanistic gender studies, a thorough understanding of how evidence is produced is an important first step toward analysis and interpretation.

This approach, we believe, can both assist scholars in the humanities in understanding the language of statistics and social scientists in understanding the causes and consequences of global and regional shifts in migrant gender composition that have produced gender balance. Thus we draw insights from the humanities by calling attention to the constructed nature of both statistical data and the categories used to measure the relative numbers of male and female migrants, and from the social sciences by remaining resolutely and unapologetically empirical in our quantitative analysis of statistical data on binary sex. As we show in subsequent chapters, an analysis of variations in the gender composition of migrant populations reveals the importance of understanding both their causes and consequences.

═ Chapter 2 ═

Analyzing Migrant Gender
Composition with Statistical
Data on Sex

The sex ratio is the most widely used analytical category for the study of the relative numbers of males and females in populations.[1] Yet recent studies of the feminization of migration—including the 1984 and 2006 statistical studies previously discussed—do not measure the relative numbers of male and female migrants this way. Instead, they compare the percentage female among migrants over time and space. In this book, we too focus on the percentage female among migrants, and we analyze migrant gender composition rather than sex composition to explore how gender ideology and gender relations influenced migration over four centuries of human history.

One of the most important contributions of social constructivist gender studies for scholars working with quantitative methods has been its attention to how and by whom data are created, for what purposes, and how key concepts have been operationalized. As chapter 1 reveals, new data figured prominently in the discovery of the feminization of migration. This chapter examines the creation of data and analytical categories that have been central to quantitative analyses of sex, gender, and migration. It also provides an explanation for the choices—of data, categories, and measures—that structure our analysis in the chapters that follow. Acknowledging the historical construction of data, categories, and measures opens them to interpretation, critique, and revision. Such interpretation, critique, and revision are essential if gender analysis is to be combined effectively with quantitative analysis of migration.

This chapter begins with an examination of the history of data created about mobile people and their (binary) sex. It examines the use and operationalization of the sex ratio for the study of variations in the numbers of males and females in human populations, and explains why we measure migrant gender composition rather than the migrant sex ratio. It also discusses variations in gender composition—including variations labeled as feminization—and points toward data and methods, as well as diverse gender relations in sending or receiving societies, as factors influencing variations in migrant gender composition. Understanding the extent of these variations is a necessary step toward establishing a typology of gender composition that is just as valid for the analysis of seventeenth-century as twenty-first-century migrations and as useful for analyzing individual flow data as household level stock data. That typology, in turn, allows scholars to begin to consider a working definition for a key process— feminization—that has remained largely undefined by almost all scholars who have used it to frame their work.

Creating Data on Mobile People and Their Sex

As long as states have existed, they have counted their subjects and citizens. Ancient civilizations as diverse as the Babylonians, Chinese, Greeks, and Romans counted their subjects to tax them, to collect and store their grain, or to recruit them as soldiers or laborers.[2] Historically, both religious institutions and states chose, at times, to register births, marriages, deaths, and households to extract services or funds, or to foster control over and involvement in the most intimate aspects of the lives of their subjects.[3] The two often came into conflict as state power grew.[4] Because they often evaded enumeration and resisted state demands on them, people on the move seemed suspicious to agrarian societies that imagined themselves as sedentary.

State enumerations and registrations of population events such as births, marriages, and deaths created the statistical data used by the earliest state scientists. In first describing a ruler's subjects as a population, Bacon referred metaphorically to rulers as herders of men, leading to descriptions of human populations as the rulers' stock, a usage that became ubiquitous in population studies during the nineteenth century.[5] When modern states began taking regular census counts of populations in the eighteenth century,[6] statists called the information stock data.

Neither the registration of vital events nor regular census enumerations of populations automatically created knowledge about migrants. Yet in Britain, Bacon lived in a society where his neighbors shifted residence in response to political turmoil, the mobilization of armies, disease, and revolution.[7] In 1609, he recommended that Britain encourage emigration to the Americas, allowing it to create "a double community, in the avoidance of people here, and in making use of them there."[8] However, migration could be enumerated in censuses only when each individual's current residence and place of birth were both recorded. The United States began including such information for natives and aliens only in 1850, sixty years after its first census; Britain, which began recording birthplaces for natives in 1841, and most other nations lagged behind.

Even when census-takers began recording birthplaces, they counted only those migrant individuals who had remained abroad until the time of the next census. Those who had returned home or moved on to another country were not counted. Stock data thus creates knowledge mainly about longer-term migrants in receiving regions rather than their shorter-term counterparts. Nor are emigrants usually identified in census listings of sending areas. Censuses also cannot capture moves made or paths taken by individuals between the time of their birth and their enumeration. And because states generally take censuses only every ten years, stock data provide no simple measure of migration volumes. Each census population thus creates a complex demographic composite that reflects intercensal births and deaths as well as migrant exits and entries.[9] Yet, as chapter 1 shows, the UN's use of a new category of mobile persons living outside the country of their birth was nevertheless generally heralded as a significant improvement in data on international migration, largely because almost all nation-states around the world collect and report census data.

Finally, stock data inevitably reflects differing national assumptions about who belongs and who is instead an outsider.[10] For example, the United States enumerates the foreign birthplace even of individuals who have naturalized and acquired U.S. citizenship (and at times it has also noted the foreign birthplaces of the parents of each native-born citizen, too). That information would not appear in Germany's records, which take the form of elaborate and continuous residential registration systems rather than periodic censuses. In that country, which does not grant birthright citizenship, the category of alien includes both those born abroad and their children born in Germany (until they naturalize in later life) because these children at birth inherit their foreign juridical status from their parents.[11] Israel offers yet another example; the overwhelming majority of its foreign-born population are immigrants who are Jewish or have Jewish ancestry or family ties. Excluded from its census counts of the foreign born are all noncitizen foreign-born temporary workers.[12]

Historically, both merchants providing transportation services and states concerned with the size of their populations have had special incentives to instead enumerate people on the move. It was no easy task. Of all population components of interest to demographers, migration is the most difficult to enumerate.[13] Unlike birth or death, migration is not a one-time or even permanent change in individual status. A person may move many times, in many directions, for shorter or longer periods, over shorter or longer distances. A migrant may become sedentary for long periods before suddenly moving again. Both natives and foreigners can leave a country or return to it. States therefore must invest considerable resources to create distinctive spaces, usually along borders and in ports or transportation hubs, where they can control movement sufficiently to enable enumeration. Early modern Spain required all leaving for its New World colonies to depart from a single city, Seville.[14] Whether on the west coast of Africa in the seventeenth and eighteenth centuries, in nineteenth-century Macao or Bremerhaven, or at New York's Castle Garden and Ellis Island, Canada's Grosse Isle, or San Francisco's Angel Island, states, merchants, and purveyors of transportation services built slave barracoons, coolie barracks, customs offices, and emigrant or immigrant processing centers to facilitate enumeration.[15] Today, most airports worldwide have become points of entry, but the goal of controlling and enumerating migrants remains unchanged. Migrants have often had strong incentives to avoid enumeration, and record-keeping systems rarely capture migrant illegality or irregularity.

Enumerations produced in such sites are called flow data. E.G. Ravenstein was one of the first to refer to migration as a flow, and since his lifetime scholars have often commented on the ubiquity of water metaphors (waves, streams, floods) in descriptions of migration.[16] Unlike stock data, flow data counts and sometimes also lists the characteristics of individual bodies on the move. Published compilations of flow data typically aggregate the numbers of border crossers for a single year. Annual numbers of migrants counted as entering or exiting are usually considerably smaller than those of foreigners or aliens enumerated in any national census. Furthermore, states often choose to count people moving in only one direction across their borders (either exiting as emigrants, for example, or entering as immigrants). Flow data are thus very sensitive temporally, making them useful for historical analysis, but individual countries differ in how they collect these data and how they define migrants. Flow data also may exaggerate the total numbers of persons on the move, especially when movements are temporary, circular, repeated, or multidirectional. States may seek to distinguish between permanent and temporary moves, when even migrants themselves may not be able to assess their intentions at the moment they cross a border.

Aware of how immigration could build a new nation of Europeans who chose its democratic form of government, the United States began compiling migration flow data in 1820,[17] well before it began asking residents about their birthplaces—a change in census-taking that first facilitated attention to internal migrations (to the frontier but also to cities). Both forms of migration were soon closely associated with American exceptionalism.[18] A century later, the League of Nation's International Labour Organization compiled flow data that roughly resembled the U.S. series but was very aware of the uneven and idiosyncratic nature of these data collected in other countries.[19] The categories used in compiling flow data varied enormously from country to country, as did definitions of emigrants and immigrants; national states also differed in what, if any, individual migrant characteristics they recorded. As chapter 1 suggests, such discontent motivated the United Nations to shift to using stock data in the 1970s and 1980s.

This book analyzes the sex of migrants as recorded in both stock and flow data. Scholars in gender studies have particularly critiqued quantitative methods' dependence on such binary data on sex. But a careful focus on how data on sex was created suggests that statistics reflect gender relations and as such are subject to interpretation. Sex, as an analytical category, originated, as the *Oxford English Dictionary* notes, in the old French word for genitals. In fact, the largely male record-keepers who created stock and flow data rarely observed migrants' sex. Slave traders were almost alone in observing unclothed migrants, because unfortunate African captives were often "exposed naked to public view, and sold like a herd of cattle."[20] At Ellis Island, medical examinations focused more on the eyes and lungs than the genitals of entering immigrants. Census-takers have never resembled priests inspecting infant boys and girls to enumerate them or medical doctors listing causes of death as they examined unclothed corpses. On the contrary, most record-keepers have allowed migrants and foreigners to attribute sex to themselves. Notations of male or female reflected either migrants' self-ascription or record-keepers' best guesses of sex to persons engaged in fulfilling or rejecting culturally determined expectations of correct gender behavior, clothing, or performance. Record-keepers thus transformed their own notions of gender into sex as a fixed, dichotomous, and biological characteristic.

Once recorded as sex, flow and stock data made possible the invention and measurement of sex ratios. Acknowledging how gender constructed data on sex suggests that the construction of the sex ratio, too, deserves further scrutiny.

Measuring, Analyzing, and Critiquing the Sex Ratio

The first known use of the term *sex ratio* for measuring human populations was by John Graunt in 1662, who wanted to understand why populations grew or declined. By the time he wrote his book, *Natural and Political Observations Made Upon the Bills of Mortality,*[21] Graunt had started counting the numbers of boys and girls among newborns. As theologians, mathematicians, physicians, and biologists elsewhere duplicated Graunt's methods and interests, they discovered that births of boy babies routinely outnumbered births of girl babies. By the middle of the nineteenth century, statisticians had tracked sex ratios across the life course using registers of mortality. They discovered that males died at higher rates through adolescence and old age, and that women therefore outnumbered men from middle to old age. By the nineteenth century, state scientists began drawing national population pyramids or age-sex pyramids to track population composition over time.[22] Therefore, as suggested in the introduction, the relationship of age and gender remains central to the analysis of any population's gender composition.

Whether they studied animal, plant, or human sex ratios, statisticians seemed unable to agree on a standardized way to measure them arithmetically. Graunt had observed that in one rural parish, "There were born 15 *Females* for 16 *Males*," whereas in London there were "13 for 14." In 1741, Johann Süssmilch, who also believed the sex ratio to be an expression of God's divine will, reported that "For every 1000 baby girls born, there are 1050 boys."[23] Others expressed the balance of male and female as a ratio at birth of 105 boys to 100 girls or ratios such as 22:23 or 16:15.[24] Still others expressed the sex ratio by dividing the numbers of males by the numbers of females and multiplying by one thousand. In all cases, observers created an arithmetic relationship between the two sexes. Over time, individual states settled on particular measures but these continued to differ cross-nationally.

Demographers today continue to differ somewhat in how they measure the relative numbers of males and females in a population. A book that some demographers call "their Bible" describes several commonly used measures.[25] The first is the percentage of males (or females) in the population, which is called "the masculinity proportion or femininity proportion." The second is the sex ratio, measured either as a masculinity ratio or a femininity ratio of the number of one sex per hundred of the other sex. The third is also a proportion but of the "excess or deficit of males" (or occasionally females) to the total population.[26] The authors note a preference for the masculinity ratio in technical discussions, but offer no explanation for that preference. They also acknowledge that some nations have preferred other measures, including a femininity ratio. India, for example—a country that has historically expressed concerns about high mortality among infants, girls, and women—expresses the sex ratio as the number of females per thousand males. Nor has the sex ratio itself lacked critics. For example, Éric Brian and Marie Jaisson suggest that sex ratios are "ill-founded on the mathematical level," and might better be expressed "in terms of 105 boys out of 205 births—51.2 percent—or its complement of 100 girls out of the same total, which is 48.8 percent."[27] Without agreement on how to measure the sex ratio arithmetically, sex ratios cannot easily be compared across populations—clearly a necessity for comparative or global studies.

One small way that quantitative studies of migration have responded to the challenge of gender studies has been to question both the hegemony of the sex ratio as an analytical category and its measurement as a masculinity ratio. Marion Houstoun and her colleagues analyzed the migration sex differential, but most studies since discuss the gender differential.[28] In addition, although Donato in 1992 examined the sex composition among migrants, she and her coauthors in subsequent publications instead focus on gender composition.[29] Donna Gabaccia examined sex ratios in 1996 but fifteen years later argues for analyzing gender ratios.[30] These changes in terminology reflect awareness that gender relations and not sex determine the relative numbers of male and female migrants.

Those who study migrant gender composition also measure it as a percentage female or femininity proportion—that is, the number of women in relation to the total population, and not in relation to the number of men. We too prefer this measure; not only is it analogous to comparable measures of the distribution of class, socioeconomic status, religion, race and ethnicity in other populations, it is also more easily grasped by scholars without any specialized training in statistics. Unlike sex ratios, proportions expressed as percentages are also uniform across cultures. Throughout this book, we therefore explore variations in migrant gender composition using the percentage female rather than analyzing migrant sex ratios measured by a masculinity ratio.

Understanding Variation in Migrant Gender Composition

To identify how gender relations produce variations in migrant gender composition, we acknowledge that many factors, and not just gender, may affect migrant gender composition. Other factors to be considered include the size of populations analyzed, the spatial scales of analysis pursued, the age structures of populations studied, and the type of data analyzed.

It is clear that the size of the migrant populations analyzed affects variations in gender composition across time and space. At the global level, variation in proportions female among foreign stock after 1960 was just 3 percentage points. In the UN stock data that Zlotnik discusses, the gender composition of those living outside the country of their birth varied more across macro-regions—from a low of 40.6 percent female (among foreigners living in sub-Saharan Africa in 1960) to a high of 52.6 percent female (among immigrants living in North America in 1980) or variation of 12 percentage points.[31] Examining national-level stock micro-data, Donato and Amada Armenta document still greater variation. For the United States, migrant gender composition varied over time from a low of 38 percent to a high of 68 percent female (a range of 30 percentage points); for foreigners living in South Africa gender composition by country of origin varied from 28 to 42 percent female (a range of 14 percentage points).[32] In their analysis of historical flow data, Donna Gabaccia and Elizabeth Zanoni show that in some years, national-level flow data described women and girls constituting less than 10 percent of emigrants, whereas in national-level data on immigration, they were more than two-thirds—a spread of more than 50 percentage points.[33] In historical flow data, too, the degree of variation—though greater than in stock data—diminished at macro-regional and global levels.

Population size generally increases with spatial scales, and larger populations vary less across time in their gender composition than smaller populations do. Aggregated annual counts of male and female border crossers or in foreign-born populations can thus be expected to exhibit the smallest variations at the global level simply because these are the largest possible populations measured by either type of data. Variations in gender composition across large world regions exhibit larger variations than global variations, and the largest variations are in analyses of national or subnational level data. Similarly, because national flow data for any year describes a much smaller population than census data that compile the results of many years of entry, variations across time or space in gender composition as measured in flow data also predictably surpass (often considerably) variations measured in stock data.

Demographers' very long-term study of population sex ratios (typically as measured with stock data) has also produced a clear understanding of predictable variations in gender composition associated with the changing age structure of a population.[34] Populations with many young people always have relatively more males, and those with many old people have relatively more females. Thus, according to Swanson, Siegel, and Shryock, "national sex ratios tend to fall in the narrow range from about 95:102, barring special circumstances, such as a history of heavy war losses or heavy immigration. National sex ratios outside the range of 90:105 are to be viewed as extreme."[35] Sex ratios of 95:102 are the equivalent of a population that is 49.5:51.2 percent female; the extreme sex ratios of 90:105 correspond to a gender composition that is 48.8:52.6 percent female. Demographers have also developed a statistical method, *age standardization,* to control for the impact of differential mortality in aging cohorts on changes in intercensal gender composition. Demographers have used age standardization to interpret the gender composition of internal migrations for at least fifty years but students of international migrations have done so only occasionally.[36]

Had Ravenstein considered the predictable variations in gender composition caused by age distribution, he might not have proclaimed with such certainty the relation of sex, distance, and migration he labeled as a law. Using full-count micro-data for the 1881 U.K. Census, demographic historians have found that age standardization eliminated almost all the sex differences in mobility that Ravenstein claimed to have observed.[37] Only among unmarried adolescents and the very old were women in fact more mobile than men. The Irish anomaly among long-distance migrants also probably reflected the fact that the Irish were the oldest of Great Britain's long-distance migrants, having begun entering Britain in the eighteenth century or earlier.[38] This meant that older people were presumably well represented in the Irish migrant population by the 1870s: if elderly Irish women outnumbered elderly Irish men—as they almost certainly did—then females could have formed a majority of the total Irish migrant population even if all earlier migrants from Ireland had arrived as young people traveling in gender-balanced or even male-predominant groups. On this point, it is important to note that flow data, unlike stock data, captures gender at the moment of migration and is thus not influenced by the impact of later mortality among migrants.

Without taking the age composition of migrant populations into account, scholars working with stock data cannot accurately measure feminization. Measures of feminization similar to figure I.1 may reflect rising proportions female among migrants. But they may also reflect other changes in population, such as the aging of the migrant proportion. With no access to individual-level stock data, the UN statisticians of the 1990s could not use age standardization to control for the impact of aging on migrant gender composition. (In chapter 6, we offer just such an analysis.)

As we show in the chapters ahead, migrant gender composition varies considerably over time, too, and some of the variations can be described as masculinization or feminization. For example, many empirical studies suggest that men are culturally defined risk-takers and most likely to migrate first.[39] Over time, the heavily male migrations that ensue often become more gender balanced because fiancées, wives, and children follow departed men and migration chains or networks develop.[40] Feminization in such cases is the result of migrant-motivated family unifications, or what scholars sometimes call the maturation of migration chains. We see such migration chains, and their accompanying feminization, as indicators that migrants are shifting the site of reproduction of both their families and ways of life from sending to receiving societies through family or marriage migrations. Labor markets also vary in their demand for labor and that demand is typically segmented by gendered understandings of appropriate male and female expectations.

Variations in migrant gender composition are also inherently temporal. Feminization often refers to increases over time in the percentage female, and masculinization to decreases over time in percentage female. Unfortunately, no scholar has ever defined feminization as an increase in 2, 10, or 20 percentage points, nor has any scholar determined whether feminization should be understood as an increase occurring over five, ten, or twenty years. We argue that twentieth-century feminization resulted in the achievement of gender-balanced migrant populations but others might understand feminization to have occurred only when female majorities resulted from increases in women's share among migrants.

Rather than focus on change in gender composition over time, the late twentieth-century discovery of the feminization of migration has most often rested on an implicit and diachronic—but only rarely empirically documented—assumption that past migrations had male majorities and that present-day migrations are more gender balanced or have female majorities. Rarely is the past assigned a specific date range. When exactly was the past to which scholars contrast the feminized international migrations after 1960? Was it in 1650, 1780, or 1890? Did the past encompass all those dates or all the dates in between them? These are important questions for us to address and they should be of interest to more than historians.[41] One example illustrates why this is so. If migrant gender composition in 2005 is compared with 1960, then the feminization of migrations occurring over the intervening forty-five years was— as Zlotnik argues—a relatively modest increase of 2.9 percentage points.[42] If 2005 is compared instead with 1900 or 1910, feminization appears far more dramatic because—as the next chapters demonstrate—migrations around 1900 included lower percentages female than either the migrations that preceded or followed them. In fact, however, a comparison of 2005 with 1910 cannot easily be made, at least at the global level, because no published compilation of global stock data for the gender composition of persons living outside the country of their birth in 1910 exists.

Those scholars who are most explicit and careful in their comparisons of past and present contrast contemporary, feminized migrations to the migrations occurring during the decades surrounding the year 1900.[43] In doing so, they choose a moment in time when male predominance among migrants was at its peak. Although such comparisons of past and present are useful for many purposes, they do not explain feminization, masculinization, or other population dynamics over time.[44] Until questions about migrant gender composition are posed over a longer history and larger geography, it will be impossible to determine when—or why—the twentieth-century global shift toward gender balance began, how unprecedented or unusual it was, and what consequences it may have had. Therefore, we have good reason to present some of our analysis in a form that Nancy Foner has called "then to now."[45] This type of longitudinal or diachronic analysis is, for historians, the most common way of studying the past, even if most historical studies do not extend their analysis to the present.

Analysis of the past and change over time is not uncommon in demography. Although variations of age and sex in national population pyramids cannot easily be aggregated to the global level or tracked over very long periods, demographers have devoted considerable energy to identifying progressive, long-term, and unidirectional temporal variations in population structures labeled as transitions or—sometimes—as a single demographic transition.[46] They have particularly focused on the shift from an earlier demographic regime characterized by high-fertility and high mortality to a modern regime of low fertility and low mortality.[47] They have attended to the description and analysis of a long-term fertility transition but have also sometimes discussed a mortality transition.[48] They also debate the possibility that the developing countries of the late twentieth and twenty-first century are undergoing the same kind of transition as countries that industrialized and urbanized more than a century ago. Some demographers suggest that the wealthiest countries are now experiencing a second demographic transition—to such low fertility rates that population declines must—in the absence of migration—be anticipated.[49]

Only recently have scholars interested in migration begun to explore whether and how temporal variations in migration rates may relate to such demographic transitions. A few scholars link the feminization of particular occupations to a second demographic transition,[50] calling attention to how sinking fertility and aging populations in wealthy countries contribute to the feminization of Third World labor that Saskia Sassen-Koob first noted.[51] Certainly, the possibility that the shift toward migrant gender balance is related to other long-term transitions seems worthy of exploration.

Given the many possible sources of variation in migrant gender composition, the development of a clear definition of feminization as a temporal phenomenon posed complex problems for our analysis. Both flow data and stock data measures of variations of migrant gender composition are as subject to diverse interpretation as any other measures. In the section that follows, we develop a typology briefly described in the introduction and based on the analysis we present in chapters 3 through 7, which examine variations of migrant gender composition over time and a variety of spatial scales. We also suggest a number of somewhat differing ways of defining feminization, including a definition based mainly on our typology.

Defining Feminization: A Typology of Migrant Gender Composition

By considering predictable sources of variation, we have developed a typology of gender composition that distinguishes between predictable demographic variations and other increases or decreases in the percentage female. Although they often use the same terms to describe findings about the gender composition of immigrants, specialists in different disciplines reach different conclusions about the variations in gender composition they observe. For example, when sociologists and historians compare present-day migrations with those occurring a century ago, historians typically emphasize continuities or similarities. Sociologists instead often describe the present as a unique product of sharp and recent rupture from the past.[52] We attempt to take such disciplinary differences into account with the goal of creating a typology that is flexible and that can help us identify the most significant variations in migrant gender composition across time and spatial scales.

Prior studies that compare past and present suggest a very simple typology composed of only two categories—historical male-dominant and contemporary balanced or female-dominant migrations. Feminization is a shift from the first category to the second and masculinization, which is almost never discussed, a shift from the second to the first. Such a simple typology largely ignores the predictable sources of variation in gender composition caused by changing age structure, the type of data used, or the size of the population studied. It also lacks the necessary complexity to convey how variations reflect diversity in gender relations and in gender ideology.

Based on our distinction between predictable demographic variations in gender composition and variations that result from gender dynamics and ideology, we present a typology that allows comparisons of migrations with male and female majorities but labels them as male predominant and female predominant rather than male or female dominant. (As we note briefly in the introduction, dominant describes a political not an arithmetic relation; it is defined by the *Oxford English Dictionary* as "exercising chief authority or rule: ruling, governing, commanding; most influential.") Furthermore, we do not assume that greater numbers automatically deliver greater power; on the contrary, following Guttentag and Secord, we acknowledge the possibility that the larger group of either males or females may be disadvantaged in their dyadic relations.[53] We recognize that gender relations involve the exercise of power, but we are not yet sure how the relative numbers of male and female migrants empower or disempower either group. Therefore we use the term *predominant* and define it in a strictly numeric sense to create a typology of migrant gender composition.

Our typology extends beyond a simple one of male predominant and female predominant. We create a third category for gender-balanced migrations, but do not insist that it occurs only when the numbers of males and females are exactly equal. Because few migrations are exactly 50 percent female, we define gender-balanced migrations as those in which the gender composition ranges between 47 and 53 percent. In the past, demographers' descriptions of predictable variations in gender composition, or the product of equally predictable variations in the age structure of populations, define a reasonable but narrow range of gender composition (from 49.5 to 51.2 percent female), which are likely when using stock data for gender-balanced sedentary populations. However, because flow data vary considerably more than stock data, because variation increases at lower scales of analysis, and because we do not want to create separate typologies for stock and flow data, we define a more generous range as constituting gender balance. In the chapters ahead, we define male-predominant migrations as less than 47 percent female, gender-balanced migrations as 47 to 53 percent female, and female-predominant migrations as greater than 53 percent female.

In addition, because historical migrations are documented largely with highly variable flow data, the range of male-predominant migrations that we identify also proved to be a very large one, varying from 0 to 47 percent female. The range of female-predominant migrations was smaller, varying from 54 to approximately 70 percent female. Especially when analyzing historical flow data, it seems problematic to insist on the use of a single broad category, especially for male-predominant migrant populations. Is there any reason to assume, for example, that the lives of men and women in migrations that were only 10 percent female closely resembled the lives of men and women in migrations that were 47 percent female? Although few might disagree that 10 percent female constitutes an overwhelmingly male migrant population, the upper end of this category is harder to establish. Eventually, we hope that studies documenting the consequences of male-predominant migrations will make it possible to identify a sensible upper limit based on the analysis of documentable consequences of gender imbalance. But for now, we have added only two additional categories to our typology. Heavily male predominant is defined as any migrant population that is less than 25 percent female. Migrations that were more than 75 percent female, though extremely rare in both past and present, are defined as heavily female predominant. Both categories may need future refinements as scholars better understand the consequences of variations in migrant gender composition.

As the chapters ahead demonstrate, evidence exists for heavily male-predominant, male-predominant, gender-balanced, and female-predominant migrations for almost every time period, every spatial scale, and every part of the world described by flow data. Migrant gender composition in stock data (widely available only for the second half of the twentieth century) more often falls within only two categories— male predominant and gender balanced. Many of our chapters focus particular attention on heavily male and on the gender-balanced or female-predominant migrant populations, using them as case studies of the diverse gender relations that produce variation in gender composition. Often our choice of case studies was influenced by the existence of scholarly literatures that are rich enough to allow us to situate heavily male and gender-balanced and female-predominant migrations in a particular social or historical context, identifying the types of gender relations in sending or receiving societies associated with each category.

By creating a typology of migrant gender composition, we also hope to more accurately and concisely define feminization than prior studies.[54] In this book, we suggest and use three definitions of feminization. Our most generous simply defines it as any multiyear rise in the percentage female among migrants. In the chapters ahead, we show there were many periods of short-term and temporary feminization of migrant populations followed by years of masculinization. Our second definition is based more narrowly on our typology of gender composition: any shift from one category to another (from heavily male to male-predominant, or from male-predominant to gender-balanced) is considered as feminization just as any shift from female-predominant to gender-balanced, or from male-predominant to heavily male-predominant is considered masculinization. Finally, a third definition identifies feminization as any increase in the proportion female that has demonstrable consequences for migrants, for their homelands, or for the new societies they enter.

In this book, we present considerable evidence from flow and stock data for a twentieth-century feminization that was sustained over a much longer period than the many earlier short-term feminizations that historical flow data identified. Based on these data, we can also show that the outcome of feminization has been gender-balanced migrant populations and not long-term female predominance. We must, however, leave open the question of whether the relatively balanced gender composition of current migrant populations will persist into the future; we cannot predict whether it will eventually qualify as a form of demographic transition. Finally, although a definition of feminization based on documentation of demonstrable consequences may eventually provide the most useful and rigorous definition, scholarship about the consequences of variations in migrant gender composition remain too limited to make such a definition useful today. Scholars wishing to document the consequences of feminization will need new and different kinds of data on migration to study the consequences of variations in gender composition; only then can they analyze such consequences to revise our typology or to more carefully define feminization. Most existing flow and published census data simply cannot support nuanced analysis of such consequences. In chapter 6, we introduce the kind of individual-level census data that may facilitate an analysis of the consequences of variations in migrant gender composition matter. In chapter 7, we explore in a preliminary way the consequences of gender composition for the well-documented case of the United States. Until scholars more fully document the consequences of a 5, 10, or 20 percent increase in female proportions among international migrants across many spatial scales, our third definition of feminization will remain elusive.

PART II

ANALYZING GENDER COMPOSITION IN HISTORICAL FLOW DATA

$=$ Chapter 3 $=$

Gender and Early Modern Migrations, 1492–1867

I f indeed the "past is a foreign country" where "they do things differently," then the great vastness of that strange place poses a research
problem as large as the spatial vastness of today's interconnected
and mobile world.[1] This volume slices up the past into segments to
render it analytically manageable. We thus follow history's disciplinary conventions, linking periods of stability and change in migrant
gender composition to the periodization of global integration over four
centuries.

This chapter analyzes variation in gender composition during the
early modern era, a period that stretches from the late fifteenth century,
when two formerly isolated macro-regions (the Americas or New World
and the Afro-Eurasian Old World) became a single global network
of trade and exchange, to 1800, when many political, economic, and
migratory circuits created during previous centuries underwent significant transformation.[2] The early modern era is not the past to which
current migration patterns are compared. Scholars who have instead
compared recent migrations to those occurring a century ago select a past
moment when the presence of female immigrants was at its historical
nadir. Both in the early modern era and again in the twentieth century,
women and girls made up a higher proportion of international migrations
than during the second half of the nineteenth century. Thus, comparisons
to the years around 1900 wrongly suggest that feminization is unprecedented or new and potentially far-reaching in its consequences. We
demonstrate that gender balance and even female predominance among
migrants is neither unprecedented nor new. On the contrary, the chapters
that follow portray a persistently restless and mobile world characterized
by the pulsing rhythms of political and economic integration, followed
by collapsing interregional economic and social ties, and by considerable
variation in the volume and gender composition of international migrant
populations.

Global Integration, Migration, and the Early Modern World

Beginning between 1450 and 1500 and continuing into the early 1800s, the early modern era encompasses the expansion and then temporary contraction of consolidating European states through the colonization of the Americas, Asia, and Africa. These new Dutch, British, Spanish, French, and Portuguese empires were sea empires, founded especially on active trade routes around the Atlantic and on less-traveled and longer-distance sea lanes to a small but growing number of European-dominated port cities and islands in Asia and Africa.[3] With their new imperial system of tropical plantation production,[4] the European empires required the mobilization of millions of laborers, producing horrific levels of coercion and cruelty. Most long-distance early modern migrants in the Americas were slaves, soldiers, or servants with limited autonomy and limited control over their own destinies. As migrants, Europeans and Africans were, to differing degrees, isolated from the social networks and support that had rendered them less vulnerable in their homelands.[5] Beginning in the late eighteenth century and continuing into the nineteenth, nationalist challengers broke up parts of Europe's American empires into independent nation-states in the Caribbean and North and South America.[6] Reformers also gradually suppressed the Atlantic slave trade, thus partially unraveling the circuits of early modern global integration. Migrant gender composition changed, too.

The nation-states that create population data scarcely existed in the early modern world. It is possible to analyze early modern migrations only because historians have collectively compiled records produced during transoceanic commerce and imperial oversight. In doing so, they have understandably focused disproportionately on the foundational task of estimating the volumes of early modern migrations. Given the scattered nature of early modern records, scholars can still make at best only rough estimates of migration volumes. And because most efforts at compilation and estimation have focused on the Atlantic world of Europe, Africa, and the Americas, it is not possible to describe with much certainty the global scope or scale of early modern migrations.

Early modern scales of global integration, while significant, were not as extensive as those that would follow in the nineteenth and twentieth centuries. Global volumes of trade were relatively much smaller than they are today and both trans-Pacific and Atlantic-Pacific linkages remained limited, even in the early modern empires that straddled both oceans.[7] Certainly, however, the modern exchange of peoples, animals, plant crops, and weeds that Crosby labeled as the Columbian Exchange was both global and long term in its consequences.[8] The demographic collapse of indigenous American populations that followed conquest and the transoceanic spread of European germs also meant that European empire building could succeed only with vast new inputs of human labor, much of it coerced.

Although it was the largest transcontinental migration of the early modern era, the trans-Atlantic slave trade was not the only significant one, even in and around the Atlantic Ocean. Historians estimate that 12.5 million people were forced out of Africa in chains, ten million of whom survived to work in the Americas.[9] Documented exclusively in flow data, few African slaves gained the autonomy to circulate, return, or migrate in multiple directions. Individual slaves were thus usually enumerated once as transoceanic migrants, if they were counted at all.

Most other migration systems of the early modern era also involved coercion but were less thoroughly documented. In addition to the Atlantic slaves, an estimated six million enslaved sub-Saharan Africans were shipped across the Sahara to North Africa, western Asia, and the Ottoman empire; as many as eight million became slaves through displacement within Africa.[10] Before 1800, slaves forced out of Africa considerably outnumbered Europeans. Estimates suggest only three to four million European migrants: up to a million and a half from Spain, a million and a half from much smaller Portugal, four hundred thousand from Great Britain, one hundred thousand from Germany, twenty-five thousand from the Netherlands, and seventy-five thousand from France.[11] Eighty percent of these Europeans were indentured servants, and most of the rest were soldiers, mercenaries, and missionaries.[12] By the 1790s, both Britain and France also banished unknown numbers of poor convicts to penal colonies in the Atlantic and the Pacific.[13] In addition, historians have also estimated that approximately 107.9 million mobile Europeans crossed early modern borders within Europe, mainly as soldiers, journeymen, sailors, and vagrants.[14]

Combining these rough estimates gives a total of 138 million migrants, or an average of half a million annually, or about one-third of the annual migration volumes of the better-studied nineteenth century.[15] These 138 million made up no more than 1.8 percent of total early modern world populations (estimated at 450 million in 1500 and 800 million in 1800). Today, by contrast, migrants are about 3 percent of the world's population.

Of course, none of these estimates contain evidence of gender composition; that is simply not possible on a global scale. However, some data from the large Atlantic migrations do distinguish men and women from boys and girls, facilitating the study of variations in gender composition during this early era. The remainder of this chapter introduces the types of data available for analysis and discusses variations among both relatively small groups of European migrants and much larger groups of enslaved Africans around the Atlantic. As the best documented macro-region, the Atlantic offers—for now at least—the largest spatial scale for writing a gendered geography of early modern migrations. In addition, it reveals patterns that appear and reappear in later chapters. The recruitment of migrants as individual laborers, whether destined for plantation labor or unpaid enslaved reproductive work within households, often produced unbalanced migrant populations that were either male or female predominant. When empires instead sought migrants to reproduce biologically or spread their own cultures to new settings, migrations were more often gender balanced.

Gender, Coercion, and Colonization in Early Modern Migrations from Europe

Mobility, at least over shorter distances, was nothing new to Africans, Europeans, or North or South Americans prior to the early modern era of the Columbian Exchange.[16] Yet considerable evidence points to the possibility that few people anywhere in Europe responded with great enthusiasm to the new empires' demand for laborers in their American colonies. William O'Reilly estimates that more than "half the migrants who crossed the Atlantic before 1850 went involuntarily, the overwhelming majority enslaved Africans, and the remainder European convicts and prisoners. Many others were indentured servants, or were otherwise contracted under terms of labor debt, which meant that only 10 per cent of migrants enjoyed total independence" in choosing migration.[17] Clearly, even the migrations of early modern Europeans provide disturbing examples of the structural social inequalities still associated with global integration in our own times. No voluntary mass migrations developed before 1800 because the Americas were, at first, distant and unknown. As they became better known, so did their appalling conditions of labor, the prevalence of slavery, and harsh systems of labor discipline. In the case of Europeans, resistance to moving, high levels of coercion, and the hope that migration to the Americas might prove a temporary phase in life—as it had been for many apprentices and farm and domestic laborers in medieval and early modern Europe—combined to create heavily male European labor migrations.[18]

By contrast, scholars have identified quite rapid feminization among the minority of migrants who received land or intended to settle permanently in the New World, hoping to invest, prosper, and reproduce themselves biologically and culturally. Two examples—of Spanish migrants in the sixteenth century and British migrants in the seventeenth and eighteenth centuries—illustrate early modern divergence in gender composition between more and less coerced European migrants and between individually recruited European labor migrants (mainly men) and more gender-balanced migrations of settler colonizers. One might even conclude that migrants free enough to be attracted by opportunity were gender balanced and that those compelled by poverty and homeland hardship to consider other options were heavily male.

Spain's first or pioneer migrants to the Americas and Asia in the 1490s and early 1500s were navigators and sailors, merchants, soldiers, and missionaries. Given the very common and cross-cultural gender ideology that associated femaleness with domestic life and masculinity with risk-taking, military service, governance, and adventure, it is scarcely surprising that the earliest migrants were almost all male. But given such a beginning, some degree of feminization of Spain's migrants was also inevitable. Historians working with a variety of methods and data have created a complex portrait of Spain's earliest migrants in the 1500s, one that includes evidence of both feminization and masculinization and divergence in the gender composition of settlers and semi-coerced laborers across the sixteenth century.

Hoping to understand how Spanish language dialects affected the development of Spanish in the Americas, and working with both imperial and biographical materials from Spain and the Spanish Americas, Peter Boyd-Bowman examined data describing fifty-five thousand men, women, and children, roughly 20 percent of persons estimated to have traveled to the Spanish Indies before 1600.[19] Given the relatively small size of the migrant population, variations in gender composition were large. Among the earliest migrants (from 1493 to 1539), only 5.6 to 6.3 percent were female, but thereafter the proportion female doubled to 16.4 percent before peaking at 28.5 percent (male predominant) at the end of the century. Noting variations in gender composition among migrants of differing regional origins, Boyd-Bowman argued that migrants who traveled the longest distances to embark in Seville—Spain's imperial administrative center that governed all trade and other relations with the Americas—were the most heavily male (under 25 percent female). Migrants from the provinces immediately surrounding Seville were predominantly but not heavily male (typically 30 to 40 percent female), and migrants from the city of Seville were 42 to 50 percent female, or gender balanced, by the latter years of the sixteenth century. Boyd-Bowman estimated that fully one-third of all women migrating to the Americas in the 1500s originated in Seville.[20] The largest groups of women Boyd-Bowman describe traveled to Peru and New Spain, which were Spain's two main administrative centers in the Americas and also the most urban sites of Spain's American empire; male migrants scattered more widely.

Boyd-Bowman's evidence hinted at a gendered market for servant labor that preferred young men: well over half (58.2 percent) of migrant men but only one-sixth of migrant women listed servant as their occupation. Female migrants included a fairly even mix of unmarried and married, and an unspecified portion of the unmarried girl children of married female migrants. In a case study of emigrants from two Spanish towns in Extramadura, Altman found that significant numbers of male servants were recruited by upper status migrants, who paid the sea passages for the poorer men who served relatively short terms (less than a year) of bonded servitude.[21] Boyd-Bowman concluded that the typical male emigrant was "a poverty stricken Andalusian . . . aged 27½, unmarried, unskilled and probably only semi-literate, driven by hunger to make his way to Peru in the employ of any man who would pay his passage and had secured the necessary permit." His composite female migrant possessed strikingly different characteristics; she was "already in her early thirties . . . travelling to Peru with her 36-year old husband, two young children, a manservant, and a maid."[22] Thus, the typical female migrant enjoyed higher status than the typical male and also seemed more likely to have anticipated a long-term, if not always permanent, life in the Americas.

As women's presence among migrants rose in the latter years of the sixteenth century, Spain was experiencing an economic crisis that encouraged entire households to abandon Spain in search of better opportunities. Boyd-Bowman described letters sent back to Spain from the Americas that urged wives and other relatives to join men who had migrated earlier.[23] In fact, by the end of the 1500s, Spain had required men to reunite with their wives within a fixed period of time—a first example of how imperial strategy influenced migrant gender composition. Other scholars have instead viewed the much less well-documented seventeenth- and eighteenth-century Spanish migrations as both increasingly male and increasingly coerced, with ever more dependent, desperate, and young male servants forming the majority, perhaps as high as two-thirds, of all migrants.[24] According to Magnus Morner, the seventeenth-century Spanish economic crises also convinced servants who had anticipated short-term service abroad to remain in the Americas.[25] For the seventeenth century, Morner identified an important exception to the general masculinization of Spanish migration and it too pointed toward the power of imperial policy to alter migrant gender composition.[26] Subsidized by the Spanish crown, many families departed as settler colonizers in gender-balanced groups from the Canary Islands for Venezuela and Cuba—two colonies where Spanish population had not grown and may have been declining. The failure of earlier migrant populations to reproduce threatened Spain's political hegemony in the face of growing inter-imperial competition in the Caribbean and South America, and resulted in imperial interventions to support settler colonization by gender-balanced and reproducing family groups. A collection of letters from the 1700s showed that Spanish men already in the Americas also initiated chain migration—although they called both for wives and for nephews who could assist them in their businesses or plantations. According to Morner, these men assured "their ladies" they could now travel the Atlantic without risk and would enjoy "a marvelous reputation" (that is, free from any hint of work as prostitutes in a male-predominant population) in America.[27]

Studies of British migration to North America in the seventeenth and eighteenth centuries have revealed similar variations in gender composition.[28] Among the small group of very early English settler colonizers to Virginia after 1609, the earliest of free and voluntary migrants were more than one-quarter female, or male predominant, and servants were 11 percent female, or very heavily male.[29] A 1635 register kept by English custom officials about some five thousand migrants to the Americas described migrants to the West Indies as traveling under indenture or debt peonage: they were only 6 percent female, or very heavily male predominant. Refugees and religiously motivated Puritans destined for New England, by contrast, more often traveled in family groups; although they clearly intended to settle permanently, women and girls still made up only one-third of the Puritans.[30] Other studies have described the more voluntary Great (Puritan) Migration to Massachusetts, from 1630 to 1640, as 40 percent female, at least one ship transporting a female majority.[31]

For the much larger migrations of the eighteenth century, when hundreds of thousands of migrants, many of them indentured servants, traveled from Britain, Ireland, and Germany to the British colonies in North America, Bernard Bailyn contrasted the heavily male indentured servants (and convicts) from southern England to Scots recruited as settler colonizers by American land speculators in rural areas.[32] The latter more often traveled in gender-balanced family groups toward peripheral farming areas. Variations in gender composition thus resembled those among Spanish migrants. In addition, although Susan Matt claims that Britain's servants "never intended to remain" in North America and that one-sixth of the Pilgrim refugees eventually returned to Europe, the gender composition of early modern migrations of return remains unknown and little studied.[33]

The largest group of coerced English labor migrants of the early modern era were indentured servants who typically signed contracts submitting themselves to temporary bondage in exchange for passage to America. They (or, technically, their contracts) were bought and sold in port cities and markets; in many parts of the Caribbean and southern colonies in British North America, servants lived and worked together alongside enslaved Africans. Purchasers clearly preferred male servants for agricultural work. Because they also purchased women servants to work in their households, whether urban or rural, female servants often became pregnant, which resulted in an extension of their term of servitude.[34] Some evidence suggests that the migrations of indentured servants became more masculine over time. David Galenson described women as 23 percent of seventeenth-century servants but by the eighteenth century only 10 percent—a clear trend toward masculinization in an already heavily male migration.[35] In a detailed study of the Delaware Valley and Philadelphia, Farley Grubb demonstrated that migrant gender composition also varied with national origins. Between 1745 and 1831, women were 14.3 percent of English, 19.8 percent of Ulster Irish, and 20 percent of Scottish servants—all heavily male migrations.[36] By contrast, whereas the south Irish included 33.7 percent women and girls, forming a male-predominant group, the German servants, at 43.8 percent female, approached gender balance. Grubb also presumed that variations in gender composition reflected changing demand for male and female labor in both Europe and North America.

Although scarcely providing a comprehensive portrait of large migrant populations, data on the sex of transatlantic European migrants within the Spanish and British empires point toward a number of factors that predictably influenced gender composition. Early modern labor markets were strikingly gendered, and New World employers much preferred male to female servants and laborers, especially on plantations. By contrast, the gender composition of nonservant Europeans—who presumably had greater choice and exercised greater autonomy—was in both empires male predominant, but not as heavily so. Such variation may have reflected the quite differing "life projects" of the two groups; like most poorer young people in Europe, laborers approached migration as a continuation of the dependency and submission that characterized the lives of all young European laborers. It was a temporary moment in their life course. By contrast, settlers—and landowners and established businessmen or government bureaucrats—were older, more often anticipated a permanent migration, and traveled as families. Yet effects on the gender composition of settlement and servitude were not always the same across empires. In the Spanish empire, cities in the Americas attracted disproportionate numbers of women traveling in families; in North America, gender-balanced family groups instead migrated to frontier rural areas where they intended to farm, as settler colonizers, replacing indigenous populations. Spanish men also proved more willing than women to travel long distances to find transport to the Americas, and in Britain, it was the southerners embarking in nearby London who were most heavily male rather than the Scots, who had to travel longer distances to embark. Given that empirical differences appear to reflect the degree of freedom or compulsion migrants faced, it is easy to imagine that the most heavily coerced and largest group of all early modern migrants—African slaves—would both vary less in their gender composition and fall into the category of heavily male migrations. Yet fairly rich data on the slave trade suggests the opposite.

The Transatlantic Slave Trade, 1501–1867

The Atlantic slave trade produced slave populations in the Americas that were both less heavily male than the European laborers and, especially in its first centuries, almost as gender balanced as the European settler colonizers. Interpreting these variations requires that scholars of slavery consider not only demand for plantation labor but also issues related to reproduction and the social relations of gender that transformed free people into saleable commodities in Africa. Understanding variations in slave gender composition also requires attention to interactions between European and African gender ideologies and gender relations, and to how gender organized societies in both sending and receiving societies.

Because the enslavement of human beings posed a long-term political challenge to every new Atlantic nation-state in the eighteenth and nineteenth centuries, and because the legacy of slaves' exclusion from personhood and citizenship in those states has still not been completely overcome, Africa, Africans, and African slavery remain at the center of many recent histories of early modern global integration.[37] But the underlying assumption that slaves may be analyzed as migrants, comparable in at least some respects to other migrants, is still a somewhat controversial assertion. The early exclusion of the slave trade from migration studies ended only as historians shifted their attention from U.S. immigration to migration and mobility in Atlantic and global history[38] and to the demography of early modern migrations,[39] broadening historians' typology of migrations to include forced and voluntary movements.

This analysis of slave gender composition is largely based on the Trans-Atlantic Slave Trade Database, described in the introduction.[40] Painstakingly integrating thousands of ship, port, and customs records into a single, and now digital, data source, these data code commonly available variables for transatlantic voyages into eight categories. For analysis of slave migrant gender composition, the most salient of these categories are the itinerary and outcome of voyages, the numbers transported, dates of arrival or departure, and individual characteristics of the transported slaves.

As one might expect of records created by a diverse and often barely literate group of men, the Trans-Atlantic Slave Trade data are far from perfect. Some records of slave trading were extremely rich and included even the names of the slaves transported,[41] whereas others provided only the barest notations of departure and arrival dates, names of ships, and total numbers of slaves transported. The majority of these records contained no description of individual characteristics, including sex and age.[42] However, a subset of records includes data on sex; 3,404 documented voyages distinguished men from women and boys from girls, 811 distinguished sex

Figure 3.1   Annual Disembarkations of Slaves from Africa, 1501–1867

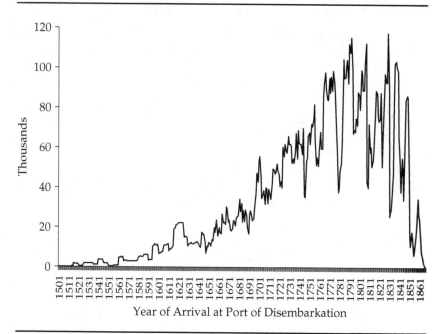

Year of Arrival at Port of Disembarkation

Source: Authors' compilation based on Voyages 2012.

separately for adults and children, and 484 noted the numbers of males and females without reference to age. These 4,699 voyages constitute 13.4 percent of all voyages in the database (or 9 to 11 percent of the editors' estimate for all slave ship journeys).[43]

The *Trans-Atlantic Slave Trade Database* thus provides a valuable, if only partial, sketch of the dynamics of the slave trade over 350 years. Although data on the sex of migrants are quite limited for the years before 1650 (when migrations were still small), evidence improves as slave transports grew after 1650. Figure 3.1 tracks disembarkations and nicely illustrates the considerable dynamism and temporal variability characteristic of historical flow data. The disembarkations recorded in the *Trans-Atlantic Slave Trade Database* were somewhat smaller in number—in part because of mortality during what was called the Middle Passage (the trans-Atlantic journey)—but otherwise closely followed the dynamics of embarkation.[44] Before the mid-seventeenth century, the documented annual totals of slaves shipped from Africa rarely exceeded twenty thousand. Between 1650 and 1700, the numbers doubled and then—as the cultivation of sugar in the Caribbean and Brazil expanded—ballooned to one hundred thousand each year, and continued at that level until almost 1840. Only after 1840 did the numbers begin to drop, first in response to the first abolition of the trade (by Britain in 1807 and the United States in 1808) and then to the abolition of slavery itself (first in Haiti and then, after 1810, in post-colonial Latin America). The United States finally abolished slavery in 1865; Cuba and Brazil followed only in the 1880s.[45]

Until scholarly collaboration produced the Trans-Atlantic Slave Trade Database, scholars had summed up the gender composition of the slave trade quite simply as "two men for every woman."[46] This meant that approximately one-third of all forced into the Middle Passage were presumed to be women and girls. This conventional reckoning placed the slave trade firmly within our category of male-predominant migrations, but it also meant that the slave trade was not as heavily male as most contemporary coerced migrations, such as servants or prisoners from Europe. This simple 2:1 ratio nevertheless allowed historians of slavery to imagine the enslaved African as a slave man, and to ignore female slaves as a minority. In the historiography on Atlantic slavery, studies of female slaves and of slave society gender relations developed only with the rise of feminist scholarship after 1970;[47] they raised some of the same complaints found in feminist studies of more voluntary forms of migration.[48]

Figure 3.2 tracks the percentage female among slaves from 1532 to 1864. By illustrating variation in slave women's presence at its highest spatial scale—that is to say, for the entire Atlantic—this figure nicely illustrates what Jennifer Morgan calls the "radical potential" of demographic evidence to revise sweeping generalizations about historical gender relations.[49] Clearly, the gender composition of African slaves was not always "two men for every woman." Gender composition varied over time. The most extreme variations (from 70.4 percent female in 1546 to only 6 percent female in 1548) reflect mainly the paucity of sixteenth-century data on sex and the overall relatively small annual totals (approximately one thousand yearly in the database). Still, during these poorly documented early years, gender balance, female predominance, and heavy female predominance characterized six of the ten years for which annual totals are available. The small size of the captive populations recorded is not, by contrast, a sufficient explanation for the many later years of female-predominant or gender-balanced composition revealed in figure 3.2. Even after 1650, as the numbers of slaves increased into the tens of thousands, sixteen of the forty years for which we have data on sex remained female predominant or gender balanced.

After 1700, as the numbers of slaves approached one hundred thousand annually, male predominance became the rule. Variation in gender composition diminished, and for much of the next century, male

Figure 3.2   Female Slave Trade Embarkations, 1532–1864

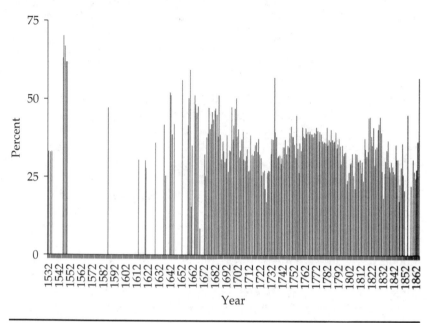

Source: Authors' compilation based on Voyages 2012.
Note: This figure combines all data recorded about sex from voyages in the *Trans-Atlantic Slave Trade Database*. If necessary, we transposed percentage male into percentage female, and if two measures, such as the percentage female and percentage of women and girls were given, we chose to present the higher percentage female though the difference was never more than a few percentage points.

predominance meant that yearly shipments of slaves included between 30 and 40 percent females—or very roughly two males for every female, just as earlier studies had assumed.[50] Variation in gender composition increased again as the impact of abolition spread around the Atlantic, and especially as enslaved children began to replace enslaved adults after 1800.[51] As Morgan and others argue, the slave migrants of the Atlantic were thus more gender balanced than either the much smaller early modern migrations of Americas-bound European indentured laborers or the voluntary mass migrations of Europeans and Asians during the second half of the nineteenth century (a topic we engage in chapter 4).[52]

Scholars have significantly revised earlier scholarly portraits of slave migrant populations as a result of the *Trans-Atlantic Slave Trade Database,* and Morgan has offered a useful summary of these revisions. Rather than assign the 2:1 ratio of male predominance to the entire period of Atlantic slave trade, historians now recognize that "prior to the eighteenth century, women and men arrived in near-balanced numbers to many parts of the Americas, and as slave traders shifted toward the import of children in the waning years of the trade, adult men ultimately constituted a minority of all those transported."[53] Of these two assertions, the first is the most compelling because the final years of the slave trade were also heavily male, even if slaves were more likely to be young boys than adult men at that time.

The obvious question to be answered is why the most coerced of the early modern labor migrations included relatively more women and girls than either European or other later labor migrations. As laborers, enslaved Africans worked long hours on plantations; they produced the sugar, rum, tobacco, and indigo and extracted some of the precious metals that made Europe's Atlantic empire building financially worthwhile and successful.[54] European landowners had long employed both male and female workers and servants, especially on large estates; African women, too, often worked in agriculture. Yet archival sources on American plantations confirm a pronounced European preference for male slaves as well as male European servants.[55] Ships captains visiting the coast of Africa were routinely and explicitly instructed to "buy as few females as in your power, because . . . Females are a very tedious sale."[56] In almost all coastal ports in western Africa, adult males fetched the highest prices as commodities.[57] European purchasers in the Americas also expressed strong preferences for male laborers and paid higher prices for them there.[58]

A comparison of Atlantic slave trade migrations with other contemporaneous Afro-Eurasia migrations highlights how unusual it was for women and girls to be a minority among slaves, as they ultimately were in the Atlantic. Although statistical data on the sex of slaves remains extremely limited outside the Atlantic, the two-volume collection, *Women and Slavery* (2007), provides some comparative evidence. For example, Paul Lovejoy describes the trans-Saharan migration slave system as 75 percent female, and Gwyn Campbell, Suzanne Miers, and Joseph Miller suggest that two-thirds of slaves traded away from eastern Africa were female.[59] These authors attribute the different gender compositions of slave populations to the different function of slavery in and outside the Atlantic. In Afro-Eurasia before and after 1500, slavery was largely a system for organizing household domestic production and reproductive labor; in such household-based societies, slavery created demand for slave women as domestic workers and as child-bearers and child-minders. (Enslaved males more often worked in navies and armies.) The families, households, and lineages of slave purchasers in Afro-Eurasia expanded their power through control over slave women's reproductive work, not limited to but definitely including their fertility. Outside the Atlantic, then, purchasers of slaves preferred women because, in nonstate societies, slavery served familial, lineage, domestic, and reproductive ends.

For the Atlantic, historians have explored two possible explanations for the relatively more gender-balanced composition of African slaves than European servants. One suggests that concerns about the reproduction of their slave workforce also influenced New World purchasers of slaves during the early years of the Atlantic slave trade. The second points toward African gender relations and ideologies that influenced the supply of labor available for sale in slave markets that attracted both trans-Saharan and Atlantic purchasers. These two explanations seem connected since both Africans and Europeans associated fertility, reproduction, and reproductive work with females in ways that shaped both the supply of slaves and the demand for them.

Jennifer Morgan provides a convincing argument that the reproduction of their slave workforce was an early and, in some places, ever-present concern among European purchasers of slaves.[60] Using data collected from early European images and reports that constructed the fertile and lactating bodies of African women as exotic oddities, she suggests how the association of femaleness with fertility and reproduction influenced the development of markets for slave labor.[61] Pointing to numerous cases of gender balance among slaves imported into English-speaking slave societies in the Caribbean and North America, she argues that slave purchasers were as concerned about the reproduction of their property as they were about the labor needs of their plantations.[62] As the legal status of slaves stabilized throughout the Americas, transforming children born to enslaved mothers into slaves themselves, the owners of slave property also viewed women and their fertility as sources of wealth.[63]

Evidence from the Trans-Atlantic Slave Trade Database provides some support for Morgan's argument that demand from the Americas balanced reproductive and labor concerns. Table 3.1 reveals that receiving societies in the Americas selected roughly similar slave populations, and that sending societies in Africa exported somewhat more diverse slave populations. However, these data also suggest that the supply side of the slave labor market influenced gender composition more than the demand side. To explain such variations in the supply of male and female slaves, we chose to explore gender relations in several slave populations that fell outside the eighteenth-century Atlantic norm of "two men for every woman."

Table 3.1   Female Slaves Exported and Imported, 1532–1864

Sending (Exporting) Regions in Africa		Receiving (Importing) Regions	
Senegambia/Offshore	35.6	Europe	40.5
Sierra Leone	33.5	North America	30.7
Windward Coast	36.7	Caribbean	35.3
Gold Coast	33.9	Spanish North	35.3
Bight of Benin	37.6	America	
Bight of Biafra/Guinea Islands	41.6	Brazil	33.8
West Central Africa/St. Helena	32.6	Africa	32.2
Southeast Africa/Indian Ocean Islands	26.5	Other	40.1

Source: Authors' calculation based on Voyages 2012.
Note: All numbers in percentages.

Within the Atlantic system of slavery, table 3.1 shows that the Bight of Biafra stood out among African regions for exporting slave migrants with higher than average female representation (41.6 percent female) over a long period. In contrast, West Central Africa distinguished itself for its low representation of women (32.6 percent female).[64] A comparison of slaves departing from these two regions shows them to have been roughly comparable in numbers; the dynamics of migration from the two regions are also quite similar.

Gender composition from both regions varied over time. Before 1600, the very small populations of people captured and exported from both regions were gender balanced. However, as the volume of the slave trade increased after 1600, incidences of gender-balanced and female-predominant yearly shipments from West Central Africa (an area sometimes known as Kongo or Angola) diminished but remained common from the Bight of Biafra. Even as the slave trade reached its peak and became more masculine for the entire Atlantic between 1700 and 1800, the Bight of Biafra continued to see occasional years characterized by gender-balanced and female-predominant shipments. After 1800, gender composition of slaves shipped from the two regions converged toward greater male predominance, even though for these last years of the slave trade, West Central was more likely to ship heavily male cargos (often of younger males) than the Bight of Biafra.

Studies have sought to explain the differing patterns of enslavement that developed in the two regions, and the origins of variations in the gender composition of slaves shipped to the Americas from each. The Bight of Biafra was a relatively modest arena of slave capture and export until the 1730s. Most of those enslaved were either individuals marginalized from their own kin groups or had been kidnapped as individuals.[65] The area had greatest importance for English slave traders and the region seems to have been an important early source of slave labor for the English-speaking colonies in the Caribbean and North America.[66] In his study of the Bight of Biafra, Ugo Nwokeji argues that men played a more important role in agriculture in the Bight of Biafra than they did elsewhere in West Africa,[67] where agricultural labor was generally understood to be female work.[68] In Biafra, men were the main cultivators of yams, the preferred and symbolically most central food for ethnic groups living in the region. Women cultivated crops imagined to be lesser in value, making females more dispensable as household members and thus easier to transform into saleable commodities.[69]

Nwokeji argues further that the shift in Biafra toward male majorities in the middle and later years of the eighteenth century accompanied the expansion of a new lineage group, the Aro (a non-Muslim trading diaspora), that sought to incorporate ever-greater numbers of females into their lineage groups to reproduce and expand their influence in the region without recourse to military action.[70] For the Aro, slavery was a strategy for expansive reproduction and growth, typical of Afro-Eurasian slave systems, and one that increasingly kept women enslaved locally.

Finally, according to Nwokeji, the Bight of Biafra sent relatively more women into Atlantic slave trade because it had not been firmly incorporated into the trans-Saharan slave trade.[71] Offering higher prices for female captives, the African and trans-Saharan slave markets drew women away from Atlantic slave markets where they fetched a lower price.[72] To explain Biafra's isolation from the trans-Saharan slave markets, Nwokeji argues that the long-distance trade in kolanuts that coexisted with the trans-Saharan slave trade and that typically connected trans-Saharan societies to West African coastal regions never developed in the Bight of Biafra.[73] Among the Igbo living there, kolanuts instead enjoyed special ritual and spiritual significance so they were not exported, and local merchants either sold women to the Atlantic slave trade or at local markets (to the Aro, for example).

Male-predominant slave populations from West Central Africa were also products of highly particularistic and local gender relations. The Trans-Atlantic Slave Trade Database defines West Central Africa as the western coast of the continent south of the Bight of Biafra and west of the Cape of Good Hope. An enormous area, drained by rivers originating deep in the African interior, the region experienced repeated invasions, warfare, and political reorganization and centralization in the centuries surrounding the first incursions of European slave traders. Portuguese traders early dominated the procurement of slaves from this region and large numbers of the Africans thus acquired became slaves in Brazil, with its especially exploitative conditions of sugar plantation and mining labor systems.[74]

In a major study of the west central African slave trade in the eighteenth century, Joseph Miller describes West Central Africa as a place with a long history of enslaving cultural outsiders as household dependents; here too slavery functioned as a strategy for expanding a lineage's prestige and economic strength.[75] According to Miller, "most slaves from western Central Africa . . . reached the coasts as by-products of political-economic strategies that African kings and lineage leaders followed to attract dependents."[76] As in West Africa, these native practices created domestic slave markets that operated as alternatives to the coastal markets of the Atlantic slave trade. Unlike the Bight of Biafra, however, West Central Africans participated actively in the trans-Saharan slave trade from an early date. In the sixteenth and seventeenth centuries, most newly enslaved dependents had been captured from other lineages during periods of warfare, generating more male slaves.[77] Throughout this period, too, rising lineages sought to exchange regional products, such as guns, rather than people for the European imports.[78]

Miller and others describe a shift in governance that coincided with growing male predominance among exported slaves in the late seventeenth century.[79] No longer able to provide sufficient quantities of native products to European traders, but in continued need of European imports to pursue local warfare and political consolidation, competing leaders in the Angola-Kongo region began to sell men belonging to their own lineages and to acquire female captives as household slaves or additional wives to ensure reproduction and population growth.[80] This practice began at the so-called slaving frontiers that developed in inland areas undergoing drought dislocations or civil conflict, generating many refugees. Increasingly, kings and other leaders sold male kinsmen, prisoners, or refugee dependents to purchase imported goods. This mode of producing a largely male supply of slaves rested on the common notion that it was women more than men who propagated new generations, and so were enslaved locally. It also rested on very specific customs of warfare that released male captives from death by transforming them into slaves.[81] By contrast, in inland regions of the Bight of Biafra, Cross River Igbo traders delivered their rulers fixed numbers of heads of dead male warriors, producing a surplus of women and children captives to be sold as slaves or incorporated into the victors' lineage groups in other ways.[82]

Our analysis of data from the Trans-Atlantic Slave Trade Database, supplemented by other methods and sources, thus challenges some explanations of variations in gender composition that emerge from studies of early modern European migrants. The earliest of forced migrations from Africa were not the most heavily male, in contrast to the Spanish migrants studied by Boyd-Bowman.[83] In addition, contrary to theorists beginning with Ravenstein, neither African nor European or American sellers or purchasers of slaves were concerned exclusively with the narrowly understood productive labor of the migrants. Right or wrong, Africans, Europeans, and Middle Eastern slave purchasers alike viewed females as possessing valuable reproductive capacity whether for the reproduction of lineage groups, of slave work forces, or of human property. Given that association, they also viewed female servants who were slaves as appropriate workers and producers of goods and services in domestic and household settings.

And the Consequences?

When they have, on occasion, pondered the consequences of early modern migrant gender composition for either sending or receiving societies, scholars have focused largely on marriage patterns and reproduction. For Africa, most scholars have denied that the export of either female- or male-predominant groups of slaves had any long-term impact on Africa's population growth or development.[84] But they have debated whether gender imbalance in the slave trade promoted changes in marriage patterns. Nwokeji denies the export of women encouraged polygyny, as Lovejoy and Miller suggest.[85] Jan Vansina instead describes the emergence of a new kinship structure ("corporate matrilineality") in areas of heavily male slave exports, where "whole communities contained a preponderance a women, children and slaves, controlled by a few older and polygynous men."[86]

On the other side of the Atlantic, Carole Shammas attributes more dramatic and long-term changes in marriage and kinship to the heavily male-predominant migrations of slaves and servants, pointing toward the emergence of what she calls "marriage challenged zones," in which the majority of men "could not marry or had little incentive to do so."[87] Morgan may be right that English-speaking plantation owners viewed adult women slaves as reproducers of their wealth, encouraging gender-balanced purchases, family formation, and reproduction, but slave-owners in Brazil and Cuba instead discovered how to reproduce their workforce in a brutally different way, purchasing again and again new heavily male groups of slaves as earlier cohorts of mistreated workers died from overwork and disease.[88]

For the theorists Marcia Guttentag and Paul Secord, imbalanced sex ratios held the power to change marriage patterns at least in part because they altered the relative power of the men and women seeking to marry.[89] Yet only a handful of scholars of Africa have documented changes in gendered power, for example, in female-predominant African societies produced by the export of male slaves,[90] where at most a few elite, older women may as wives have gained influence.[91] In the Americas, Shammas finds no single or simple pattern in gendered relationships of power, although some historical studies of white indentured servants suggest that women gained modest possibilities for upward mobility through marriage to higher status men.[92] A study of the Caribbean also showed both black and white women gaining advantages in both marriage and property acquisition in the heavily male population of eighteenth-century Bermuda.[93]

Overall, then, it seems that the radical potential of demographic data on migrant sex to reveal gender ideology and relations at work has been more fully realized by scholars seeking to understand the gendered causes of migration than by those focused on migration's gendered consequences. Future research—perhaps drawing on the theoretical foundation of Guttentag and Secord[94]—should focus greater attention on how the gender composition of early modern slaves, servants, and settler colonizers mattered in the formation of colonial Atlantic societies. At the very least, studies of the colonial Atlantic confirm the much later findings of Ester Boserup: that reproductive as well as productive work—work that was associated with women around the Atlantic—was central to economic development.[95]

=== Chapter 4 ===

Global Convergence: Gender and the Proletarian Mass Migrations, 1800–1924

Writing the *Communist Manifesto* in the midst of the revolutions of 1848, Karl Marx and Friedrich Engels identified many phenomena that late twentieth-century theorists would label as globalization. In the eyes of the two dialectical materialists, "the need of a constantly expanding market for its products chases the bourgeoisie over the whole surface of the globe. It must nestle everywhere, settle everywhere, establish connections everywhere."[1] Even more than the bourgeoisie, however, it was Marx's "working men of all nations" who spread across the globe in the nineteenth century. Rates of migration surged in almost every part of the world after 1800 as a new era of European empire building began. Industrialization and the circulation of mass-produced goods and new nation-states' search for settlers to replace disparaged and marginalized indigenous populations also worked to unsettle rural farming and artisanal populations who faced diminishing opportunities to work and reproduce in their homelands worldwide. Although many in the Americas and Europe's empires celebrated the male pioneer or emigrant, often portrayed as a stalwart white man leading dependent women and children to primitive frontiers, thus ensuring the domination of imperial civilizations or republican rule in Oceania (a term often used historically for the Pacific Islands, including Australia and New Zealand), Africa, and the Americas, the most ubiquitous migrant of the nineteenth century was Marx's working man. Recognizing that it was the search for wage labor that motivated the migrations of the immediate past century, International Labour Organization (ILO) statisticians who compiled and analyzed flow data in the 1920s labeled the nineteenth-century movements as the proletarian mass migrations.

Statisticians Walter Willcox and Imre Ferenczi also noted how heavily male the proletarian mass migrations were.[2] Women formed a significant contingent among settler colonizers in the nineteenth century, as they had in the early modern era. But wage-earners not only outnumbered them, they were also much more heavily male. By the later nineteenth century, women formed a smaller proportion of long-distance migrants than they had in the past or than they would again in the future. Because few nation-states attempted to restrict entry during this period, and rarely distinguished among types of migrants, direct comparisons with migrants of the present cannot easily be made. But one characteristic of the proletarian mass migrations clearly pointed toward the future. Quite suddenly, in the second and third decades of the twentieth century, global convergence toward heavily male migrations reversed and more migrations became gender balanced and even female predominant.

This chapter examines migrations of settler colonizers and wage-earners who crossed both imperial and national boundaries—increasingly linking the Pacific, Indian, and Atlantic Oceans into a global labor market that stretched from the South China Seas to the Caribbean—and seeks to explain a convergence toward first male predominance and then gender balance that accompanied its formation. It suggests how labor markets, war, and the imposition of growing numbers of restrictions on mobile laborers worked together to affect women's representation among migrants. Over time, the effect was cumulative. Masculinization marked rising levels of migration; feminization began as global volumes of migration plummeted.

Global Integration and International Migration in the Nineteenth Century

Scholars concur in finding globalization again advancing after the middle years of the nineteenth century.[3] Historians have described the transition from early modern to nineteenth-century interregional connections, though still mainly around the Atlantic.[4] Happily, the Atlantic slave trade did not survive the nationalist, anti-imperial revolutions that began in British North America in 1776 and continued until the collapse of Spain's worldwide empire in 1898.[5] Collectively, these revolutions not only produced dozens of new record-keeping nation-states but also spurred the eventual abolition of slavery in all of them.[6] In the late eighteenth century, political upheaval, along with the anti- and inter-imperial warfare that produced it, at first diminished long-distance trade in goods and the traffic in humans. But while oceanic travel faltered during the years of American, Haitian, and French revolutions and during the intra-European Napoleonic wars, data on both trade and human mobility describe the hiatus as a temporary one.[7]

This new era of global integration reflected both a second round of European empire building,[8] notably through the extension of plantation agriculture and mining into Africa and Asia,[9] and the transformation of subsistence farmers migrating to the former grasslands of North and South America and southern Russia as settler colonizers and producers of wheat, sugar beets, and other crops.[10] Imperial trade routes connected the far-flung colonial mines, plantations, and forests by steamship and rail to urban centers of industry scattered through Europe and North and South America.[11] Trade in raw materials, foodstuffs, and industrial products increased rapidly and at a global scale.[12] Viewed from the perspective of world systems analysis, trade and empire building increasingly integrated peripheral rural dwellers into a global economy as producers, consumers, and—so historians of migration suggest—as the people who raised, educated, and reproduced the global workforce for core regions. This is why John Bodnar labels immigrants to urban industrial America as children of capitalism, even though they emerged from and often returned to rural homelands in peripheral corners of the world.[13] Whereas early modern laborers had to be coerced through slavery, indenture, and penal transportation to move long distances, the conditions of nineteenth-century capitalism created new nations and empires that in turn created multiple incentives for more voluntary, but still risky and exploitative, migrations.

Once again, massive population relocations accompanied global integration. Millions of Asians and Europeans resettled the interiors of Asia and North and South America and connected older routes of trade and older labor markets into an increasingly integrated global migratory system.[14] Some scholars focus on the new slavery that funneled thirty million indentured laborers (coolies) from India to colonial plantations in the Caribbean, Africa, and Asia,[15] but even these highly exploited workers enjoyed more control over their destinies than enslaved African laborers of the early modern era.[16] And though migrations from Europe to settler colonies in the Americas and Antipodes (Britain's term for Australia and New Zealand) continued across the nineteenth century, most migrants by the end of the nineteenth century were—like colonial and nineteenth-century indentured workers—labor migrants seeking wages, not land. For the hard-pressed peasants of both Asia and Europe, temporary and circulatory migrations to work as seasonal or precarious factory or farm hands or "arms" (braceros-braccianti) opened temporary possibilities to stabilize household-level, subsistence production at home.[17] It was in this context that migrant gender composition began to converge and to become decidedly more masculine.

In a first effort to compile and interpret migration data on a global scale, Adam McKeown estimates the total numbers of transcontinental migrants between 1846 and 1940 at 155 to 172.5 million.[18] Approximately fifty-five million people, he notes, left Europe and the Middle East and about three million left East Asia and India to move to the Americas. Another fifty million departed from South Asia and South China, and five million from the Middle East and other places in China left to transfer to Southeast Asia,

Australia, and other destinations in Oceania. Fully forty-eight million migrants left from East Asia for frontier areas in Central Asia, Siberia, and Manchuria. McKeown did not estimate international moves within Europe but these international and inter-European movers certainly equaled, if not greatly surpassed, the fifty-five million Europeans who migrated to the Americas.[19] Including inter-European migrants could easily raise these global estimates to well above two hundred million migrants between 1846 and 1940.

This more generous estimate of two hundred million approximates 17 percent of the world's population of 1.17 billion in 1840, about 9 percent of the 2.1 billion a century later. Even McKeown's more modest estimates come to slightly less than 1.5 to 1.7 million migrants annually, or three times the early modern rates, and are roughly equal to or somewhat larger than rates of migration at the end of the twentieth century.[20] Ferenczi reports only 1.6 percent of world populations in 1930 as living abroad, about half the figure for 2000, but this number is based on a narrower group that excludes the millions of immigrants who had changed their nationality through naturalization in the Americas.[21] Clearly then, these comparisons allow for quite different descriptions of the long-term dynamics of international migration.

According to McKeown, long-distance migrations across all major migratory circuits crept upward until 1870, slowing somewhat in the mid-1870s before picking up after 1880 and then escalating rapidly between 1895 and the onset of World War I.[22] After declining sharply during the war, migrations increased again temporarily. Thereafter, those to Northeast and Southeast Asia continued to grow until World War II but those to the Americas stagnated and declined sharply after 1930 in response to nationalist restrictions and the advent of the Great Depression. It was during these tumultuous swings in volume that the transition from nineteenth-century masculinization to twentieth-century feminization began.

Nineteenth-Century Flow Data: An Assessment

We assess the gender composition of immigrant populations in the nineteenth century using data from *International Migrations*.[23] These data are spatially far more extensive than available data for the early modern era. Because nineteenth-century record-keepers more often noted the individual characteristics of migrants, including their sex, we can evaluate migrant gender composition at the global level for the first time. Where possible, we also supplement data in *International Migrations* with additional flow data from Asia and the Americas and with scholarly case studies of gender and nineteenth-century migration for China, the United States, and Europe.

Figure 4.1   Emigrants and Immigrants, 1820–1924

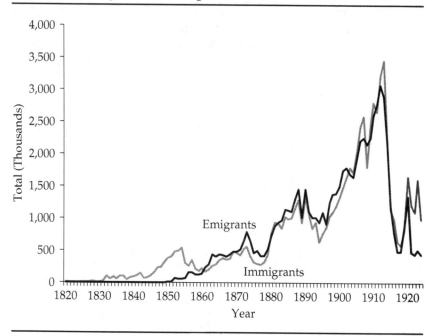

Source: Authors' compilation based on Willcox and Ferenczi 1929.
Note: These data refer only to those that have breakdowns by sex.

The 1929 compilation of international flow data used in this chapter was a product of the National Bureau of Economic Research's collaboration with the ILO of the League of Nations in Geneva. Quite different from the flow data of the *Trans-Atlantic Slave Trade Database*, the nineteenth-century flow data allow—indeed require because they were enumerated separately—comparative analysis of the gender composition among emigrants and immigrants. *International Migrations* provides sex-specific data for approximately 45 to 50 percent of McKeown's conservative estimate for the total volume of nineteenth-century migration.[24] It offers data by sex for emigrants from forty-two sending areas and data by sex for immigrants to thirty-nine receiving areas, totaling 75,885,635 emigrants and 77,022,665 immigrants. Thus, in this chapter, we analyze an unknowable but sizeable fraction of nineteenth-century international migrants.

Although enumerated in different locations, figure 4.1 shows that the dynamics and volume of emigration and immigration documented in *International Migrations* closely overlap. But the gender composition of emigrants and immigrants varied a bit more than that. The percentage female among all nineteenth-century emigrants was 30.8 percent, and among immigrants 32.9 percent. Still, over the entire century, emigrations and immigrations were both male predominant and only slightly above the upper limit defined by our category of heavily male predominant.[25]

International Migrations includes data from every region of the world but suffers from several large, if predictable, lacunae that complicate any analysis of migrant gender composition and its consequences, especially at the global level. For example, data for emigrants from and immigrants to Africa were limited once the slave trade became illicit and large parts of Africa fell under the direct rule of European empire builders who recorded only their own comings and goings. For both Africa and the Asia-Pacific areas, the best and most continuous data in *International Migrations* documented British and other European immigrants to the Antipodean British settler colonies and to Hawaii, along with departures from these places.[26] *International Migrations* included little emigration data from other British colonies even though India and the south China hinterland of Hong Kong, Canton, and Macao were major nineteenth-century sending areas.[27] Finally, although migrations into and out of Africa and Asia were underrepresented, migrations to the United States were overrepresented. As a result, global analyses of immigrant gender composition based on *International Migrations* mirror U.S. patterns far more closely than is warranted, pushing female shares higher.

Our analysis of the gender composition of the proletarian mass migrations examines three main issues. First, it treats the first half of the nineteenth century as a period of transition from the heavily male coerced European indentured servant migrations and the later slave trade migrations of the Atlantic to an era of somewhat more voluntary and also more gender-balanced settler colonizer migrations. Second, it compares the gender composition of immigrants and emigrants for macro-regions and individual countries, suggesting that migrations of settler colonizers remained consistently more gender-balanced than labor migrants. As in chapter 3, we compare exceptional migration cases that were either gender balanced and female predominant or, alternatively, heavily male to better understand the causes of such variations. Finally, it analyzes a shift from masculinization to feminization of labor migrations as increasing proportions of families of earlier male migrants shifted their homes or sites of reproduction to the Americas.

Gender Composition Among Slaves, Labor Migrants, and Settler Colonizers, 1800–1860

The abolition of slavery destroyed one of the most important and horrific circuits of early modern global integration. New migrations of both settler colonizers and labor migrants—from the more coerced indentured

Figure 4.2   Percentage Female African Slaves and Immigrants, 1800–1860

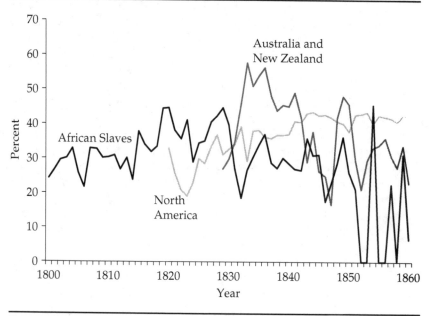

Source: Authors' compilation based on Willcox and Ferenczi 1929 and on Voyages 2012.

servants of Asia to the European laborers able to pay their own passages—were both responses to the abolition of slavery. These more voluntary migrations marked the global integration of the nineteenth century as quite different from that of the early modern era. As Harriet Friedmann demonstrates, even the most independent European settlers colonizing imperial and national frontiers grew grains destined for international sale and export.[28] Rather than being subsistence producers isolated from global markets, these migrant yeomen farmers quickly became dependent on either hiring waged workers (during harvests, for example) or their sons and daughters as wage workers. In addition, even nineteenth-century contract laborers, recruited under varying degrees of coercion such as indenture or debt peonage, ostensibly worked for wages and were deeply enmeshed in cash economies.

Figure 4.2 suggests that settler colonizer migrations entwined in complex ways with the abolition of slavery during the end of European indenture and the rise of wage-earning on a global scale in the first half of the nineteenth century. Migrations to North America became more female after 1830 as laws forbidding indentured servitude for Europeans were passed.[29] The decline of penal transportations to Australia also resulted in a more profound feminization. The juxtaposition of these three apparently unrelated migrations also provides intriguing if limited evidence for the integration of Atlantic and Pacific labor markets and for a convergence in migration gender composition across regions—an integration that most historians and economists usually date to the second half of the century.[30]

Before 1835, women's share of slave trade, North American, and Antipodean immigration increased and decreased in tandem. That the gender composition of the two Atlantic labor migrations varied together is no surprise because that had been true since at least 1700. The contemporaneous rise of Anglo American abolitionist movements in the 1790s and termination of the slave trade by Britain and the United States in 1807 and 1808 thus had important long-term consequences for the gender composition of migrants. In the United States, abolitionism so problematized any kind of servitude for Europeans as potential citizens that most states forbad indentured labor;[31] one consequence was that few Europeans traveled under contract to the United States after 1830.[32] In addition, although in the Atlantic free migrants for the first time also outnumbered slaves, in the Pacific the synchronicity of slave and immigrant gender composition persisted longer.[33]

In the mid-eighteenth century, the British Empire had already connected the Atlantic and Pacific macro-regions through its colonization of India and its efforts to limit the imperial expansion of France and the Netherlands in the southeastern Pacific.[34] Beginning in 1788, Britain had organized sizeable and coerced transportations of its paupers and prisoners—who before 1776 had been sent to North America—to Australia. Although *International Migrations* includes no data on these earliest penal transportations to New South Wales, most scholarly studies have described male convicts as outnumbering female convicts by a factor of five or six until the 1830s.[35] If they were indeed 18 to 20 percent female, then such convict migrations easily fell within the category of heavily male migrations.[36] By 1830, men released from servitude in New South Wales in Australia may have outnumbered women by as many as ten to one.[37]

Rising percentages of women and girls accompanied the waning of European indentured and penal migrations, but feminization proceeded in somewhat different fashion on the opposite side of the world. The proportion female among European immigrants to the United States increased steadily from 1820 to 1840 and then stabilized at just above 40 percent—still slightly male predominant but considerably more balanced than during earlier eighteenth-century Atlantic migrations. Not only did settler colonizers in both centuries more often travel in family groups and expect to settle permanently and to reproduce themselves, they also found themselves after 1800 welcome to do so and to claim western lands as free white subjects or citizens-to-be.[38]

Despite this generally positive correlation between the enhanced liberty of European migrants as settler colonizers and the feminization of migration, studies of antebellum immigration to the United States also provide a sober reminder that some nineteenth-century migrants from Europe remained extremely poor. They included, for example, the extremely vulnerable and often starving and ill survivors of the Irish potato famine between 1845 and 1852. Coerced to leave but able to choose among several destinations (Canada, the United States, Great Britain, and Australia), many of the poorest Irish were women who settled disproportionately in East Coast U.S. and Canadian cities. Called paupers and stigmatized by both Americans and Canadians, these poorest migrants lacked the resources to become settler colonizers. But they could find wages in textile mills or as domestic servants in middle-class households. Among the Irish settled in American cities, then, gender composition was actually more likely to be gender balanced than in rural and frontier areas.[39] Both gender ideology about appropriate work for women and the familiarity of family farm labor on the settlers' frontiers contributed to the modest feminization of North American immigrants after 1820.[40]

On the other side of the world, the gender composition of immigrants instead shifted after 1830 from heavily male to female predominant. As critiques of convict transportations mounted in Britain after the Napoleonic wars, Britain's imperial strategists hoped that the migration of the unmarried middle-class women they regarded as ladies might lead to higher morality and higher rates of marriage in Australia, rendering governable the heavily male ex-prisoner populations.[41] Middle-class emigration societies especially focused on assisting female migrations,[42] and the men of Australia loudly disparaged lady newcomers and demanded good plebeian women with practical skills. The British crown's financial support for female migration quickly produced much higher proportions female than among North America's settler colonizers.[43] Eventually, earlier migrants also provided financial support for the migration of sisters, brothers, and potential wives.[44]

When schemes to assist emigration to Australia ended abruptly in the face of economic crisis in 1841, the gender composition of European migrations to North America and to the Antipodes diverged sharply, terminating the short period of gender-balanced Antipodean immigration and providing a first indicator—appropriately, from the Pacific—of a renewed masculinization that would soon characterize almost all labor migrations worldwide. Even the discovery (in Great Britain's 1851 census) of the so-called surplus of unmarried adult women[45]—which produced renewed calls to assist four hundred thousand unmarried middle-class ladies as potential emigrants—failed to produce a second era of gender-balanced migration to Australia.[46] In Australia, the swift masculinization of immigration followed the discovery of gold in 1851. Whether Chinese, South American, or European, gold-seekers in Australia and subsequently in North America were not settlers expecting to reproduce themselves, their families, or familiar ways of life.[47] Such short-lived rush migrations to newly opening mining areas were the cutting edge of largely male movements of seasonal laborers in construction, lumbering, mining, commercial and plantation agriculture that defined the proletarian mass migrations worldwide.[48]

Adding data on Africa, Asia, and the Caribbean in *International Migrations* brings the masculinization of the nineteenth century into even sharper focus. Several scholars have challenged earlier histories that contrast a new slavery among racialized Asian coolies and privileged, white European settler colonizers.[49] Instead, they describe a complex middle ground of more and less secure and more or less coerced and indebted wage-earning labor migrants from many origins, traveling long distances to work temporarily for low wages. That the indentured laborers coming from Asia in the nineteenth century were much more heavily male than early modern slaves seems to confirm their point.

Almost all scholarly studies describe Asia's indentured workers as heavily and persistently male.[50] The migrations of Chinese and Indian laborers developed in quite different ways, however, and had somewhat different gender composition.[51] The British abolition of slavery in 1838 and the subsequent British Opium Wars with China (which began in 1839) created exploitative recruitment practices in part because locally knowledgeable and connected Chinese contractors and middlemen played central roles in recruiting and managing overwhelmingly male workers.[52] In contrast, given its long history of penal transportations from Britain to Australia and from India to Mauritius, British imperial administrators saw regulation of gender composition among Indian indentured laborers as essential to the maintenance of colonial order.[53] British regulations required fixed proportions of women, from 15 to 40 percent, to travel among male laborers from India.[54] By 1870, both Chinese and Indian laborers worked in places such as Panama, Peru, Malaysia, Australia, Trinidad, British Guiana, Jamaica, and British Honduras.[55] But in the British Caribbean, only 14 percent of Chinese were women—far lower than among the Indians.[56] Well into the twentieth century, China generated some of the most unbalanced and heavily male of the proletarian mass migrations, whether the Chinese traveled under indenture to Southeast Asia or, more freely, to North America. Including data on the undercounted and uncounted Indians and Chinese contract and indentured laborers would accentuate further the global masculinization of migrant populations first evident for Australia in figure 4.2.

Variations in Gender Composition
Across Spatial Scales, 1860–1924

After 1860, the emigration and immigration data included in *International Migrations* become both more comprehensive and more continuous. Gender composition among both emigrants and immigrants still varied impressively, with occasional cases of gender-balanced and female-predominant migrations standing out among the growing majority of male-predominant and heavily male migrations. Variations at a number of spatial scales point toward structural inequalities, gender relations, and forms of gender ideology that influenced the gender composition in both sending and receiving societies. At least for the nineteenth century, it is easier to identify a narrow range of factors that encouraged heavily male migrations than those that resulted in gender-balanced or female-predominant migrations.

Figures 4.3 and 4.4 trace the gender composition of emigrants and immigrants for regions with long series—at least thirty continuous years—of sex-specific data. Figure 4.3 focuses on the gender composition of immigrants to three important and well-known destinations: South America (represented by Argentina and Uruguay), the United States (including Hawaii), and Oceania or the Antipodean British Pacific (Australia and New Zealand). Figure 4.3 also adds to these well-known destinations several less well-known but important northern European ones (Belgium, the Netherlands, and Sweden).

Gender composition of immigrants to these four regions varied from a one-time low of 15 percent female to a one-time high of more than 60 percent female, with most annual flow data falling within the range defined as male predominant, that is, between 25 and 43 percent female. Overall, before 1890, immigrants to Europe and to the United States included higher proportions of women and girls than immigrants to Latin America or to Australia and New Zealand did. Proportions female among immigrants to the United States fell very sharply after 1890, however. Then, during the beginning decades of the twentieth century, immigration to all four destinations suddenly feminized.

Figure 4.4 shifts attention to the gender composition of emigrants from Japan, southeastern European (Austria, Italy, and Portugal), and northeastern Europe (Great Britain, Germany, Ireland, the Netherlands, and Sweden). These data are supplemented by flow data on Chinese emigrants.[57] Figure 4.4 shows that in 1870 and 1880, Chinese emigrants were a completely male group.[58] Yet by the first decades of the twentieth century, all emigrations also feminized.[59]

What is most impressive about figure 4.4 is its evidence of very heavily male emigration, especially in the late nineteenth century. Emigration

Figure 4.3   Percentage Female Immigrants, 1860–1924

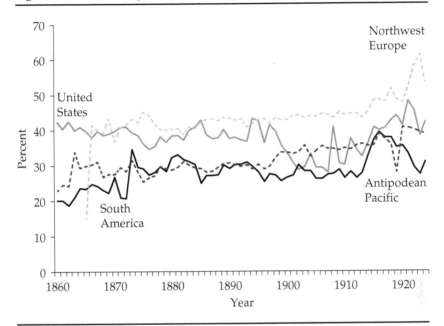

Source: Authors' compilation based on Willcox and Ferenczi 1929.
Note: Although the number of immigrants to northern Europe countries were far smaller than the number traveling to the Americas, they have been the subject of considerable scholarly study (Moch 1992; Bade 2003). McKeown excludes migrations within Europe from his calculations. In Willcox and Ferenczi's (1929) data, migrants to European countries (many of them possible return migrants) constituted about 9 percent of global totals across the entire century. For some sending societies, European destinations were very important, almost half of all migrants leaving Italy went across the Alps to European destinations and not to the Americas (Gabaccia 2000). France, Germany, the Netherlands, and the United Kingdom all attracted significant numbers of immigrants from other European countries.

from Japan and from southeastern Europe before 1890 usually fluctuated between only 15 and 25 percent female. The actual percentage female was undoubtedly much lower; recall that *International Migrations* included no emigration records for the many millions of mainly male emigrants leaving India for Africa and Southeast Asia.

Both figures 4.3 and 4.4 offer fascinating, if limited, evidence of global synchronicity in gender composition across the nineteenth century. Before 1890, the dynamics of gender composition of immigrants to European countries inverted the dynamics of gender composition among

Figure 4.4   Percentage Female Emigrants, 1860–1924

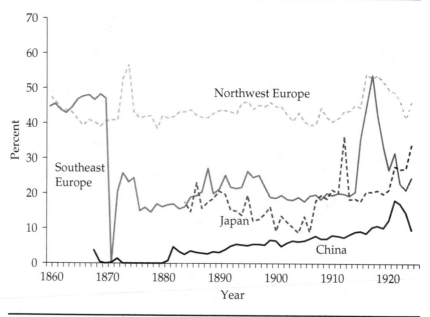

Source: Authors' compilation based on Willcox and Ferenczi 1929 and on unpublished port data for Chinese travelers made available to us by Adam McKeown and compiled by Elizabeth Sinn.

immigrants arriving in the United States. After 1890, immigration to the United States quickly and sharply masculinized (with the percentage female dropping to less than one-third), and the proportions female among Australia's immigrants (which had fallen sharply after 1850s) rose. Dynamics in gender composition like these suggest that northwestern Europeans viewed other European countries, the United States, and the Antipodes as alternative and competing destinations, their choices likely influenced by an inverse cycle of employment and investment documented by several Atlantic economic historians.[60] By contrast, feminization characterized all emigrations and immigrations documented in figures 4.3 and 4.4 after 1910.

Scholars have sought to explain the more gender-balanced composition of immigrants to the Americas and to northern European countries and the heavily male emigrations from southern and southeast Europe and from China and Japan. The latter especially emphasize that male emigrants from southeastern Europe and Asia lacked the resources to become settler colonizers; as laborers they frequently encountered discrimination and thus took temporary or seasonal work. The most heavily male migrations were sojourners with very high rates of return to their homelands.[61] In the case of Asian sojourners, natives' racism resulted in shockingly frequent incidences of anti-Asian violence and the increasing imposition of laws aimed at restricting Asian workers' autonomy and mobility.[62] Asian and European sojourners included a mix of married and single men traveling without families but as part of groups of male friends and kinsmen, often under the leadership or control of a labor recruiter boss known as a padrone or snakehead.[63] Case studies of Chinese and Italians suggest further that men's desire to provide infusions of cash for their families, through short- or longer-term wage-earning campaigns became the foundation for reproducing peasant households and ways of life associated with subsistence agriculture in peripheral areas of the world economy.[64]

Analyzing immigrants within Europe, Marlou Schrover argues that gender balance was the norm among both European emigrants and immigrants in the nineteenth century.[65] But her analysis also points to even greater variations in gender composition than is revealed in figure 4.3. For example, before World War I, both Great Britain and Russia attracted male-predominant immigrants—heavily so in the case of Russia. Schrover argues further that short periods of rapid feminization often followed years of heavily male migrations, pointing to state policies that sometimes prohibited or limited the immigration of one sex or the other. In addition, a sizeable literature documents that female wage-earners became immigrants to neighboring European countries largely to seek work as domestic servants.[66] Finally, Johanna Leinonen and Donna Gabaccia argue that international marriages—including those between European natives and North Americans and with the American children of returned emigrants—sometimes also produced gender-balanced immigrant populations, for example in Sweden.[67]

Two U.S. immigrant groups with relatively balanced gender composition—Russian Jewish and Irish immigrants (see figure 4.5)—were the product of very different migrant motivations and gender relations. Both groups have sometimes been compared with twentieth-century refugees—the Irish driven into exile by famine and the Jews by pogroms.[68] Such homeland experiences certainly could encourage permanent departures, with migrants intending to reproduce their families and cultures elsewhere—a common foundation for gender-balanced migrations. But this explanation better fits the case of Jews from Russia and eastern Europe, who typically migrated in family groups or quickly reunified after the arrival of male pioneers; they included considerably higher than average proportions of married women and minor children.[69] By contrast, the vast majority of immigrants from Ireland—male and female, before, during and after the famine of the 1850s—were young, impoverished, and unmarried labor migrants seeking wage employment.[70] Irish immigrant women worked in very large numbers in domestic service, much like their counterparts in Europe, but their Jewish counterparts rarely did. Unmarried Jewish women gravitated instead toward factory employment while living within family households. In contrast to the very high rates of marriage for Jewish immigrant women, Irish immigrant women had very low rates and often postponed marriage into late life. In short, quite different gender relations and gender ideologies may produce gender-balanced migrations, even among those with strong incentives to leave their homelands.

Scholars of immigrants to the Americas most often attribute variations in migrant gender composition to ethnicity and cultural difference, putting special emphasis on patriarchal control exercised over female mobility in Mediterranean and Asian cultures. On the whole, the proportion female among southern European immigrants and Asian immigrants in Latin and North America certainly was low.[71] However, Frid di Silberstein's study of Italian immigrants arriving in Argentina between 1881 and 1911 identifies several periods of gender balance, in the early 1890s and 1900s, when total immigration volumes fell during periods of economic contraction.[72]

Demand for male and female wage-earners in the U.S. labor market, government regulations of land and thus settler colonization, and restrictive entry policies also influenced gender composition. Gabaccia argues that the sharp, late nineteenth-century drop in female proportions among U.S. immigrants was the result of the simultaneous closing of the American frontier (and thus the declining importance of relatively gender-balanced settler colonization migrations) and the rising importance of labor market demand for unskilled and largely male wage-earners in construction and the extractive heavy industries (such as steel and machinery manufacture).[73] According to Gabaccia, although demand for female labor in textiles, garments, and food processing also increased, demand for domestic servants—the largest labor market for female wage-earners—stagnated. Overall, immigrant gender composition was more balanced in cities such as New York or Chicago (with their large garment factories and many domestic servants) than in mining areas or in urban centers of heavy industry such as Detroit or Pittsburgh. Gabaccia does not deny that gender composition varied with national origin. Between 1820 and 1928, migrant gender composition varied from 36 to 48 percent female among northern and western European immigrants (with gender balance among the Irish), but from 10 to 46 percent among southern and eastern Europeans. Among Asians, the percentage female was lower, varying from 1 percent among those from India to 33 percent among those from Japan. Immigrants from Mexico, at 32 percent female, and from Canada, at 39 percent female, more resembled European than Asian immigrants. But Gabaccia's work also points toward other causes of variations in migrant gender composition.

Figure 4.5   Percentage Female Irish, Hebrew, Italian, and Chinese
Immigrants, 1856–1924

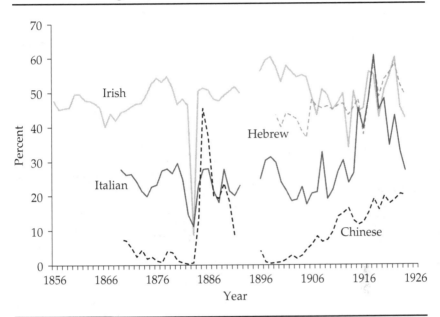

Source: Authors' compilation based on Willcox and Ferenczi 1929.

For example, increasing state restrictions imposed on migration after 1870 may have influenced U.S. immigrant gender composition. Figure 4.5, calculated from U.S. flow data, contrasts the gender composition of immigrants from China, Italy, and Russia—all groups that faced increasing restrictions after 1870—to the Irish, whose migrations were never as heavily restricted. As we observe, these restrictions had complex effects on all four national-origin groups.

Figure 4.5 describes sharp and temporary shifts in gender composition among Chinese and Irish migrants around 1882. That the proportion female among the Irish dropped precipitously just as it increased sharply among the Chinese suggests that both groups of men responded almost immediately to the Chinese Restriction Act of 1882. The volume of male Chinese migrant laborers sharply declined while Irish migration increased and temporarily masculinized. Progressive feminization of Chinese migration did not develop until twenty years later and therefore does not seem to have been an immediate response to restrictive laws imposed between 1882 and 1924. Note also that figure 4.5 does not include data on Japanese immigrants, but many studies have pointed to an increase in female proportions after 1907, when the so-called Gentlemen's Agreement between the United States and Japan imposed restrictions on Japanese laborers but exempted their proxy brides.[74] This so-called picture bride era of Japanese migration continued until 1917. In that year, the United States also restricted the immigration of all illiterates but exempted spouses of naturalized immigrants living in the country, with the result that the proportion female among both Irish and Italian increased. Both Gabaccia and Marion Houstoun and her colleagues provide convincing evidence that the exemption of wives and dependent children of naturalized immigrant citizens from the restrictive provisions of the 1924 laws also encouraged the rapid feminization of immigrants.[75]

Although evidence of global convergence toward the masculinization and subsequent feminization of international migrations seems convincing for individual nations and macro-regions, trends at the global level are harder to describe. Gabaccia and Elizabeth Zanoni reveal conflicting patterns of masculinization and feminization in nineteenth-century emigration and immigration data.[76] In their analysis, the percentage female among immigrants first fell (from over 40 percent) toward heavily male levels (about 25 percent female) during the 1860s and early 1870s but after 1880 began to rise to 35 percent. Emigration on a global scale suggested a very different dynamic sequence with the percentage female consistently above 25 percent. Women were the least well represented before 1860, but their proportions rose steadily to 38 percent during the 1920s. Both emigration and immigration data point toward masculinization followed by feminization, but the timing and levels of these dynamics differed.

Our analysis of the flow data in *International Migrations* suggests that the feminization of migration also reflected overall volumes of emigration and immigration. When global migration volumes increased in the nineteenth century, so did the percentage male; when they dropped, more often the proportion of women and girls rose. This suggests that periods of economic crisis and increasing state restrictions on immigration worked mainly to alter the choices open to male labor migrants. Migrations motivated by settlement and reproduction, including large shares of women, varied less and were less influenced by rising global demand for male labor or growing restrictions. And, as the case of the United States suggests, restrictions could even encourage feminization when they exempted women and children deemed to be dependent on those earlier male migrants who had committed themselves (through naturalization) to more permanent settlement.

Figures 4.6 and 4.7 examine the relationship of volume and gender composition among immigrants and emigrants enumerated by sex. In these figures, too, trends in gender composition among emigrants and immigrants differed significantly. Figure 4.6 describes a century of

Figure 4.6   Global Emigration, 1840–1924

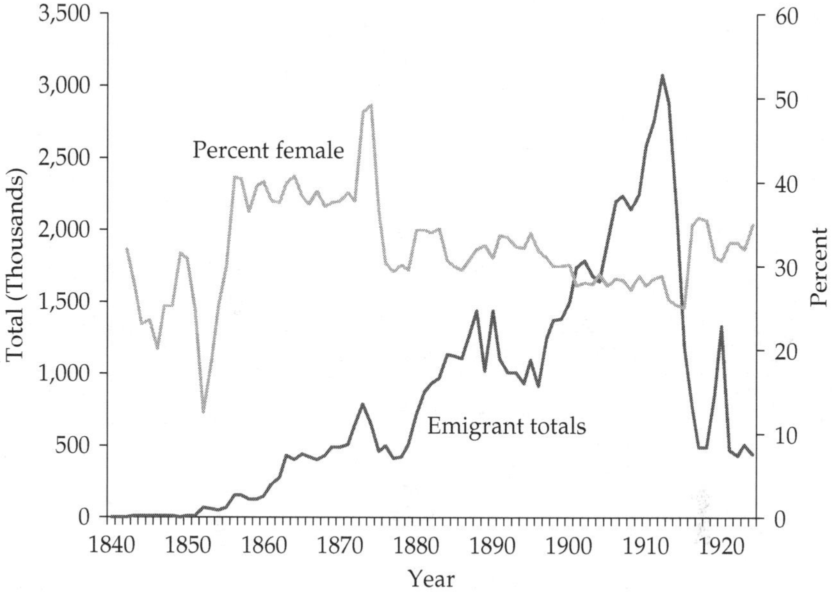

Source: Authors' compilation based on Willcox and Ferenczi 1929.

emigration that began (as we argue in this chapter) with a short period of feminization that pushed global emigrations toward gender balance around 1870. An equally sharp masculinization followed as migration increased worldwide: global migrations became most heavily male (around 75 percent) just before World War I. A modest feminization occurred among emigrants as migration volumes subsequently dropped: by 1924, women and girls made up only 30 percent of global migrants.

Figure 4.7 suggests feminization among immigrants in the years before 1840, followed by rapid masculinization to less than 30 percent female by century's turn. Furthermore, twentieth-century feminization also appears as quite modest. The gender composition of both global emigration and immigration fluctuated dramatically in the decade between 1914 and 1924. Although the dynamics of gender composition among emigrants and immigrants at the global scale differed, the relation between female shares and volumes of migration held in both cases, especially after the onset of immigration restrictions in the late nineteenth century. Schrover, de Frid Silberstein, and Gabaccia all also find evidence of this inverse

Figure 4.7   Global Immigration, 1820–1924

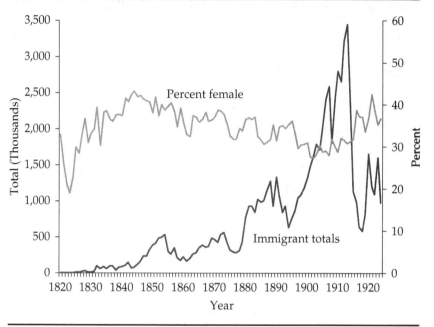

Source: Authors' compilation based on Willcox and Ferenczi 1929.

relationship of gender composition and migration volume in their studies of individual countries.[77]

Another possibility is that male migrants responded more directly to business cycles of investment and employment than female migrants did.[78] Such cycles better capture demand for paid, male labor than demand for unpaid reproductive or paid domestic work by women migrants. The possibility of an inverse relation between gender composition and migration volumes at the global level certainly provides an important starting point for analysis of twentieth-century feminization because global migrations are widely understood to have plummeted in the face of immigration restrictions, international warfare, and worldwide economic depression after 1930. Chapter 5 explores that possibility.

And the Consequences?

For the nineteenth century as for the early modern era, the consequences of variations in migrant gender composition are poorly understood and explored almost exclusively for the most heavily male emigrations and immigrations. Much research thus remains to be undertaken. In China and in parts of southern and eastern Europe, the same patriarchal and extended family kinship systems that released young male workers to migrate usually also guaranteed that the living places, lives, and work of women and children changed little with the migration of young men: women worked and remained subordinated within patriarchal families. Widespread ownership of small homes or small pieces of land allowed— in the absence of males—for the continuation of subsistence production by family labor, including wives, sisters, and daughters. Madeline Hsu, Dino Cinel, Bruno Ramirez, and Gabaccia all also note the fairly conventional and traditional uses to which migrant men's remittances were put.[79] The emotional consequences of the long separations of married men and their wives, and the possibilities for migrant men to escape homeland marital obligations or to form second families while abroad are also duly noted, but cannot be evaluated quantitatively.[80] By contrast, Linda Reeder argues that the absence of migrant men empowered women to approach governmental officials for new forms of assistance, and required them to manage household affairs and property with enhanced authority, encouraging rising rates of literacy.[81] Both Reeder and Maddalena Tirabassi note the development of moral panics among bourgeois Italians concerned about migrating peasant men's supposedly diminished control over rural women's sexuality—exactly the kind of moral disparagement of women Guttentag and Secord predict in female-predominant populations characterized by male structural power.[82] Evidence shows, however, that illegitimate births were less common, and the rate of such births often declined, in Italian regions with heavily male migrations.

Solid evidence suggests that receiving societies also feared the impact of heavily male migrations. Both Chinese and Italian migrants faced suspicion that their emigrations were less freely entered into and more coerced or strategic and less informed or rational than migrations with higher representations of females, for example, among the settler colonists.[83] Most host societies, much like Britain's imperial strategists, also saw heavily male migrations as threats to social order and morality, and sometimes also to local women.[84] Repeated claims by natives that migrant men threatened native women with their uncontrolled sexuality and introduced new moral threats such as homosexuality or raised rates of criminality have received little or no confirmation from empirical research. At most, historians have called attention to sexual jealousies and despair among heavily male Asian migrant populations leading to frequent suicide.[85]

Heavily male migrations almost certainly influenced women's work and marital choices by both sexes in societies with many immigrants. The development of a new domestic arrangement called boarding—male kin and friends paying immigrant women for their domestic services—is well documented for the United States.[86] But though some feminist theorists of the 1960s positively associated increased wage-earning with greater female autonomy, most studies of immigrant women in the heavily male migrations find instead that women wage-earners were young and unmarried and—working as they did at low-pay, exploitative jobs—either sought an escape into marriage or pursued autonomy through consumption.[87] Josh Angrist also argues that though heavily male migration increased nuptiality rates among the daughters of immigrants, it also diminished women's labor force participation, an outcome he attributes to the empowerment of the outnumbered girls to make desirable and early marriage choices.[88]

Marriage patterns, especially intermarriage or out-marriage (exogamy), offer perhaps the best documented consequence of heavily male migrations, at least for the United States. Scholars began to study immigrant intermarriage as a measure of assimilation in the 1940s.[89] Historically, at least, immigrant men were far more likely than immigrant women to choose partners from a different cultural group—a predictable consequence in heavily male migrations—and their marriage partners were most often natives of the destination country.[90]

Even this commonsensical consequence of heavily male migrations is not without its scholarly critics, however. Suzanne Sinke describes the way men's transnational ties to their homelands allowed them to escape the kinds of dyadic disadvantage in seeking marriage partners that Guttentag and Secord predicted as a consequence of heavily male populations.[91] Sinke notes that when migrations were heavily male, women from their homelands migrated to marry—sometimes because of an explicit invitation from a particular migrant man, sometimes based on their realistic assessment of marriage options at home and abroad. According to Annemarie Steidl, rates of out-marriage among the heavily male Austro-Hungarian empire immigrants to the United States were quite low because so many were able to choose the transnational option in finding a spouse.[92] Leinonen and Gabaccia instead find that heavily male northern European immigrant groups were very likely to out-marry and especially to marry native-born women.[93] Older migrant men also typically married native women who were much younger than themselves.

About the consequences, if any, of female-predominant migrations much less is known. Leinonen and Gabaccia identify and compare migrant female majorities among groups from several North Atlantic countries in the years around 1900. They argue that female-predominant migrations did not produce significant out-marriage (as was common among men in heavily male migrations) but rather a tendency among women (perhaps because they frequently worked as domestic servants) to marry late (and then to a fellow countryman) or not to marry at all.[94] Studies of the occasionally female-predominant Irish migrations[95] and historical studies of migrant domestic servants[96] tend to view the postmigration lives of women more as a consequence of their culture or their work as domestics than as a result of migrant gender composition itself. Nevertheless, it is striking that at least two studies of female-predominant migrations echo Guttentag and Secord's predictions. Diner also described a female immigrant Irish culture that expected high rates of female wage-earning, and that openly acknowledged considerable male-female tensions within the group and expression of open gender hostility.[97]

Several desiderata emerge from this brief review. First, scholars have explored many of the consequences of gender imbalance—patterns of marriage, in particular—that theorists such as Guttentag and Secord identified more than twenty-five years ago.[98] They have not, however, devoted enough attention to how gender imbalances may have influenced gender relations and fertility (whether among those separated by migration or unified in homelands or new destinations). Second, further study is needed of the consequences for sending and receiving regions of the anomalous but fairly common nineteenth-century cases of female-predominant migrations. Both female labor and family migrations may produce gender balance and female predominance, as this chapter's comparison of Russian Jewish and Irish immigrants in the United States suggests. Case studies of these nineteenth-century migrations may provide a foundation for understanding the consequences of the feminization of migrations in the early twentieth century.

= Chapter 5 =

The Twentieth Century: Migrant Gender Composition After 1918

Convergence toward heavily male migrations was a distinguishing characteristic of nineteenth-century global economic integration. Feminization, by contrast, would characterize the entire twentieth century. Beginning with the unraveling of an earlier global economy around 1920, the feminization of migration finally attracted attention during a renewed period of global integration at century's end. This made it easy for scholars and policymakers to assume that what they called globalization had caused feminization. The statistical record suggests otherwise, however. Instead, the much longer-term shift toward gender balance reflected the impact of new regulations and restrictions imposed on migrants by national states and international organizations around the world. Constructed during the 1920s and 1930s, a new international regime regulating human mobility pushed international migrations toward gender balance as the global economy extended into the twenty-first century.

In the twentieth century, countries increasingly sought to control, manage, and govern massive and formerly largely unregulated migrations by controlling their international borders and limiting rights to residency and work. Many countries had seen the proletarian mass migrations as threatening to the stability and the cultural or ethnic homogeneity believed to be the foundation for effective governance. The turn toward regulation and restriction of migration was thus itself, in part, a growing nationalist reaction against global integration that produced, historians argue, the great age of nationalism.[1] Even in the final decades of the twentieth century, when the free movement of capital, trade goods, and communication provided new and often celebratory symbols of recent globalization, international migration, though increasing in volume, remained tightly regulated.

Neither forced like early modern slaves, nor lured like settler colonizers, nor free to move about as they pleased like the European proletar-
ians of the nineteenth century, recent migrants have had little choice but
to navigate a complex thicket of rules and regulations. They accumulate
stacks of documents as they flee from harm or pursue positive plans for
marriage, study, work, or reproduction. As the next two chapters demonstrate, gender balance among migrants was not the result of any single
economic or political change. It was the outcome of millions of migrants
seeking ways to match their personal, economic and social desires, needs,
and plans to the migration rules of almost two hundred nation-states
around the world.

National efforts to manage human mobility also challenged international plans to collect data on global migrations. Restriction and regulation
generated new and changing typologies of migrants as, for example, guest
workers, skilled and unskilled workers, refugees, family migrants, international students, war brides, or asylum seekers. Such categories differentiated those persons a country was willing to tolerate or welcome from
others who, unable to gain permission and the necessary papers, went
uncounted or found themselves stigmatized as undesirable, criminal, or
stateless. As global integration again altered relations between richer and
poorer parts of the world in the latter decades of the twentieth century,
changing labor demand under an international regime of migration control guaranteed that women seeking wages as caregivers and assembly
workers numbered among the temporary workers who in the past had
been more often heavily male. Gender balance continued to characterize
those migrants who formed or joined kin already living abroad and those
refugees fleeing immediate violence or persecution. Male majorities persisted among the most desperate of undocumented asylum seekers and
those seeking to move without papers.

Compiled at the international level, flow and stock data could not
easily be organized around the exceedingly diverse migrant categories that individual nation-states created to regulate migration. Truly
systematic comparisons of gender composition among different types
of migrants are therefore not possible. Still, data on the gender composition of international migrants do exist. This chapter offers the first
scholarly analysis of flow data collected on international migrations
across the twentieth century; these are the only data that document
migrant gender composition, and thus feminization, before 1960. We
also assess stock data measures of migration and gender composition,
and suggest that the stock data gathered by the United Nations (UN)
in the 1980s and 1990s had their own, often unacknowledged, limits;
these limits often resulted in a misunderstanding of the origins and
extent of feminization.

Twentieth-Century Data
on International Migration

Scholars have described international migrations before 1920 and after 1960 in considerable detail, especially for nations of immigrants such as the United States, Canada, and Australia.[2] But aside from noting how restriction, depression, and wars diminished international mobility mid-century, few studies examine the years between 1920 and 1960. This scholarly silence may reflect the assumption that small migrations had little impact or that no reliable data existed to document them or their gender composition.[3]

Fortunately the last assumption is false. Flow data on migrant sex composition, as noted in chapter 4, became available in the 1920s as the new League of Nations made the compilation of data the responsibility of the International Labour Organization (ILO). Data collection then expanded steadily, first under the League of Nations and later under the United Nations. Only after UN demographers began to shift their attention toward the analysis of stock data in the 1970s and 1980s did the regular publication of flow data again diminish.

In 1953, the UN published a compilation of ILO flow data for the inter-war years. *Sex and Age of International Migrants: Statistics for 1918–1947* included data for a group of countries that was 50 percent larger than *International Migrations* had provided for the nineteenth century. Overall, about one-third of its data came from Europe and another third from North America, the Caribbean, and South America. Although only ten to twelve places in Africa and seven to eight in Asia reported data, this was an improvement over the available data for the nineteenth century.[4]

Despite their continuing work to compile data, demographers remained unsure how to define migrants. The ILO was interested mainly in labor migrations and the League of Nations struggled to devise policies to assist refugees.[5] Few countries distinguished between these categories in their record-keeping. The League of Nations sponsored a world conference to begin to map a typology of migration, but it mainly deepened statisticians' understanding of how nationalism and restrictions shaped national record-keeping.[6] Under Imre Ferenczi's eye, the standardization of flow data internationally remained a concern.[7] As in the past, many countries failed to differentiate aliens or foreigners from citizens or nationals in arrival and departure data. Some distinguished permanent from temporary migrants; others did not. As in the past, too, some countries counted only arrivals, only departures, or only European migrants. Furthermore, as growing numbers fled persecution and political violence in the 1930s and 1940s, the ILO became increasingly interested in refugees but it could not usually distinguish them statistically from labor migrants.[8]

When it began publishing a new series of annual flow data in 1948, the UN's *Demographic Yearbook* acknowledged the "absence of a uniform and practical definition" that differentiated migrants from short-term business travelers or tourists.[9] Intensely embroiled in controversial efforts to solve a refugee crisis in Europe, the new UN continued to deplore its inability to distinguish displacements and transfers of refugees from other migrants. But while deploring its own data, the UN also expanded collection of flow data as its membership rose from 51 to 192 countries. By 1970, the *Demographic Yearbook* included data on the sex of immigrant arrivals from more than ninety countries and of emigrant departures from more than one hundred, an increase of 50 percent over the interwar years. Collection of data from both Africa and Asia also expanded as newly independent nations emerged from colonial status.

Like the League of Nations before it, the UN struggled to select from a welter of heterogeneous national categories in which migration types should be tracked internationally. In 1950 and 1951, it identified frontier traffic as a sizeable but temporary and therefore harmless category of circulatory cross-border movement and urged countries to exclude such movements from their reports. In 1952, the enumeration of refugees was reluctantly acknowledged to be the responsibility of a separate UN agency, one that had also failed to enumerate by sex. In 1953, *Recommendations for the Improvement of International Migration Statistics* contrasted the ease of enumerating migrant sex to the impossibility of ascertaining migrant intentions or motives. By 1954, the *Demographic Yearbook* suggested counting departures alone as four separate categories.[10] Thereafter, the numbers of countries reporting emigration-departure data fell sharply. In 1959, authors admitted that migration was not a one-time well-defined event comparable to birth, death, or marriage, and suggested a simplified definition of migrant that distinguished between temporary (called short term, less than one year) and permanent (called long term, greater than a year) migrations.[11] Almost ten years later, the *Demographic Yearbook* admitted that the UN had been unable to create a standardized and universally accepted definition of *migrant*.[12] Then in 1976, new guidelines recommended that stock data could supplement flow data.[13] With evidence of increasing migration worldwide, flow data problems that had once appeared merely vexing seemed insurmountable. After 1985, UN publication of flow data became irregular. Our analysis therefore ends with that date.

However flawed, the flow data compiled internationally between 1918 and 1985 neither ignored sex nor routinely excluded women; even under the direction of the ILO, the data were not limited to counts of male labor migrants. Figure 5.1 shows that dynamics of emigration (departures) and immigration (arrivals) closely mirrored one another and also followed the rough patterns scholars have described for the twentieth century. Recall that figure 4.1 described global volumes of

Figure 5.1   Global Emigration and Immigration, 1918–1985

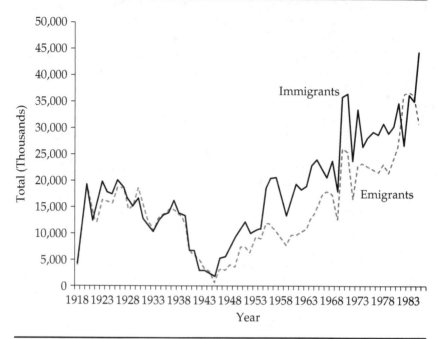

Source: Authors' compilation based on United Nations, Department of Social Affairs, Population Division, 1953, and United Nations, Department of Economic and Social Affairs, 2014.

migration from 1900 to 1920 as being between 2.0 and 3.5 million annually. Figure 5.1 shows that high volumes of emigrants and immigrants early in the century gave way to declining migrations after 1920, slowly rising migrations after 1950 and more rapid migration increases after 1960. Figure 5.1 also suggests why the United Nations struggled to find a way to enumerate refugees. Although enumerated migrations for the early 1940s fell under five hundred thousand yearly, scholars have estimated the number of stateless refugees at more than six to eight million in Europe alone in 1945.[14]

Data from *Sex and Age of International Migrants* enumerated 35,604,644 departures and 36,936,347,928 arrivals between 1918 and 1947.[15] These migrants constituted about 1.9 percent of the world's population in 1920 and about 1.6 percent in 1950. These estimates are close to the ILO's 1936 estimate of foreigners enumerated in stock data; in 1930, it was 2 percent of global population. Because UN stock data (for 150 countries from 1945 to 1955) described foreigners as making up 5 percent of the world's population, we believe that the sex-specific flow data in *Sex and Age of International Migrants* described roughly half of all migrants worldwide—about the same proportion captured in *International Migrations* in 1929.

After 1945, the dynamics of the two data series published in the UN's demographic yearbooks remained roughly similar but differences in how migrants were counted by individual nations produced greater disparities in the total volumes of arrivals and departures. In particular, the number of departures enumerated between 1945 and 1985 (65.6 million) were considerably lower than the numbers of arrivals (88.2 million).[16] Worldwide, immigrant arrivals equaled about 3 percent of the world's population in 1950, approximately 1.6 percent of that in 1990, which is slightly below UN estimates of about 3 percent of all persons living outside the country of their birth (LOCOB). For the 1960s and 1970s, we compared flow data with decadal estimates of global migrations and found that departure flows constituted a much lower share (41 to 54 percent) than arrival flows (63 to 72 percent).[17] Flow data otherwise documented rates of increases in migration comparable to global stock estimates of 32.3 million of LOCOB worldwide in the 1960s, 42.1 million in the 1970s, and 42.5 million in the 1980s. The 1990s saw another rapid increase in LOCOB, to 54.1 million.

Although Asia remained undercounted between 1918 and 1985, flow data nevertheless reinforce Adam McKeown's contention that migration was global in its dimensions and directions long before 1945.[18] Table 5.1 compares the distribution of immigrants-arrivals flow data with UN estimates based on the modeling of stock data for 1990 and 2013. As migration volumes diminished after 1920, Europe, Asia, North America, and South America all remained the important destinations they had been in the nineteenth century. Table 5.1 also underscores McKeown's observation that migrations to southeast and northeast Asia continued into the 1930s as migrations to European and American destinations diminished sharply.[19] As race-based restrictions were eliminated after 1945 and replaced by restrictions on other grounds, the share of Asians among emigrants again increased. European emigrants became Europe's guest workers and South America disappeared as an important migrant destination, replaced in part by Australia and New Zealand (Oceania in table 5.1).[20]

International migrations were global in the early twentieth century and remained so throughout the century. Better coverage of Asia and Africa in UN stock data for 1990 and 2013 suggests that either earlier flow data may have underestimated the historical importance of Africa as a migrant destination, or that both Asia and Africa were becoming more important as migrant destinations by the end of the twentieth century. Europe also replaced the United States as the largest receiver of migrants. Although available flow data do not allow scholars to compare

Table 5.1   Distribution of Immigrants, 1917–2013

	1917–1947 Immigrants- Arrivals 36.94 million	1945–1985 Immigrants- Arrivals 88.2 million	1990 LOCOB 154.2 million	2013 LOCOB 231.5 million
Asia	29.50	22.12	32.00	30.60
Oceania	2.20	8.61	3.00	3.00
South America	19.80	2.77	(includes Caribbean) 4.60	(includes Caribbean) 3.69
Caribbean	4.60	.057		
North America	23.60	21.65	18.00	22.93
Europe	17.30	41.94	32.00	31.29
Africa	3.00	2.34	10.00	8.00

Source: Authors' compilation based on United Nations, Department of Social Affairs, Population Division, 1953, and United Nations, Department of Economic and Social Affairs, 2014.
Note: LOCOB: Living outside country of birth. All numbers in percentages.

refugee, labor migrants, and other types of migrants over time, they provide adequate documentation for the gender composition of those who were counted as they crossed international boundaries. Feminization must therefore be understood as a long-term transition and not as a development of the late twentieth century.

Describing Migrant Gender Composition in the Twentieth Century

By tracking migrant gender composition with flow data and by comparing it when possible with broad stock data patterns for the years after 1945, we describe global convergence toward gender balance and offer tentative explanations for it. As in earlier chapters, we seek explanations for feminization in variations in migrant gender composition across time, macro-region, and nations. Our explanation for gender balance as a long-term, twentieth-century trend traces it to the intersection of the international regime of migration management and restriction with the restless dynamics of the twentieth-century global economy and changing gender ideologies.

Figure 5.2 tracks the percentage female among emigrants-departures and immigrants-arrivals between 1917 and 1985. Much like their nineteenth-century counterparts, these data describe the gender composition

Figure 5.2   Emigrants and Immigrants, 1918–1985

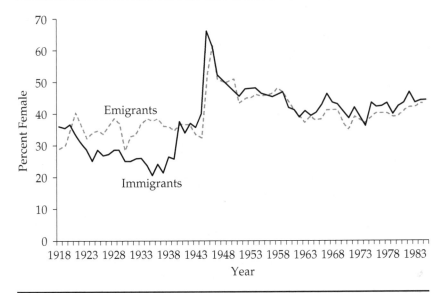

Source: Authors' compilation based on United Nations, Department of Social Affairs, Population Division, 1953, and United Nations, Department of Economic and Social Affairs, 2014.

of global departures and arrivals somewhat differently. Data for arrivals and immigrants show a decline in the percentage female toward low nineteenth-century levels, but only temporarily—to under 30 percent—in the 1920s and 1930s. In contrast, data on departures and emigrants show the percentage female remaining well above nineteenth-century levels for the entire century. Moreover, both data series point toward significant feminization in the decade between 1937 and 1948 and toward a very modest masculinization thereafter. Even with this modest masculinization, migrant populations in both series vacillated between 40 to 45 percent female for most of the second half of the twentieth century and approached—but did not reach—the lower limit of migrant gender balance, 47 percent.

Stock data instead describe international migrations as gender balanced in the decade after World War II. Published in the *Demographic Yearbook,* census data on foreign-born populations in 132 countries described postwar LOCOB as 48 percent female.[21] The UN data later describe women as 47 to 49 percent of migrants worldwide after 1960.[22] That stock data revealed slightly higher percentages female than flow data is a predictable outcome given the limits of stock data, but has rarely been acknowledged in the scholarly literature on feminization.[23] As chapter 2 emphasizes, stock data excludes temporary migrants (often heavily male) who arrived and departed in any intercensal period; it also reflects the feminization that always accompanies the aging of populations. The aging of a large cohort of earlier migrants produced the higher proportion female in stock data, compared with flow data, especially in countries with long histories of immigration. Difficulties in controlling for the impact of age on measurements of migrant gender composition in stock data have plagued analysis of sex and migration since the work of E. G. Ravenstein.[24] The aggregated census data compiled and made available by the UN could not take into account the impact of changing age structure on the gender composition of migrant populations. By juxtaposing the very modestly male-predominant migrant flows of the 1950s to stock data's portraits of migrant gender balance, we suggest that the presence of aging migrants produced a somewhat exaggerated measure of feminization in the UN data, a possibility we consider further in chapter 6.

Although the flow data summarized in figure 5.2 described twentieth-century migrations as modestly male predominant, they also revealed considerably higher proportions female than found in the nineteenth-century labor migrations. At 40 percent female or higher, twentieth-century migrations more resembled the migrations of early modern and nineteenth-century settler colonizers and refugees and the earliest years of the Atlantic slave trade than they did the migrations of slaves and individually recruited labor migrants in the eighteenth century or contract workers and other proletarian migrants of the nineteenth century. Again, in figure 5.2, feminization began early and persisted as a long-term phenomenon.

Variations in gender composition across regions provide additional evidence of global convergence toward gender balance for the twentieth century. Table 5.2 shows that every region of the world attracted higher proportions of female migrants in the early twentieth century than they had in the nineteenth. Migrations to every region of the world also feminized across the twentieth century. Increases in female shares of migration were especially dramatic in the Caribbean, Asia, and Europe. They also characterized migrations to both regions that were gaining (Asia, Europe) and those that were losing (Caribbean, Latin America) their importance as migrant destinations. Although the proportions female documented by flow data rarely exactly matched the evidence of feminization in stock data from the latter decades of the twentieth and twenty-first centuries, they seem impressive enough to conclude, again, that feminization began early and persisted as a twentieth-century trend.

Stock data for a few individual countries before 1960 confirm that—predictably—feminization was even more dramatic at the national level. In the paradigmatic nation of immigrants, women and girls were 43 percent

Table 5.2   Percent Female Immigrants, Arrivals, and Foreign Born, 1917–2013

	1917–1947 Immigrants-Arrivals 36.94 million	1945–1985 Immigrants-Arrivals 88.2 million	1990 Foreign Born 154.2 million	2013 Foreign Born 231.5 million
Asia	26.90	38.41	45.60	41.20
Oceania	43.10	47.70	49.10	50.24
South America	35.50	43.77	(includes Caribbean) 49.82	(includes Caribbean) 51.60
Caribbean	31.00	54.75		
North America	43.70	52.26	51.06	51.22
Europe	36.30	55.00	51.45	51.87
Africa	41.20	49.25	46.60	45.86

Source: Authors' compilation based on United Nations, Department of Social Affairs, Population Division, 1953, and United Nations, Department of Economic and Social Affairs, 2014.
Note: All numbers in percentages.

of the 13.5 million foreign-born immigrants living in the United States in 1910. Marlou Schrover's recent study of Europe shows approximately the same proportion female—between 43 and 44 percent—among foreigners living in Germany between 1890, when they numbered four hundred thousand, and 1910, when they numbered more than a million.[25] By 1950, the gender composition of the somewhat diminished foreign-born population of the United States (ten million) had risen to 49 percent female, an increase of 6 percentage points. Increase in the percentage female was even greater in Germany. Immediately after World War II, 54 percent of the 3.3 million foreigners living in western Germany and fully 58 percent of the 1.3 million in eastern Germany were female.[26] The populations of the two German states had feminized by ten to fourteen percentage points between 1910 and 1950. Yet, even at the national level, feminization went almost completely unremarked by social scientists and policymakers. No one ever suggested such demographic changes might bring consequences, nor were there any scholarly studies of what those consequences might be. Because the changes went unremarked, they also went unexplained. Our hunch is that the aging of earlier immigrants (always accompanied by a rising female presence in a population), the increasing importance of refugee movements (especially in Germany), and a changing economy that created more service and clerical jobs historically taken by women explain some part of these increases.

Figure 5.3   Gender Composition of Global Emigration, 1918–1985

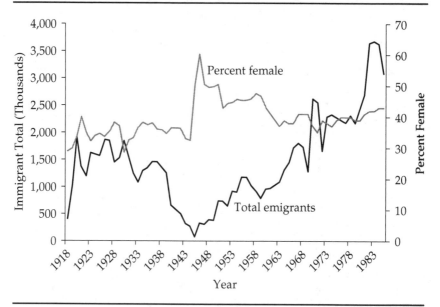

Source: Authors' compilation based on United Nations, Department of Social Affairs, Population Division, 1953, and United Nations, Department of Economic and Social Affairs, 2014.

Twentieth-century feminization began and pushed migrant gender composition toward gender balance as total volumes of international migration fell sharply after 1925. This correlation of rising percentages female and plummeting migration levels was visible in the nineteenth-century data. Figures 5.3 and 5.4 track the percentage female and global volumes of emigration-departures and immigration-arrivals as documented by twentieth-century flow data. Both suggest that before 1970, feminization generally accompanied decreases in global volumes of migration and masculinization was more common when migrations volumes rose. After 1970, however, the correlation became much weaker. Although both emigration and immigration increased after 1970, migrant gender composition remained relatively stable, at over 40 percent, after that date. Many studies of feminization and the Alcalá report on women's migration worldwide all also pointed toward increasing levels of female migration after 1990.[27]

Considering the flow data variations in gender composition across time while incorporating insights from the scholarly literature on the twentieth-century world and its migrants, we now offer a tentative explanation for

Figure 5.4   Gender Composition of Global Immigration, 1918–1985

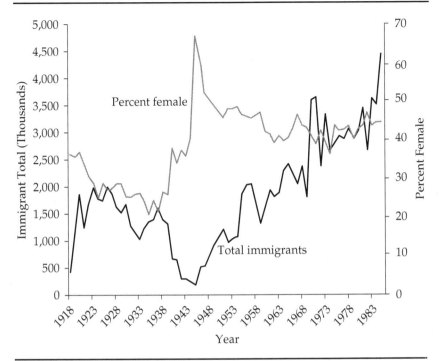

Source: Authors' compilation based on United Nations, Department of Social Affairs, Population Division, 1953, and United Nations, Department of Economic and Social Affairs, 2014.

the feminization of migration. It both acknowledges the early onset and long twentieth-century history of feminization and considers the possibility that somewhat different gender dynamics, including those in global labor markets, may have produced migrant gender balance before and after 1970.

Explaining the Twentieth-Century Global Convergence Toward Gender Balance

In the 1920s and 1930s, countries in the Americas and Europe imposed new limits on human mobility, thereby encouraging some kinds of movement and discouraging others.[28] This new migration regime departed decisively from both the laissez-faire liberalism and imperial contract labor recruitment programs of the nineteenth century.[29] Legislators and government administrators usually pointed to fears of cultural diversity and class conflicts and to concerns about national sovereignty and security (especially during World War I) and troubled national economies (notably during the depression of the 1930s) as motives for increased regulation.[30] Although scarcely coordinated with other movements hostile to past forms of global integration (such as growing anti-imperial mobilizations in Asia and Africa or the rise of fascist and authoritarian nationalist states in Asia, South America, and Europe), a spreading international regime of regulation and restriction nevertheless worked to unravel one of the key integrating ligaments of the nineteenth-century global economy.

Whether increasing regulation or disintegrating global labor markets was more important in causing the plummeting levels of international migration documented in figures 4.1 and 5.1 cannot yet be determined. But it seems certain that the powerful correlation of feminization and declining migration revealed in figures 5.3 and 5.4 had complex origins. It is possible that volatile demand for male labor relative to the more fixed demand for women's reproductive labor, paid or unpaid, continued to matter.[31] The social dynamics of migration, women migrants following earlier male labor migrants after they decided to settle, may have also mattered. In addition, new humanitarian arguments emerging from the League of Nations—that refugees deserved special consideration in the face of growing national restrictions and postwar ethnic cleansing in new nations—may have encouraged feminization because gender balance had historically often characterized migrants seeking refuge.[32] In any case, the work of the League of Nations' High Commissioners charged with oversight of the stateless and displaced, beginning with Fridtjof Nansen (1861–1930), did not trouble themselves with the creation of data about gender composition. And aside from studies of Jewish refugee movements—which were gender balanced—scholars have also not analyzed the gender composition of stateless persons and refugees in the 1920 and 1930s.[33]

Certainly, feminization had frequently accompanied declining migrations even in the absence of restrictions during past economic crises. To give one example from the United States, as demand for male U.S. labor dropped during the 1907 financial crisis, immigration plummeted in only one year from 1.3 million to 780,000 and the proportion female jumped from 27.6 to 35 percent.[34] Continued feminization in Asia until 1937 also occurred independent of the kinds of restrictions imposed increasingly in Europe and the Americas. It is thus possible that feminization after 1920 reflected the extreme volatility of demand in largely male labor markets, and that the migrations of women simply continued, undisturbed, as an occasional but stable minority of encumbrances on male labor migrants, as Ravenstein imagined. We believe, however, that comparison of relatively unregulated Asian immigrations to immigration in other regions after 1920 supports a different conclusion: for even as they feminized, immigration to Asia remained far more heavily male than immigration in Europe or the Americas.[35] The ongoing but relatively small movement of family settlers to Manchuria may have been almost alone in driving the modest feminization of Asian immigration.[36] If so, it is worth considering the possibility that Asian immigration feminized more slowly than elsewhere because no governmental regulations or restriction yet intervened in regional labor markets.

Outside Asia, regulation and restriction of migration encouraged feminization without dictating its course in any straightforward fashion. As chapter 4 demonstrates, Britain had already in the nineteenth century sought to increase the presence of women in Australia and to secure women's presence among India's contract laborers as strategies for governing heavily male populations. In the 1920s and 1930s, concerns about migration governance also figured prominently in the creation of restrictions on migration.[37] Few countries after World War I explicitly restricted or regulated migration to include women or to increase the numbers of female migrants. Many, however, sought quite consciously to reduce the nineteenth-century labor migrations that had been heavily male, to encourage permanent (if smaller and more selective) settlements of future migrants and to promote the integration and reproduction of earlier male migrations through provisions for the unification of families. In the United States, special provisions for family unification formed part of restrictive laws beginning in the late nineteenth century.[38] After 1921, spouses and dependent children of immigrant men who had naturalized and acquired U.S. citizenship could enter independent of discriminatory numerical caps imposed on other migrants of European origins.[39] Donna Gabaccia argues that the most heavily restricted migrants (those from southern and eastern Europe) subsequently experienced higher levels of feminization than groups that were either less heavily restricted (those from northern and western Europe) or completely free from numerical migration caps (those from countries in the Americas, especially Mexico and Canada).[40] Later, in the 1950s and 1960s, these restricted immigrants became the most enthusiastic supporters for the expansion of family reunification opportunities for immigrants. Thus, after 1920, migration restrictions created enhanced expectations of permanent settlement among migrants, ending the proletarian mass migrations of largely unregulated male movements. In the nineteenth century, too, states had viewed female migration and gender balance, which promoted marriage and family formation, as mechanisms for rendering more governable the heavily male populations, which were viewed as unruly and potentially dangerous. However, with enhanced expectations of permanent settlement by smaller and more selective groups of immigrants also came the expectation of, and possibilities for, reproduction in the receiving society—factors associated with migrant gender balance since the early modern era.

Outside the Americas, too, states had sought to bring proletarian and largely male mass migrations under control already at the end of the nineteenth century. The most common strategy in Europe was to recruit workers for short periods—issuing, for example, permits that allowed workers from Poland to be employed seasonally on Prussian or French farms. In Africa, programs that recruited exclusively male groups of African laborers for temporary work in European-owned mines continued into the twentieth century and contrasted sharply with the Europeans who, as documented in flow data, arrived voluntarily in Africa as gender-balanced settler colonizers.[41]

Cindy Hahamovitch describes the rapid spread of temporary labor programs—the forerunners of guest worker programs—through Germany, France, Switzerland, and other European countries in the years after World War I.[42] The intention of these programs was in part to prevent temporary workers from gaining access to the expensive social services provided by new European welfare states.[43] But even the United States, which scarcely possessed a welfare state before the late 1930s, experimented with the creation of temporary worker programs.[44] Most early guest worker programs also apparently recruited heavily or exclusively male laborers. When countries then also excluded these temporary workers from their counts of arrivals or of resident foreigners (as some but not all did), percentages female among migrants inevitably rose.

After 1937, the outbreak of warfare and its escalation into global conflict shows how other kinds of migrant regulation at both the national and international levels encouraged feminization. Warfare simultaneously discouraged voluntary labor migrations, generated growing populations of displaced and refugee people, and shipped millions of young male soldiers to locations far from their homes, where many of them found spouses they wished to accompany them home.

The dangers and violence associated with warfare certainly raised risks of travel, and figures 4.1 and 5.1 reveal international migrations falling to their lowest levels during the two world wars. The consequences for migrant gender composition during World War II and its aftermath (1937–1948) varied across regions, however. Emigration from Europe and Oceania feminized dramatically, if briefly, during World War II. By contrast, wartime emigration from Asia and the Caribbean masculinized. The available flow data cannot tell us whether masculinization during World War II reflected the recruitment of temporary workers, as in the United States through all-male braceros.[45] However, we do know that agricultural employers avidly supported such programs. Scholarly studies of the laborers brought to Germany from Ukraine and other conquered territories show that these migrations were more likely gender balanced in part because the Nazis recruited nannies and cleaners as well as factory workers and agricultural laborers.[46] Clearly, there is still much to be learned about the relation of gender and free or coerced labor migrations during wartime, given escalating demands for labor and shifts of many male workers into military service.

The same must also be said about the gender composition of the displaced persons and refugees generated by warfare. Although it is quite likely the displaced persons of Europe were a gender-balanced group, no systematic data confirm this assumption. Whereas the ILO had collected data noting the sex and age of migrants throughout the interwar years, UN initiatives with refugees at first produced little systematic data—understandable perhaps given the conditions of their work, but nevertheless a problem for understanding global convergence toward gender balance. For example, neither the 1951 Provisional Intergovernmental Committee for the Movement of Migrants from Europe (PICMME)—formed to tackle the European refugee problem, it would eventually evolve into the International Office for Migration (IOM)—nor the UN High Commissioner on Refugees (UNHCR) reported regularly on the sex or other demographic characteristics of those they served.

In contrast, scholars have focused considerable attention on the so-called European, Korean, German, and Japanese war or military brides who married Canadian, Australian, and U.S. soldiers during and after World War II and the Korean War.[47] The numbers of migrating brides may not have been large enough to alter gender composition on a global scale but they worked their influence at the regional level. The data in *Sex and Age of International Migrants* confirms findings made by historians that migrations driven by intercultural marriages (for example, American and British migrants with Swedes in the nineteenth century)[48] routinely produced female predominance because women were expected to take up residence in the homes of their husbands. The power of large U.S. military bases to produce female-predominant migrations continued throughout the twentieth century, even as gender expectations about marriage roles came under feminist challenge.[49]

Global inequalities remained pronounced in the 1950s and 1960s, sparking popular discussions of conflicts among First (NATO, capitalist, and democratic), Second (Warsaw Pact and communist countries), and Third (unaligned, largely postcolonial) Worlds.[50] Such inequalities produced rising migrations internationally, as figure 5.1 documents. Still, no dramatic re-masculinization of migrant populations occurred after World War II. The most likely explanation for relatively stable migrant gender composition in the postwar era was that regulations and restrictions continued to spread and to encourage gender balance as they had in earlier decades. It is also possible that some countries excluded the shortest term guest workers from their statistics.

Although advocates of free trade gained influence after World War II, no countries advocated a return to relatively free migration and even newly independent countries in Africa and Asia began patrolling their borders (and counting those who crossed them) as they established sovereignty. Neither did the abandonment of racially based migration restrictions (most famously in the United States) signal the abandonment of restriction and regulation. The same 1965 immigration act that eliminated discriminatory national origins quotas in the United States extended numerical limits on migration to the Americas for the first time.[51] Even the UN's Declaration on Human Rights acknowledged mainly that a person had a right to leave his or her country and to request asylum elsewhere but gave no guarantee that it would be granted. In the context of the Cold War, the relocation of religious and political refugees remained an important focus of migration regulation both internationally and at the national level.[52] Worldwide, however, the UNHCR counted only 1.6 million refugees living in camps in 1960 and 2.5 in 1970. The gender composition of refugees was not often documented but presumably they were gender balanced.

Regulations like those in operation between 1920 and 1940 prevented the postwar reemergence of heavily male labor migrations from producing any pronounced global masculinization. Scholars have exhaustively studied the postwar guest worker migrations of both Europe and the United States.[53] Both movements were heavily male. But many of the guest worker programs of Europe did allow the spouses and dependent children of workers to join them once they had established permanent residence. Naturalization, by contrast, was rarely an option. Scholars have also pointed out that in Europe, women, albeit a minority, were sometimes also recruited as guest workers.[54] Canada too recruited foreign domestic workers who then had the right to obtain the status of permanent residence and sponsor the migration of family members.[55] And, while the United States provided no provisions for the reunification of Mexican braceros' families, revisions to its immigration laws in 1952 and 1965 actually increased the availability of visas for family reunification (at least for naturalized citizens and permanent residents) and refugees relative to the number of visas available for labor migrants.[56]

After 1970, the same factors—including warfare, the search for refuge from discrimination and political violence, and the privileging of family unifications—continued to encourage gender balance within a rapidly changing world. With the deindustrialization of Europe and North America and the rise of powerful new industries in east and west Asia, the collapse of the Soviet Union and Warsaw Pact in 1989, and the spread of new digital technologies and modes of communication, popular and scholarly discussions of a thoroughly globalized world proliferated in the 1990s. This new era of global integration—much like earlier such epochs—generated increased if also changed demands for labor across the world's regions. For the first time, however, rapidly expanding global markets for labor had to work within an international regime of migration restrictions. As a result, migrations remained roughly gender balanced but the recruitment of women earning wages to do reproductive work, in both domestic and institutional settings, also attained an importance they had not had since the early modern slave trades of Afro-Eurasia.

Warfare and political violence associated with the building of post-colonial and postsocialist states in Africa, Asia, Europe, and Central America continued to guarantee that the numbers of refugees increased worldwide from 8.4 million in 1980 to 15.6 million in 2010. As the UNHCR began also to track internally displaced migrants, the numbers of these coerced migrants increased to more than forty-three million. The UNHCR reported gender balance (46 to 49 percent female in the 2000s) and con-cluded that "women and girls comprise about half of any refugee, inter-nally displaced or stateless population" a decade later.[57] Of the people who instead avoided the UNHCR system of refugee camps and formal procedures for group relocation and sought asylum as individuals, often undertaking arduous or dangerous journeys across the Mediterranean to Europe or across the Pacific to Australia to do so, however, only one-third were female.

In both Europe and in the United States, where the recruitment of male guest workers for industry and agriculture had been terminated in the 1960s and 1970s, marriage migrations and the unification of families remained the most important mechanisms for migration, facilitating the largest shares of international migrations in both places. At least since the 1970s, the largest group of female immigrants to the United States arrived with visas allotted to those reunifying families.[58] Providing far fewer visas or work permits for unskilled and semi-skilled male workers, both Europe and the United States noted the rise of irregular, clandestine, undocumented, or illegal arrivals.[59] From one million migrants without documents in 1970, the numbers in the United States rose to more than 11.7 million in 2012.[60] Estimates suggest that approximately 40 percent of adults were female.[61] In the European Union, clandestine migrants have been estimated at three to five million, but estimates of the female share are not available.

A vast and increasing scholarly literature documents further that female labor migration, including both married and unmarried women traveling as part of temporary labor recruitment schemes, has become more common during the most recent round of global integration. In the 1980s, Saskia Sassen-Koob notes changes in the gender practices of indus-trial labor markets in global cities and in Asia.[62] In newly industrializing parts of Asia or Central and South America, and in declining U.S. indus-trial cities, employers often preferred women for textile production, meat processing, and electronic assembly work.[63] But whereas Mexico's maquiladora plants along the U.S. border drew largely from internal migrants, meat processing in North Carolina and garment shops in Los Angeles or New York had largely immigrant female workforces. And although textiles, garments, and food processing remained important niches for migrant female labor internationally (so-called heavy industries such as oil or steel instead drew male migrants), migrant women—again, mainly from a country's interior—also dominated many electronic assembly plants, such as in coastal China. Still, most studies of autonomous female labor migrants focus on domestic and care or service workers working under temporary contracts.[64] Indeed, one distinguishing characteristic of the world economy of the late twentieth and early twenty-first centuries has been the rise of paid reproductive labor by migrant women originating in a macro-region increasingly defined as the Global South.[65] They are employed in the corresponding macro-region called the Global North, which includes parts of east and west Asia as well as North America and Europe, often as employees of wealthier wage-earning women who have moved into professional work. The demographic aging of many countries in Europe with falling fertility rates further increased demand for female service workers, especially where welfare services for young and old were being cut as a result of neoliberal reforms.[66] Overall, the rise of the temporary female labor migration originates in the shift of both Global North and Global South women's labor from unpaid to paid work, with migrant women doing paid reproductive work under strictly regulated and often highly exploitative conditions in homes, hospitals, and elder-care.

Concerns about trafficking of women and children, including sex trafficking, have accompanied awareness of women's labor migrations but statistics on these—like other forms of illicit migration—vary enormously. Estimates of trafficked labor of all sorts suggest between twelve and twenty million coerced and trafficked workers worldwide, but these numbers emerge mainly from advocacy groups and are widely rejected by scholars who point to the absence of reliable empirical data. The UN, for example, tracks mainly legislative and policing responses at the international level—not estimates of trafficked persons.[67] Policing records suggest that most trafficking does not involve sex work but rather exploitative labor conditions. Estimates of sex trafficking of women specifically vary enormously, with estimates of approximately one million globally appearing and reappearing in reports, often without citation to empirical evidence.[68] Given more than two hundred million migrants worldwide and more than one hundred million female migrants, and many popularly cited figures the product of speculation and exaggeration, it is clear that sex trafficking is not driving the feminization of migration, as some have feared.[69]

In the first half of the twentieth century, then, a new international regime of restricting and regulating migrations, exacerbated by global depression and warfare, diminished and transformed the heavily male labor migrations of the previous century. It did so largely by limiting male laborers to short-term guest worker programs and by privileging the unification of families separated by male migration to encourage settlement. In the second half of the century, international programs for the relocation of refugees housed in camps organized by the UN Human Rights Commission further encouraged the settlement of reproducing family groups. Global reorganization of both production and reproduction saw the creation of guest worker programs for both male workers in construction and industry and female workers performing paid reproductive work in richer countries, creating for the first time greater gender balance among global labor migrants. Only among migrants lacking proper documentation or seeking asylum were international moves still heavily male predominant, with sex trafficking a possible exception to the pattern.

Migrant Gender Composition in Flow and Stock Data: An Assessment

We have sought explanations for the feminization of migration in the analysis of both flow and stock data; to understand the resulting gender balance, however, scholars need to keep in mind the limits of both types of data and their availability across time. In 2013, in a somewhat surprising move, demographers in the Population Association of America requested that the UN return to the collection of "comprehensive data on annual flows of migrants across international borders,"[70] the kind of data the UN had increasingly abandoned after 1970. This suggests that scholars are reconsidering the usefulness of stock data, acknowledging its weaknesses, but also reconsidering the kinds of knowledge that flow data produces. Should the UN follow up on the suggestion, it will again however face the struggle of defining migrants and counting their sex. The 1996 *Demographic Yearbook* that published a decade of recent worldwide flow data provided no breakdown by sex as it routinely had done thirty years earlier. Recent UN flow data—for example on the "outward mobility ratio" of international students or on tourists entering and departing countries worldwide—also fails to record sex, making gendered analyses of these global flows almost impossible.[71]

Rather than ignore flow data or dismiss it as too flawed to use, this chapter analyzes it to present a richer and more historically accurate description of the feminization of migration and global convergence toward migrant gender balance. Although our analysis of how restrictive migration policies, global labor markets, and changing gender ideologies intersected to produce gender balance must be regarded as tentative, we believe our most important point—that gender balance was produced in several different and changing ways across the century—will survive critique. By juxtaposing and considering the somewhat different portraits of migrant gender composition that emerge from flow and stock data, the chapter also suggests that stock data may have overestimated the extent of recent feminization.

If analysis of migrant gender composition is to advance, scholars must also consider how stock data on international migrations have been created. When it abandoned the publication of flow data to analyze stock data, UN demographers were convinced stock data was more easily available, defined migrants more clearly, and provided a broader and more inclusive snapshot of migrant gender composition. They were only partly correct. The UN Population Division rightly emphasized the large number of countries that reported the sex of persons living outside their birth country and described having access to 913 censuses (enumerated between 1945 and 2001) from 228 countries.[72] However, only 158 of those countries reported data from more than one census. UN reports on gender and migration thus provided estimates of migrant stock for many countries based on observed trends rather than empirical data. One online report acknowledged that "for countries having information on the international migrant stock for at least two points in time, interpolation or extrapolation was used to estimate the international migrant stock." And for countries reporting only one census, "estimates for the reference years were derived by assuming rates of growth or decrease for the migrant stock in the years preceding or following the only observation available." For the eighteen countries that had never reported any census data, "a model was used to estimate the international migrant stock assuming that the proportion of international migrants in the total population would vary inversely with the size of the total population, as was observed in countries with data available."[73] To a considerable degree, then, estimates and statistical modeling had replaced empirical data.

Scholars associated with the University of Oxford's Migration Observatory have also emphasized limitations that scholars must keep in mind when interpreting UN stock data on gender and migration.[74] The first is that data collection practices and categories continue to differ cross-nationally even in stock data. Seventy percent of countries report census enumerations to the UN, but 17 percent (mainly in Europe) report data collected from population registers, and another 13 percent report data from surveys of representative population samples. These three types of data are not completely comparable. Neither do censuses, population registers, or surveys use the same standardized categories of analysis. For example, 80 percent of countries collect and report data on foreign-born residents (whether they have naturalized as citizens or not) but the remaining 20 percent count foreign nationals or aliens. The former is a more capacious category; in the latter, persons of foreign origin become invisible—the statistical equivalent of nonmigrants—when they change their citizenship. In countries such as Switzerland, where children inherit the nationality of their foreign parents, the numbers of aliens can grow even in the absence of new migrations. The birthplaces of aliens are also still not included in all national censuses despite pleas from international planning groups to include them.[75]

A second more general problem is that no stock data capture current migration patterns and trends. They reflect instead the accumulating effects of earlier migrations, along with intercensal changes caused by births and deaths. The only way to capture recent patterns and longer-term trends migrations in stock data is to include a census question about the date of migration as well as the place of birth—something few countries do. A related problem is that when countries' geographic and political boundaries change, people who have never moved may be reclassified as international migrants.[76] Finally, although refugees who were absent from the flow data of the late 1940s and early 1950s were eventually counted as immigrants or arrivals in censuses after their relocation, refugees living in camps (usually in Africa or Asia) are not often counted in either population registers, censuses, or sample surveys. And, as noted, data on refugees, asylum seekers, and displaced persons have not always included systematic information about sex, limiting the use of the kind of gender analysis we offer in this book. To these limitations of stock data we add that some nations, such as Israel, Egypt, and others in the Middle East, do not even enumerate noncitizen migrant workers as foreign-born persons.

In short, the kind of data collected and produced affects what scholars can know about migrant gender composition and thus about gender and migration. In the chapters that follow we introduce new forms of stock data to offer fresh insights into the causes and the consequences of migrant gender composition after 1970. Digitized, micro-level data from the University of Minnesota's IPUMS-International allow us to examine for the first time the characteristics of individual migrants, controlling for the impact of age on migrant gender composition. These data and analyses permit us to explore new explanations for migrant gender composition across sending and receiving regions and countries.

PART III

ANALYZING MIGRANT GENDER COMPOSITION WITH MICRO-LEVEL STOCK DATA

= Chapter 6 =

How and Why Migrant Gender
Composition Varies, 1970–2010

In this chapter, we examine recent variation in migrant gender composition by analyzing stock data while taking into account the age structure of migrant populations. In previous chapters, we describe some of
the relative strengths and weaknesses of stock data. Here we note several
additional issues that may matter especially to scholars interested in gender and migration. First, because past estimates of migrant gender composition have not paid attention to population age structures, they may also
have exaggerated both the degree of migrant feminization and the extent
of female presence among recent migrants, especially for countries with
long histories of immigration. Second, any analysis of stock data means
focusing on those foreign-born persons who remain long enough in a
receiving country to be enumerated by a census taker, thereby precluding
assessment of impacts of migrant gender composition on origin societies.
Such data may also render invisible certain types of migration, especially
seasonal or temporary moves that have most often—in many parts of the
world—been heavily male in the past. These are serious concerns to keep
in mind when analyzing stock data because together they suggest limits
on our ability to understand the long-term dynamics of migrant gender
composition save in the few countries, such as the United States and a
small group of North Atlantic countries, for which historical stock data
are available.[1]

This chapter complements analyses in earlier chapters with an analysis
of stock data since 1960. It reveals considerable global variation in migrant
gender composition, a global upward shift of women among immigrants,
and sustained gender balance among U.S. immigrants into the twenty-
first century. No longer, we argue, does the foundation for understanding
migrant gender composition need to be based on either flow or stock data.
This book couples analyses of both types of data so that our understanding of contemporary migrant gender composition links the past to the
future. Our findings reveal continued convergence toward gender balance

in the composition of migrant populations, not only in the United States, Canada, and Europe, but also in many other nations around the world.

We focus on the post-1960 era, when international migration began to grow—once again—worldwide. Building on insights from earlier work, we generate age-standardized estimates of the gender composition of migrant populations in as many nations as possible because stock data are extremely sensitive to age.[2] In fact, without attending to the age structure of stock migrant populations, the United Nations (UN) and others have likely overestimated the degree of migrant feminization. We also examine regional and national variations in these shifts, and ask whether and how migrant gender composition varies by different national origins in particular host countries.

Stock Data in the Age of the Computer

As contemporary scholars of migration of the past and present, we must remember that these types of analytic tasks, undertaken today, are not possible without individual-level micro data. Yet analyses of such data also require computing power and technology that developed for widespread use only in the second half of the twentieth century. In the United States, the Census Bureau was the first civilian agency to use an electronic computer to process data in the 1950s. That it spearheaded the first computer applications should not be a surprise given how central census data have been to state sciences and national missions since the early 1800s.[3] However, in light of the emergence of computer technology and related innovations, having micro data to analyze is the singular element that makes age standardization of the gender composition of foreign-born populations possible.

By the analytic standards of the early twenty-first century, digitized individual and household micro data have become critical and luckily, for demographers and historians alike, faculty at the Minnesota Population Center recognized this earlier. In the early 1990s, they received National Science Foundation (NSF) funding to develop the IPUMS-International project, the goal of which is to collect and distribute global census data that are documented, harmonized, and freely disseminated to the public.[4] These data create a global portrait of recent migrant gender composition and permit us to consider factors related to heavily male and female-predominant migrations during the most recent era of globalization. But how did the IPUMS-International emerge and why did it not do so before the 1990s? Answering this question requires attention to the blending of research interests among historians and demographers, and to how these interests intersected with earlier but less recognized efforts of demographers in Latin America, ultimately leading to the development of IPUMS-International.

In 1959, the Centro Latinoamericano de Demografía (CELADE) in Chile initiated "one of the most ambitious international sample census micro data projects of the twentieth century, the Operación de Muestras de Censos

(OMUECE)."[5] Long before IPUMS-International, CELADE developed "the largest, best documented" census micro data depository for the nations in Latin America and the Caribbean; it included the 1960 censuses from fifteen nations plus Puerto Rico, and the 1970 censuses from these same places in addition to all other Spanish-speaking nations in the region except Cuba and Peru. Although the 1960 census samples ranged from just 1 to 3 percent and the 1970s samples from 5 to 25 percent, five nations also housed data tapes that contained their complete census micro data. CELADE archived and standardized the data, and created detailed documentation to facilitate use. By 1980, however, because of reduced funding, the censuses in that year were not standardized, though CELADE still houses census data from the region to the present. Meanwhile, a Ph.D. student in history, Bob McCaa, arrived at CELADE in 1968 with some pre-doctoral training in demography at the University of Pennsylvania and working knowledge about how to computerize vital registration data for his dissertation.[6] This early connection between McCaa and CELADE was serendipitous and would later pave the way for the IPUMS-International project.

In the 1970s and 1980s, other demographers also worked on projects that aimed to preserve and standardize historical census data. In the 1980s, Samuel Preston received federal funds from the National Institute for Child Health and Development to create and analyze data from a public-use data file with census records from the 1910 U.S. Census. Others were also working on archiving census micro data for other parts of the world and periods of time, including Charles Hirschman, Robert Retherford, Etienne van de Walle, and Nikolai Botev. In 1985, as many gathered at a panel that Bob McCaa organized on micro computers for historical research at a national conference, he met Steve Ruggles, another historian interested in using historical data to study long-term change in U.S. family structure.[7] This was another important moment of connection because it occurred during a period in the discipline of history that has been described as extremely antiquantitative. Eventually, Ruggles was hired in the History Department at the University of Minnesota, where Bob McCaa was also a historian. After Ruggles continued to work with historical U.S. Census data, he and Bob received NSF global infrastructure funding in 1998 to go global. One reason for the proposal's success was the deep contacts and knowledge McCaa had about census data worldwide; for the proposal, he obtained many letters from nation-state representatives who agreed to participate and deposit census data in IPUMS-International.

Data and Analytical Plan

Our use of stock data permits us to employ more sophisticated methods than those often used to analyze historical flow data. Rather than describe the relative gender composition of immigrants and emigrants, the stock data used in this chapter yield estimates of the gender composition of immigrant populations while considering the age structure of these populations. Stock data thus permit us to use additional empirical social science methods as we continue to focus on our central concerns about gender and immigrant gender composition.

Although approximately 232 million persons (or about 3.1 percent of the world's population) currently live outside their country of birth, this population is not enumerated in any existing data set.[8] We use individual-level census data from the Integrated Public Use Microdata Series (IPUMS-International and IPUMS-USA) for three important reasons. First, they represent the largest population data base in the world and measure the stock of foreign-born persons living in particular countries at certain times. In contrast, only forty-three countries report flow data about international migration to the United Nations and less-developed nations report little to no data.[9] Second, although neither IPUMS nor UN data cover the entire world, IPUMS data offer us more leverage because they include information that extends beyond nativity and gender. By doing so, we can consider the methodological complexity that results from different age structures of male and female populations and ensure that our results are not related to higher mortality among aging foreign-born men than women. Third, these data yield more conservative measures of migrant gender composition than flow data and, across countries, are integrated with comparable variable names and codes, making them user-friendly. Therefore, rather than use flow data that are available only for a small share of nations worldwide and often aggregated across the sexes, IPUMS data permit us to examine the factors that influence immigrant gender composition and its consequences.

IPUMS data offer a global view of the gender composition of international migrant populations after 1960, including more than five hundred million people from censuses that have vast geographic and chronological coverage. Table 6.1 lists the countries, population counts, foreign-born breakdowns, and censuses available for each country. We rely on data that contain nativity information from a total of sixty-seven nations; of these, most have more than a single census' worth of data, for a total of 179 censuses. Although geographic coverage in the IPUMS samples is uneven, the data cast a very wide geographic net. Small and large nations span all world regions and cover census years from as early as 1970 to as late as 2010. For the United States, data are available for the entire period between 1850 and 2010. Unfortunately, other countries have either less extensive or no data.[10]

For this analysis, to avoid combining women and children, as others have done in the past, we focus on immigrants who are eighteen years and older.[11] Scholars have had a keen interest in whether women who migrate are autonomous or dependent on men. Unfortunately, these data do not permit us to directly assess the issue of autonomy but by focusing on those eighteen years and older, we are able to remove dependent

Table 6.1   Foreign-Born Populations and Gender Composition, Most Recent Census Year

Country	Population	Percent	Foreign Born in Population			Percent Female	Recent Census Year	Other Census Years with Nativity Variables
			Female	Male				
Argentina	39,662,450	4.4	945,900	808,800		54.4	2010	2001, 1991, 1980, 1970
Armenia	3,265,600	9.3	178,760	124,790		59.8	2001	
Austria	8,034,710	12.5	520,660	482,530		49.7	2001	
Belarus	9,907,060	11.5	617,830	522,060		54.8	1999	
Bolivia	8,276,920	1.1	45,430	47,950		47.9	2001	1992, 1976
Brazil	193,861,160	0.2	197,660	235,680		45.7	2010	2000, 1991, 1980, 1970, 1960
Burkina Faso	14,178,240	4.8	359,610	327,320		54.6	2006	1996
Cambodia	13,401,210	0.6	38,750	43,800		46.9	2008	1998
Cameroon	8,972,110	2.8	112,390	141,870		42.9	1987	1976
Canada	29,668,704	19.3	2,959,815	2,754,259		52.1	2001	1991, 1981, 1971
Chile	15,139,140	1.3	100,960	97,110		51.6	2002	1992, 1982, 1970
Colombia	40,061,680	0.2	36,650	39,300		48.8	2005	1993, 1985, 1973
Costa Rica	3,815,000	7.8	148,310	149,860		49.9	2000	1984, 1973
Cuba	11,187,670	0.1	8,640	7,000		56.8	2002	
Ecuador	14,482,330	1.3	95,620	99,580		49.2	2010	2001, 1990, 1982, 1974
Egypt	72,824,340	0.2	75,940	83,700		47.5	2006	1996
El Salvador	5,743,640	0.7	19,960	17,750		53.5	2007	1992
Fiji	843,230	1.6	6,340	6,850		50.0	2007	1996, 1986, 1976, 1966
France	60,000,000	12.7	3,910,455	3,709,527		51.3	2006	1999, 1990, 1982, 1975
Ghana	18,941,330	0.9	91,020	88,880		49.3	2000	
Greece	10,288,840	10	514,660	510,000		50.8	2001	
Guinea	7,290,710	5	190,950	174,630		55.0	1996	1983

(Table continues on p. 126.)

Table 6.1 (Continued)

Country	Population	Foreign Born in Population			Percent Female	Recent Census Year	Other Census Years with Nativity Variables
		Percent	Female	Male			
Haiti	8,380,450	0.2	8,670	8,090	52.9	2003	1973
Indonesia	236,000,000	0.1	108,890	127,260	44.4	2010	2000, 1990, 1980, 1971
Iran	64,991,250	1	286,050	381,600	44.4	2006	
Iraq	19,442,780	0.5	42,360	58,330	39.8	1997	
Ireland	4,403,140	14.9	315,900	340,500	47.9	2006	1991, 1981, 1971
Israel	5,563,650	32.3	964,520	831,280	54.3	1995	1983, 1972
Italy	59,814,780	3.9	1,266,880	1,090,920	54.7	2001	
Jamaica	2,051,790	0.9	9,770	9,420	52.2	2001	1991, 1982
Kenya	38,419,350	0.9	176,210	175,470	51.2	2009	1999, 1989
Kyrgyz Republic	5,649,860	4.5	149,460	102,600	60.3	2009	1999
Malawi	13,419,770	1.6	113,580	104,360	52.4	2008	1998, 1987
Malaysia	21,765,000	6.9	694,950	809,200	45.2	2000	1991, 1980, 1970
Mali	9,913,300	1.7	80,510	86,350	48.7	1998	1987
Mexico	119,000,000	0.7	425,240	431,720	49.4	2010	2000, 1990, 1970
Mongolia	2,437,250	0.3	3,660	4,490	42.1	2000	1989
Morocco	25,731,280	0.4	51,980	45,960	54.1	1994	1982
Nepal	22,759,868	2.6	392,502	189,656	70.3	2001	
Netherlands	15,810,417	8.4	720,083	613,083	55.2	2001	1971
Nicaragua	5,154,850	0.7	16,170	17,740	61.6	2005	1995, 1971
Pakistan	60,442,875	9	2,503,582	2,961,583	49.4	1973	
Palestine	2,270,670	5.5	71,050	54,480	59.5	2007	1997
Panama	3,411,180	4.2	71,130	72,370	60.2	2010	2000, 1990, 1980, 1970

Peru	27,458,950	0.3	38,650	39,700	50.1	2007	1993
Philippines	74,178,100	1.7	608,680	637,870	65.8	2000	1990
Portugal	10,340,520	6.2	326,560	316,160	58.6	2001	1991, 1981
Puerto Rico	3,541,600	8.9	169,200	144,500	50.1	2005	2000, 1990, 1980, 1970
Romania	21,379,670	0.6	66,070	58,810	54.5	2002	1992, 1977
Rwanda	8,433,920	4.4	182,920	188,670	48.4	2002	1991
Saint Lucia	133,820	4.3	3,000	2,820	27.7	1991	1980
Senegal	9,945,620	2.2	100,700	115,670	45.0	2002	1988
Sierra Leone	4,942,980	1.8	40,940	48,980	40.3	2004	
Slovenia	1,796,320	8.2	71,020	75,770	72.1	2002	
South Africa	52,382,850	2.1	440,250	642,850	39.9	2007	2001, 1996
South Sudan	7,753,786	0.3	11,129	15,000	39.9	2008	
Spain	40,785,480	5.3	1,066,480	1,081,400	49.9	2001	1991, 1981
Sudan	29,803,118	0.2	32,006	32,006	47.8	2008	
Switzerland	7,281,720	21.4	808,920	752,080	51.2	2000	1990, 1980, 1970
Tanzania	37,327,350	0.6	119,950	106,800	50.5	2002	1998
Thailand	60,451,900	0.4	112,100	146,600	41.5	2000	1990, 1980, 1970
Turkey	68,889,120	1.8	657,480	613,520	67.6	2000	1990, 1985
Uganda	24,974,490	1.6	200,540	199,030	50.5	2002	1991
United Kingdom	61,450,833	7.3	2,355,767	2,140,633	49.9	2001	1991
United States	306,169,200	12.6	20,136,100	18,516,600	51.1	2010	2000, 1990, 1980, 1970
Uruguay	2,568,660	0.6	6,690	5,210	58.2	2006	1996, 1985, 1975
Venezuela	23,064,890	4.3	493,910	497,610	57.6	2001	1990, 1981, 1971

Source: Authors' compilation based on Minnesota Population Center 2014.

children from the analysis. This also brings our analysis of data into better dialogue with the theoreticians Maria Guttentag and Paul Secord, whose work articulates effects of female or male predominance for working-age, child-bearing populations.[12]

The analysis presented here relies on the key variables of age, gender, nativity, and national origin.[13] Our consistent measure for migration status relies on place of residence and place of birth, which classify adults as foreign born or native born.[14] Because the objective is to examine gender migrant composition by creating conservative and reliable estimates, we use weighted age-standardized estimates of the sex composition of foreign-born populations.[15] Age standardization is widely used in demographic analyses, and it permits us to compare populations at different points of time by controlling for sex differences in longevity. This ensures that any observed changes in migrant gender composition do not result from the sex differences that emerge and often grow as populations' age. Although a salient characteristic of populations, and one that is central to an understanding of immigrant gender composition, recent UN estimates of stock data are not standardized by age (see 2006 as an example).

Our analytic strategy provides a broad map of global shifts and variations in the gender composition of migrant populations. For as many nations as possible, we first investigate whether and how variation in the gender composition of international migrants has shifted. We then examine national-origin variation in the gender composition of international migrants in a variety of host societies.

On a technical note, we use direct standardization, which permits the standard population to vary across census years. For each year of age, we calculate age-standardized estimates by taking both the number of women in the native-born population and the percentage of men who were foreign born; multiplying these two to calculate the expected number of foreign-born men, for example, age-standardized estimates of foreign-born men; obtaining the actual number of foreign-born women; and using the expected number of foreign-born men and actual number of foreign-born women to determine the proportion of the foreign born who are women. The procedure removes the effects of differences in mortality between men and women of the same age and standardizes male population estimates to the female age structure.

Recent Shifts in Global Gender Composition

Two key findings emerge from the analysis. First, some nations that have attracted large numbers of migrants, such as the United States and Canada, have not witnessed a substantial upward trend toward higher proportions of females among migrants since 1960. This contrasts with the inverse relationship between the percentage female and volume of

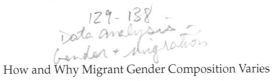

immigration observed at the end of the nineteenth and early twentieth centuries for proletarian mass migrations. However, among other nations, most proportions female among global migrants have shifted upward in the direction of gender balance. Second, variation is considerable in migrant gender composition when we examine movements from particular national origins to host countries. For example, in Ireland, women's presence among immigrants from the top three national origins ranges from 37 to 55 percent, in South Africa from 25 to 43 percent, and in Nepal from 53 to 70 percent. This range of variation permits us to consider the factors that link to heavily male and female predominant, and gender balanced, migrations, after 1960. Of course, what is not clear is whether and to what extent these variations have significant consequences for host societies, a question we examine in chapter 7.

We begin by showing standardized and nonstandardized estimates of the gender composition of global migrant populations. Figure 6.1 summarizes the average estimates for each year across all countries. It reveals that standardized estimates of migrant gender composition are more conservative than unstandardized ones, and that the average temporal variation between 1960 and 2010 is modest at best. However, the figure also illustrates a key finding about recent global feminization: that it has been largely gender balanced. Both lines in the figure begin and end within a range that we define as gender balanced; standardized estimates range from 47 to 48 percent and unstandardized ones from 48 to slightly more than 50 percent. The latter also overstate the former (see how the triangles, or standardized estimates, are consistently below the circles, or unstandardized estimates).

Figure 6.1 also shows considerable variation in migration gender composition. Among the outliers, for example, are the Netherlands in 1960 (61 percent), Nepal in 2001 (70 percent female), and South Africa in multiple years (34 to 36 percent female). These are important because they reflect country-specific dynamics that are gendered, such as the mid-twentieth century influx of refugees to the Netherlands, marriage migration practices in South Asia, and regional circular migration to and from South Africa. For example, the distinctly female-dominated immigrant population in the Netherlands was likely driven by both the decolonization of Indonesia and Suriname, which motivated return migration among Dutch expatriates, many with Indonesian or Surinamese brides,[16] and by a mid-twentieth century influx of refugees. The Nepali case is related to marriage migration practices in South Asia, and the South African one reflects the long-standing tradition of regional circular migration.

Although global shifts since 1960 are modest, we also examine shifts in immigrant gender composition in a diverse set of countries that have at least two censuses and are part of one of six regions: Africa, Asia and the Middle East, Central America and the Caribbean, Europe, North America,

Figure 6.1   Estimates of Gender Composition of Immigrant Populations, 1960–2010

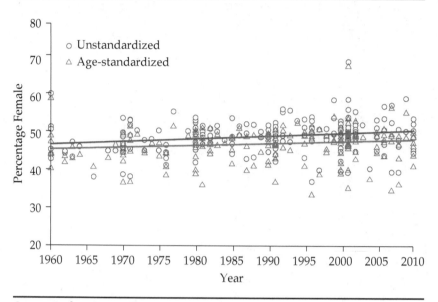

Source: Authors' compilation based on Minnesota Population Center 2014.

and South America. For the nations in these regions, we measure women's presence among immigrant populations using age-standardized estimates. In each figure, we order countries according to the proportion of their total population that is foreign born in the most recent census year.

Figure 6.2 describes upward shifts in the gender composition of foreign-born populations in thirteen African nations. For example, women's share of Guinea's foreign born (which was 5 percent of its 1996 population) grew from 44 to 52 percent, or from male predominant to gender balanced, between 1983 and 1996. Similarly, women's share among immigrants grew in five other African nations. It also rose in Senegal, from 42 to 44 percent between 1998 and 2002; in Uganda, from 45 to 50 percent between 1991 and 2002; in Tanzania, from 47 to 51 percent between 1988 and 2002; and in Morocco, from 48 to 53 percent between 1982 and 1994. In Cameroon and South Africa, nations where immigrants were predominantly male, women's share also rose modestly, from 39 to 40 percent between 1976 and 1987, and from 33 to 35 percent between 1996 and 2007, respectively. Women's rising presence among immigrants is likely related to growth in Africa's refugees, a population that includes many women as spouses and children, since the late 1970s. As Veronica Fynn documents, twenty-one nations in Africa experienced internal conflict, war,

Figure 6.2   Gender Composition of Foreign Born in Africa

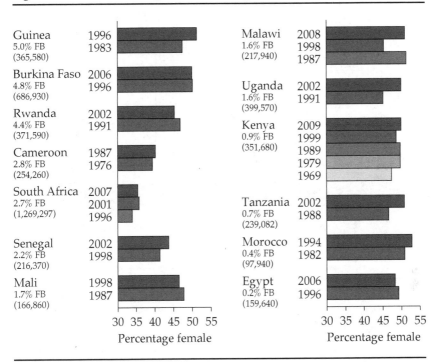

Source: Authors' compilation based on Minnesota Population Center 2014.

or political crisis in the 1990s, and Guinea, Senegal, Uganda, Tanzania, Morocco, Cameroon, and South Africa were host nations for refugees during this period.[17] In addition, women's rising presence in some nations, like Senegal, may derive from family reunification.[18]

Although these African nations saw upward shifts in women's representation, others witnessed declines during the same period. For example, Rwanda underwent significant political upheaval in the 1990s when eight hundred thousand men, women, and children were killed in the country's genocide, resulting in civil war and a downward shift in the presence of women among immigrants, from approximately 47 to 45 percent between 1991 and 2002.[19] Similar yet smaller declines occurred in Mali between 1987 and 1998 and in Egypt between 1996 and 2006. Malawi and Kenya, however, were special cases. In Malawi, women's presence among immigrants began as gender balanced in 1987, dropped in 1998, but then recovered in 2008—shifting from 52 to 45 to 51 percent female. In Kenya, shifts in immigrant

Figure 6.3   Gender Composition of Foreign Born in Asia and Middle East

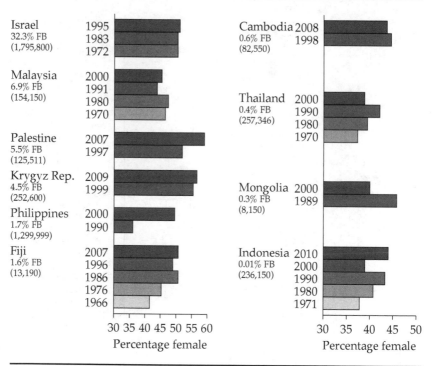

Source: Authors' compilation based on Minnesota Population Center 2014.

gender composition were smaller, from 47 to 50 percent between 1969 and 2009, maintaining gender balance throughout the period. In many African countries, these shifts were related to political instability, limited economic opportunities, and very high rates of HIV/AIDs infection, especially among women.[20]

We also see substantial variation in the gender composition of migrant populations in Asian and Middle Eastern nations. Figure 6.3 shows that the Philippines witnessed the most dramatic shift. In just one decade, the 1990s, the country's immigrant gender composition went from male predominant (approximately 36 percent) to gender balanced (50 percent).[21] This is likely related both to growth in the size of the country's immigrant population as well as diversity in the types of immigrants who settle there. Since the 1990s, the Philippines has attracted many Chinese, Koreans, Indians, and Americans, and most were students, professionals, or missionaries—populations that are more gender balanced than traditional labor migrants, who are likely to be either male or female predominant depending on the needs of the labor market.

. In Indonesia, the gender composition also feminized, from 38 percent female in 1971 to 44 percent female in 2010. Historically, many Chinese families migrated to Indonesia in gender-balanced groups. Estimates suggest that this shift was caused by the very large number of Chinese Indonesians (which is the largest Chinese population outside China). In Israel, where one-third of its population was foreign born in 1995, women's share of immigrants also modestly rose, but on the whole it has remained gender balanced since 1975 (percentage female shifted from 52 to just less than 50 and then to 51 during the period). This certainly reflects the type of immigrants that Israel attracts; often families and older immigrants, many are refugees or migrate for reasons of religious faith and ethnicity rather than for labor demand.

Malaysia's immigrant population shifted slightly downward from 47 to 45 percent female. Thailand's share of women immigrants, however, reversed between 1970 and 2000, growing from 37 to 43 percent female between 1970 and 1990 and then declining to 39 percent in 2000. These shifts are undoubtedly related to the labor demand for immigrants that has emerged since the 1970s. Since then strong economic growth has occurred in both nations related to export-led development.[22] Both Malaysia and Thailand are considered "countries of origin and destination" where illegal immigration is common.[23] In Thailand, many migrate from Myanmar-Burma as care workers.[24] From North Korea, they migrate as refugees and, according to Jiyoung Song, are mostly women.[25] In addition, the gender composition of Mongolia's immigrant population has shifted toward more men between 1989 and 2000, a period that captures this nation's shift to a democratic society and market economy. Since its first free elections in 1992, Mongolia's political and economic liberalization has led to employment growth in sectors that have long been the domain of men, such as mineral mining, energy generation, and food and textile manufacturing.[26]

In Central America and Caribbean nations (see figure 6.4), the same range of variability also appears. In Puerto Rico, where 9.2 percent of the 2005 population was foreign born, migrants became solidly gender balanced—shifting from 47 to 51 percent between 1970 and 1980 and remaining at approximately 51 percent thereafter.[27] In Costa Rica, where the foreign born represented 7.8 percent of the 2000 population, the gender composition shifted from male majority to gender balance—43 percent female in 1973 to 49 percent in 2000. Although Nicaraguans in the past were largely driven to Costa Rica by political instability, recent immigrants are motivated by better job prospects in the agricultural industry and the social programs that Costa Rica offers.[28] In addition, because the United States has a strong trade, military, and diplomatic relationship with Costa Rica,

Figure 6.4   Gender Composition of Foreign Born in Central America and Caribbean

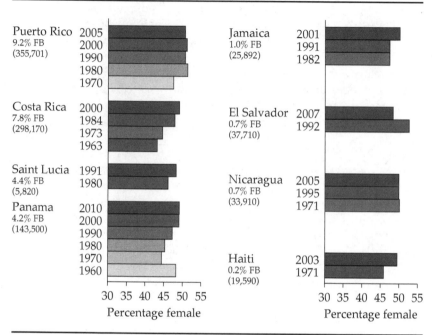

Source: Authors' compilation based on Minnesota Population Center 2014.

many American immigrants in Costa Rica are families. Women's presence among immigrants in Panama and Jamaica also grew and achieved gender balance. However, Nicaragua's immigrants remained roughly on the line between male majority and gender balance, at 46 percent female in 2005. El Salvador also transitioned toward fewer women among immigrants, but by 2007 women's share remained at the low-end of a gender-balanced population, or 48 percent, versus 53 percent in 1992. Therefore, although most of the variation is within the gender-balanced range, the variation from country to country remains impressive.

Among nations in Europe (see figure 6.5), the story is solidly one of gender balance and very modest shifts in women's share among immigrants.[29] For example, in Switzerland, where 21 percent of the population in 2000 was foreign born, women made up between 50 and 52 percent of immigrants in each of the four census years from 1970 to 2000. In the United Kingdom, where approximately 7 percent of the population is foreign born, immigrants have been gender balanced since 1991. Spain's

Figure 6.5   Gender Composition of Foreign Born in Europe

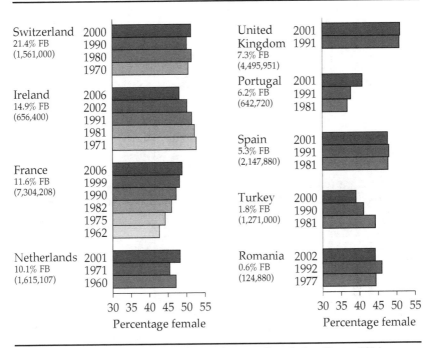

Source: Authors' compilation based on Minnesota Population Center 2014.

immigrant population also remained gender balanced, with approximately 48 percent female between 1981 and 2001. In the Netherlands, where approximately 10 percent of its 2001 population was foreign born, women's share ranged from 47 to 48 percent from 1971 to 2001. In addition, France and Portugal saw upward shifts in the share of women among immigrants. In France, the share grew from 43 to 48 percent between 1962 and 2006. This shift toward balance reflects the entry of refugees, but also the impact of restrictive laws passed in 1986 and 1993 permitting entry to immigrants only for reunification purposes, and mostly for women and children.[30]

In Portugal, women's share also grew, but immigrants remained male predominant in the latest census year, an increase from 37 to 42 percent between 1981 and 2001. In part, this upward shift reflects the increasing attractiveness of Portugal to those from Africa, Brazil, and western Europe. These immigrants were low-skilled construction workers who were male, domestic and commercial cleaning workers who were female, and professionals and semi-skilled service workers. In addition, they reflect asylum applicants who rose in the mid-1990s and claimed political persecution in African, eastern Europe, and central Asian countries.[31] In Romania, immigrants were also male predominant but shifted little over the three census years we observe, from 45 in 1977 to 47 in 1992 to 44 percent in 2002.

Only two nations in Europe reveal dramatic shifts toward masculinization of immigrant populations. Ireland is one, where women's share of immigrants declined substantially from 53 to 47 percent between 1971 and 2006 as more low-skilled migrants from nations in eastern Europe and elsewhere entered for construction and related work and as highly skilled migrants entered from outside the EU.[32] In addition, Turkey's immigrant population shifted toward more men between 1981 and 2000, dropping from approximately 45 to 39 percent female. Despite a long history of refugee resettlement, Turkey has since the late 1980s become a big receiver of irregular migrants, largely from neighboring countries who overstay visas, and who may be transit migrants who enter from the Middle East and South Asia to transit to Europe.[33]

During these years, Turkey attracted many refugees and asylum seekers from Iran and Iraq, including almost half a million Kurds as well as refugees from Albania, Bosnia, and Bulgaria.[34] In addition, although fewer in number, many irregular immigrants and trafficked people, of whom the latter were mostly women, also arrived to live in Turkey.

Figure 6.6 focuses on shifts in gender migrant composition in North America. Of the two largest immigrant-receiving nations, Canada and the United States, shifts in the gender composition were small and gender balanced. In contrast, shifts in Mexico's immigrant population suggests a gradual transition that reached the lower limit of gender balance by 2010, 47 percent female against 45 percent in 1970.

Signs of increasing feminization also appear in five South American nations—Argentina, Ecuador, Chile, Bolivia, and Uruguay (see figure 6.7). Across any two census years, one dramatic shift was in Argentina: between 1970 and 2010, women's presence jumped from 46 to 51 percent female. Also substantial was the shift for Chile, where 42 percent of the immigrant population was female in 1960 and 50 percent was in 2002. These shifts toward gender balance occurred as the forces of economic development attracted many Paraguayan and Peruvian women to migrate as domestic service workers.[35] Maia Jachimowicz also points to sex trafficking as especially important in Argentina and it may also contribute to this nation's gender balance among immigrants.[36] In contrast, Brazil experienced declines in women's presence. The significant presence of male migrants in Brazil is related to strong labor demand for manual agricultural workers, many from Portugal, Japan, and neighboring countries.[37] In Brazil, downward shifts led to a majority male

Figure 6.6   Gender Composition of Foreign Born in North America

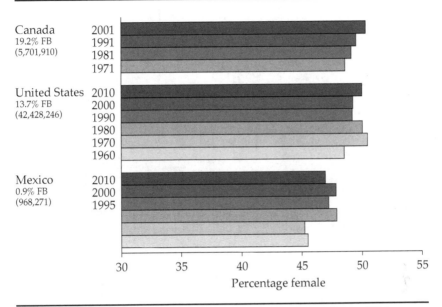

Canada
19.2% FB
(5,701,910)
2001
1991
1981
1971

United States
13.7% FB
(42,428,246)
2010
2000
1990
1980
1970
1960

Mexico
0.9% FB
(968,271)
2010
2000
1995

Percentage female

Source: Authors' compilation based on Minnesota Population Center 2014.

population in 2010, with 43 percent women among immigrants. Among those in Venezuela, Peru, and Colombia, the gender composition shifted little across census years. In Venezuela and Peru, immigrant populations were gender balanced; in Colombia, they ranged from 45 to 46 percent female between 1964 and 2005.

To sum up, two important findings about recent shifts in the gender composition of immigrant populations have emerged. First, places that have attracted many immigrants, such as the United States, Canada, Israel, and countries in Europe, have not witnessed a substantial upward trend toward higher shares of women since 1970. On the contrary, observed shifts since 1970 reflect gender balance in immigrant populations, reflecting a complex set of processes related to shifts in labor demand, civil strife, age composition, and a gendered normalization of international moves, perhaps related to increased state investment in regulating migration. Second, among destination nations with small immigrant populations, such as South Africa, the Philippines, Costa Rica, Argentina, Uruguay, or Chile, women's presence among immigrants has grown substantially. Therefore, global shifts in nations that have only recently attracted immigrants suggest more complex gender dynamics since 1970. As chain migrations mature, for example, family

Figure 6.7   Gender Composition of Foreign Born in South America

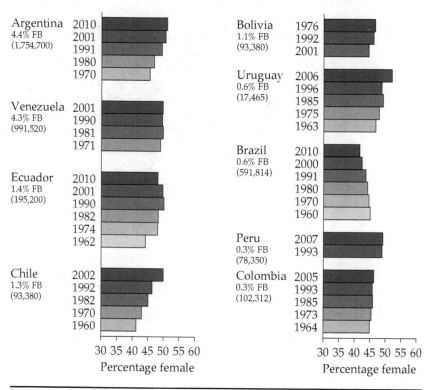

Source: Authors' compilation based on Minnesota Population Center 2014.

reunification in host societies may occur if the earliest migrants were largely male. This may be especially true when long-term male immigrant workers identify local demand for female labor that members of their own families can meet.

Variation and Convergence of Gender Composition by National Origin

Donna Gabaccia and Elizabeth Zanoni suggest that historically gender composition varied across spatial scales, with variation generally greatest at local, then regional, and then national levels.[38] As recent immigration has become more selectively female, we must also ask how much immigrant gender selectivity varies at the national level. Once again, we use data from the IPUMS-International for all nations that have national-origin information for the foreign born. We organize nations into the same six regions—Africa, Asia and the Middle East, Central America and the Caribbean, Europe, North America, and South America—and use age-standardized estimates of the sex composition. We present data from the three largest national origins of immigrants in each host society; the darkest bar refers to the top sending national origin, the medium-colored bar is the second largest, and the lightest bar is the third largest. Together, the figures suggest the extent to which migrants encounter distinctively gendered opportunities and constraints as they depart one society and enter another. Almost everywhere around the world, our analysis suggests, gender influences different occupational and social niches for migrants of differing origins.

Figure 6.8 describes substantial gender variation among immigrants for the three largest national-origin groups in African nations. For example, in Guinea, immigrants from Liberia and Sierra Leone, who were mostly refugees, were at 54 percent modestly female predominant, but immigrants from Mali, who were mostly agricultural workers, were at 60 percent male dominant. Another example is Sierra Leone, where immigrants from Guinea and Gambia were male predominant but those from Liberia were female predominant. Of the approximately eighty thousand Liberian refugees in Sierra Leone, many were entire families, displaced because of Liberia's civil war in the late 1980s.[39]

National-origin variation is larger in some African destinations, such as Rwanda, Mali, Kenya, and Uganda, than in others. Take South Africa, which attracts more male than female immigrants because of its demand for low-skilled workers for the mining industry.[40] Among those from Mozambique, the largest national-origin group, immigrants were just 25 percent female. Those from the United Kingdom, much more likely to be professional workers, were 44 percent. Those from Lesotho were 40 percent female. Malawi and Tanzania also show sizeable national-origin variations. Among immigrants living in Malawi, those born in Mozambique were 43 percent female, but those from Zambia and Zimbabwe were more heavily female, approximately 60 and 57 percent, respectively. In Tanzania, immigrants from Burundi were close to 50 percent female, those from Mozambique 47 percent, and those from Kenya 65 percent. Gender-balanced and female-majority gender migrant composition among Tanzanian immigrants has long been linked to its resettlement of Burundi refugees.[41] Similarly, among Uganda immigrants, refugees from the Congo and Sudan contributed to its gender balance. In addition, Tanzania's gender balance among immigrants is related to a strong labor demand for teachers and other professionals from Kenya, though Tanzania has recently called for their deportation.[42]

Figure 6.9 presents national-origin variation in gender composition for countries in Asia and the Middle East. Of the six nations hosting

Figure 6.8   Gender Composition of Foreign Born in Africa by Top Three National Origins

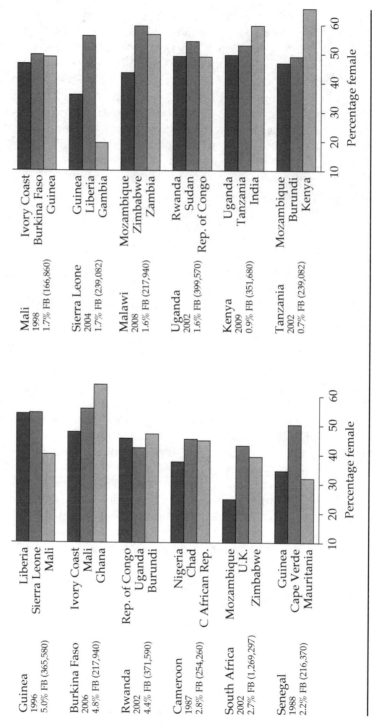

Source: Authors' compilation based on Minnesota Population Center 2014.

Figure 6.9 Gender Composition of Foreign Born in Asia and the Middle East by Top Three National Origins

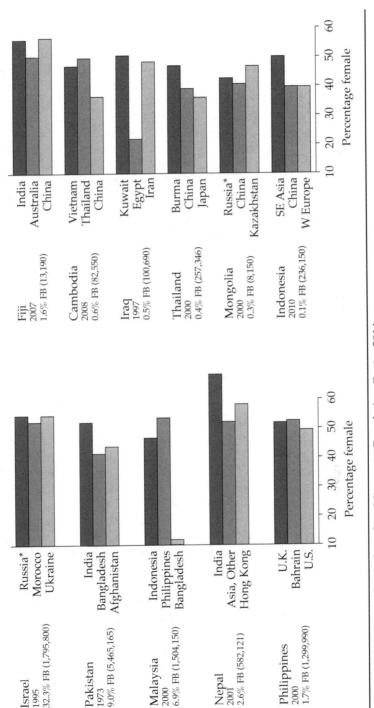

Source: Authors' compilation based on Minnesota Population Center 2014.
Note: Russia refers to Russia and the USSR.

immigrants, four exhibited considerable variability. The largest variation—for immigrants living in Malaysia—reflects how labor demand and emigration control policies that banned women's migration until very recently produced a Bangladeshi labor migration flow that was almost entirely male in 2000.[43] This compares with gender balance among Malaysia's Filipino immigrants (53 percent female), and close to gender balance among those from Indonesia (44 percent female).

We also see that variation across host countries was substantially larger for less-developed countries in Asia and the Middle East. In the most developed, Israel, which also houses the largest share of immigrants, migrants were gender balanced for all three national-origin groups. In the Philippines and Fiji, the top three national-origin immigrant groups were also gender balanced. However, among poorer nations, substantial variation exists. Nepalese immigrants from India were female predominant (70 percent), as were those from Hong Kong (58 percent) and Bhutan (54 percent). The Nepali case reflects how cultural similarities and state policies produce a distinctly gendered migration. Many Indians live in Nepal and Nepalese in India because the two nations have had an open border policy since 1950: citizens of both nations freely travel and work across borders.[44] Also contributing to women's large share is that the two nations share a religious and cultural heritage which facilitates marriage migration across the Nepal-Indian border.

Immigrants in Cambodia, Thailand, and Indonesia also display substantial variation in national origin. Immigrant gender variation varies from predominantly male for some national origins to gender balanced for others. In Cambodia, for example, Vietnamese have a long history of settlement, which the French encouraged until the 1950s.[45] Despite significant flight during the Khmer Rouge regime, many Vietnamese returned to Cambodia after the war ended. Figure 6.9 shows that in 2008, Cambodia was home to approximately 45 percent female Vietnamese immigrants and gender-balanced Thai immigrants, men working in construction-related jobs, and women in the garment industry.[46] Chinese also migrate to Cambodia in response to demand for managerial and other highly skilled workers, but were more likely to be male professionals than Chinese immigrants in Indonesia, suggesting how emigration flows from the same sending countries may reveal markedly different gender and class dynamics, in this case related to the recruitment of male workers.[47] In 2000, Burmese immigrants in Thailand outnumbered all other national-origin groups and were approximately 46 percent female. Burmese immigrants are a mix of workers in fishing, construction, and garment manufacturing seeking better economic opportunities in Thailand's fast-growing economy, and of refugees related to the religious persecution of Muslim Burmese seeking asylum in refugee camps in Thailand just across the border.[48]

In Iraq in the mid-1990s, immigrants from Kuwait and Iran were often gender-balanced refugees. The large presence of Iranian immigrants in Iraq, for example, reflected the repatriation of approximately a hundred thousand Kurds from Iran to Iraq in the mid-1970s, after Iran suppressed a Kurdish rebellion. In contrast, Egyptian-born migrants in Iran were heavily male predominant and more likely than those from other countries to be economic migrants and foreign nationals.[49] Finally, Russian, Chinese, and Kasakhstani immigrants in Mongolia were male predominant, searching for better employment opportunities. For example, since the 1990s, Chinese immigrants in Mongolia reportedly set up joint-venture companies in textile wholesale and retail sectors with partners in China and worked as traders for Chinese trading companies. Although Russian immigrants also developed joint-venture companies in the mining industry, since 1992 and the initiation of Mongolia's market economy, many Russians immigrants here became unemployed. Finally, Kazakh immigrants in Mongolia are close to being gender balanced (approximately 45 percent female) because they are seminomadic pastoralists and business owners with long histories and extended families in Mongolia.[50]

We also see variability in the gender selectivity of immigrants by national origins in Central American and Caribbean nations (see figure 6.10). In Puerto Rico, for example, migrants from the U.S. mainland and immigrants from the Dominican Republic were female predominant whereas Cubans were gender balanced. In Costa Rica, the variation was similar: Nicaraguans and Panamanians were gender balanced but El Salvadorians were female predominant. Moreover, although gender balance described the national-origin variation for immigrants in St. Lucia, immigrants in Panama ranged from heavily female among Nicaraguans to gender-balanced among Colombians and Chinese. Those in Jamaica were also gender balanced, but Hondurans living in nearby El Salvador were female predominant (60 percent female). The most dramatic example of variation is for Cuba. In 2002, immigrants in this small nation ranged from gender balanced (from Spain) to heavily female predominant (from Russia), and heavily male predominant (those from Haiti). Thus, variation by national origin across countries is significant, suggesting another regional pattern of gender selectivity related to gendered labor markets and political systems bridging national borders in very different ways for men and women.

Figure 6.11 shows that the gender composition in some European nations varied more than in others. For immigrants in Ireland, for example, those from the United Kingdom were much more likely to be women than those from Poland and Lithuania (50, 37, and 43 percent, respectively). These differences reflect the long legacy of migration between Ireland and the United Kingdom, compared with the recent movement of Poles and Lithuanians, of whom many were construction workers in Ireland's booming economy in 2006. In contrast, national origin did not

Figure 6.10   Gender Composition of Foreign Born in Central America and the Caribbean by Top Three National Origins

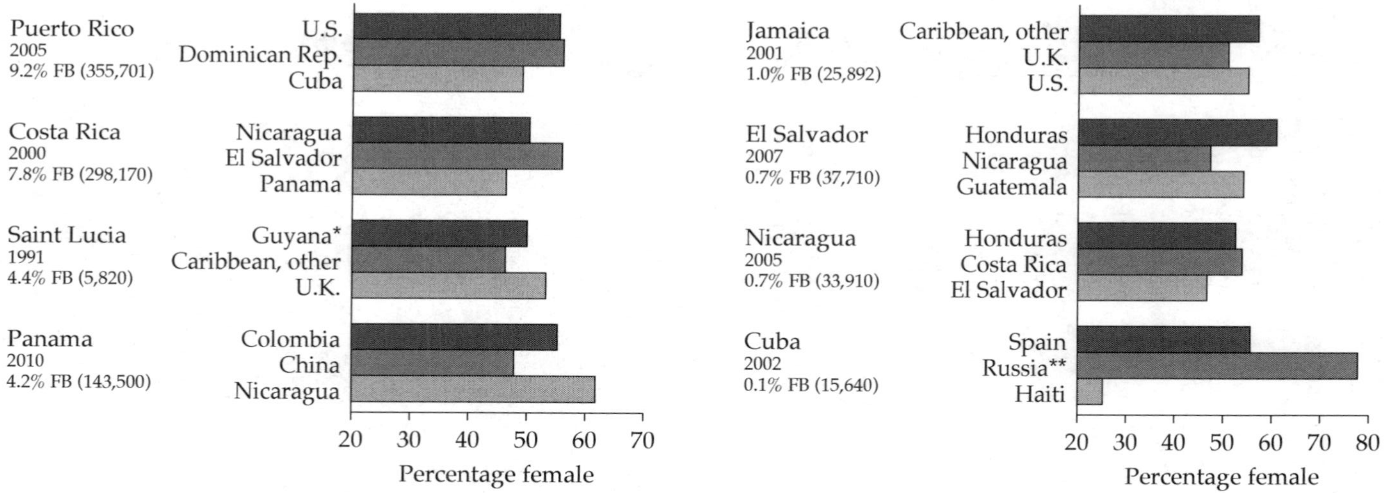

Source: Authors' compilation based on Minnesota Population Center 2014.
Note: Guyana refers to Guyana and British Guiana; Russia refers to Russia and the USSR.

Figure 6.11   Gender Composition of Foreign Born in Europe by Top Three National Origins

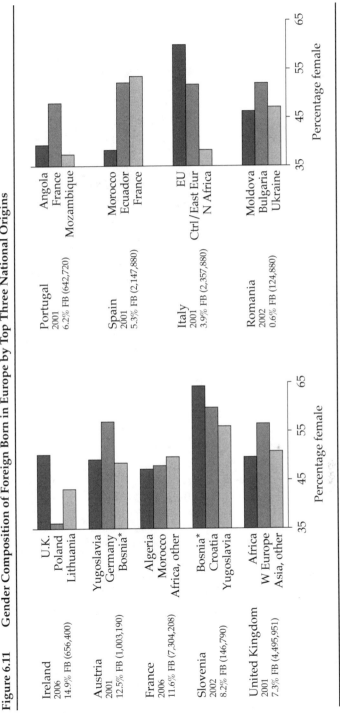

Source: Authors' compilation based on Minnesota Population Center 2014.
Note: Bosnia refers to Bosnia and Herzegovina.

Figure 6.12   Gender Composition of Foreign Born in North America by Top Three National Origins

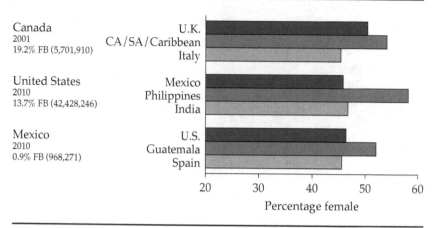

Canada
2001
19.2% FB (5,701,910)

United States
2010
13.7% FB (42,428,246)

Mexico
2010
0.9% FB (968,271)

Source: Authors' compilation based on Minnesota Population Center 2014.

dramatically distinguish the gender composition of immigrant populations in France. Although the largest national-origin groups in France were all female predominant, considerably more variation existed in the other nations in figure 6.11. Take Austria, where in 2001, Yugoslavian and Bosnian immigrants were approximately 50 percent female, but German immigrants were female predominant (with 58 percent female). Consider Italy, where immigrants from EU countries were 60 percent female, those from central and eastern Europe were gender balanced, and those from North African nations were 39 percent female.

Figure 6.12 clearly shows the national-origin variation in immigrant gender composition in the large immigrant populations in Canada, United States, and Mexico. For example, although shares of women among immigrants in Canada from the United Kingdom and China were gender balanced, immigrants from Italy were only slightly less so. In the United States, immigrant women from the Philippines substantially outnumbered those from Mexico or India. U.S. immigration policy facilitated the entry of large numbers of Filipina nurses by providing them with visas as professional workers. As the biggest labor-exporting country in Asia, the Philippines sends large numbers of women to undertake care-related jobs in developed and newly industrialized countries, including the United States.[51] In addition, the United States and the Philippines have cultural and historical links as well as bilateral military agreements—of which all have promoted strong ties between the two nations. Katharine Donato shows how U.S. military presence links to marriage-related migration of Filipinas to the United States. In contrast, U.S. immigrants from Mexico and India were mostly men, though both groups were more gender balanced than in the past.[52] Among immigrants in Mexico in 2010, those from the United States were gender balanced, reflecting a large number of U.S. expatriate retirees. Those from Guatemala were also gender balanced, but those from Spain were 46 percent female.

Finally, figure 6.13 also reveals the substantial presence of women among immigrants and variability by national origin in South America. Take Chile, where approximately 60 percent of Peruvian immigrants were women, versus 48 percent of Bolivians and 50 percent of Argentines. Immigrants in Ecuador displayed similar variation. Among Colombian immigrants, of whom many left their homes as a result of drug activity, approximately 55 percent were women. This compares with 43 percent among Peruvian and 51 percent among U.S. immigrants in Ecuador. In 2010 in Argentina, Paraguayan immigrants very likely to be domestic workers were 55 percent female,[53] Bolivians 47 percent, and Chileans 50 percent.

The three largest national-origin groups of Brazilian immigrants exhibited a wider global reach: Portugal, Japan, and Paraguay. Portuguese immigrants made up about one-third of Brazil's immigrants and were 43 percent female.[54] Japanese immigrants were similarly split, but those from Paraguay were gender balanced and approximately 10 percentage points higher. Significant immigration from Japan to Brazil reflects the unique history between these two nations, which originated in the early twentieth century when Brazil brought Japanese laborers to work on coffee plantations after abolishing slave labor.[55]

It should be clear by now that global and sizeable variations in the gender composition of immigrants exist, and that examinations of immigrants' national origins in different host countries reveals additional gender selectivity. Our findings establish that today's international migrations are gender selective, such that few if any migrant populations are heavily male.[56] Clearly, the gender selectivity we observe today is quite different from that of a century ago, even though, as we point out earlier, variation was also substantial in the gender composition of past immigrant populations. Demand for female labor in paid reproductive domestic service and other care work is much higher than it was a century ago. Where demand for paid female care workers is high, women predominate among migrants. Restrictions on migration that privilege marital and family unification and that treat refugees differently from labor migrants also often contribute to gender balance.

Despite these insights, questions remain about the processes underlying the gender composition of these populations. For example, the IPUMS data do not permit us to tease apart how gender balanced, female, or male predominant migrant populations reflect diverse and/or segmented labor

Figure 6.13   Gender Composition of Foreign Born in South America by Top Three National Origins

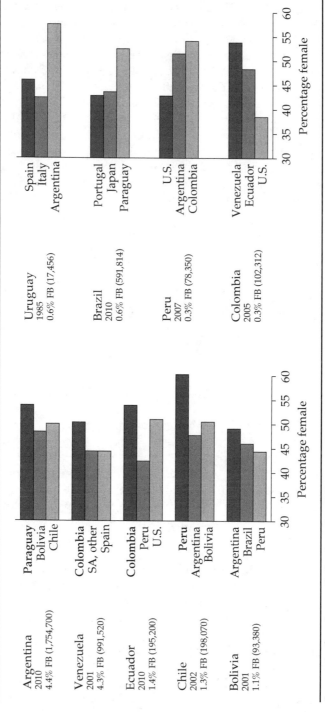

Source: Authors' compilation based on Minnesota Population Center 2014.

market dynamics in countries around the world. Instead, they assume uniformity and homogeneity in labor demand, such as for men in agriculture, as seafarers, and as oil workers, and for women in domestic, factory, and care work. Another limitation is that the data do not permit us to consider how different migrations may be related. Consider the case of Paraguayan women migrating to Argentina, which may in turn permit Argentine women to migrate elsewhere. We leave these questions for future researchers.

Scholars are interested in the feminization in part because they assume it has consequences for migrants as well as for sending and receiving societies. In the next chapter, we examine—in detail—variation in the gender composition of immigrants in the United States over the last hundred years and consider its possible consequences.

= Chapter 7 =

Consequences: A Story of Moderation and Convergence

In this chapter, we aim to open a conversation about the effects of migrant gender composition. We examine variation in the gender composition of U.S. immigrants over the last 150 years and consider its possible consequences. We focus on the United States because extensive census data are available and permit us to examine feminization and some of its consequences over a long period. The findings here do not suggest widespread consequences of increased female presence among U.S. migrants. Instead, the investigation of consequences presented here suggests that the gender balance among U.S. immigrants observed since 1970 has led to a convergence between natives and foreigners in employment-related outcomes and a modest, if any, rise in intermarriage. We hope that these findings will spur new studies about these and other consequences in the future.

Prior Literature on Consequences

Most contemporary studies about the effects of gender ratios reference a provocative, social psychological work by Marcia Guttentag and Paul Secord, who theorized about the impact of gender balances in adult life.[1] They argued that the number of opposite sex partners potentially available to women or men profoundly affects sexual behavior, marriage, divorce, child rearing, family stability, and structural aspects of society. Armed with historical case studies and U.S. Census data, they examined sex ratio effects in Athens and Sparta and in medieval Europe, among Orthodox Jews and American frontier southern and Victorian women, and among contemporary black and white Americans. A sex ratio imbalance, caused by selective migration, female infanticide or neglect, death in childbirth, or military service, results in one sex having more dyadic power because he or she has access to more alternative relationships. When men outnumber women, traditional social roles are reinforced in

150

which women are valued as wives and mothers, virginity is prized, and women's sexual morality is emphasized. When women outnumber men, moral standards loosen, divorce is common, and men often remarry. By making a strong case that sex ratios affect micro-level dyadic relationships and macro-level beliefs and behaviors, Marcia Guttentag and Paul Secord underscore how the relative numbers of men and women affect gender stratification.[2] At the same time, they recognize that dyadic power is different from structural power and that increases in men's or women's dyadic power as a result of changing sex ratios intersect differently with social structures premised on male superiority or on gender equality.

As we discussed in chapter 1, Guttentag and Secord's book led to a number of studies that examine sex ratios and their consequences, such as labor force participation, marriage formation, and racial differences in family structure. Scott South and Katherine Treat's work is a classic along these lines; they find that a nation's sex ratio led to different marriage patterns in developed and developing nations, though these effects were generally weaker than effects for socioeconomic development.[3] More recent contributions include Mattias Larsen and Ravinder Kaur, who examine whether and how male majority sex ratios in three northern districts in India affect patriarchal social structures.[4] Their findings suggest short-term shifts that encourage compromises concerning rules about clan exogamy, make dowry demand less intense, change inheritance patterns, and facilitate husbands living with their wives' parents. Women also became more aware of their legal entitlement to their parents' property, and of giving less importance to sons with respect to daughters. Erin Hofmann and Cynthia Buckley focus on cultural responses to gendered migration in the country of Georgia, and ask how women migrants navigate the tensions between deteriorating economic conditions that encourage out-migration and traditional norms promoting women's ties to home and family.[5] They find that women describe their migration in two ways: both as economically necessary (rather than a choice), and as different and unique from the migration of other women. Using these strategies had the consequence of facilitating women's return migration back to origin communities, but they may also strengthen traditional gender norms as women's out-migration continues.

To our knowledge, only a few studies examine the consequences of sex ratio variations for migrants. Analyzing micro-level IPUMS data, Josh Angrist suggests that male-predominant gender ratios among turn-of-the-century U.S. immigrants improved women's marriage prospects and lowered their labor force participation.[6] Male predominance encouraged higher rates of marriage among both men and women and was positively associated with higher spouse and couple incomes. Gender ratios also affected second- and third-generation marriage markets, where the children of immigrants were better off than their parents.

Steffen Krohnert and Sebastian Vollmer also consider the consequences of the very high rates of emigration of young women in eastern Germany, where educational achievement is higher for women than men but the demand for high-skilled female labor is limited.[7] The authors identify several important effects of this type of gender migration selectivity. First, it permits eastern German women to successfully compete for jobs in other areas of Germany. Second, it leads to intermarriage between eastern German women and comparably skilled western German men. Third, it has substantial negative effects for eastern Germany, including a downward shift in fertility, surplus of young unmarried men, and growing emphasis on traditional gender norms and extreme right-wing ideology. Findings from both the Angrist and the Krohnert and Vollmer studies are consistent with Guttentag and Secord, suggesting that higher sex ratios and more men results in stronger traditional gender norms, increases in men's competition for women in marriage markets, and other effects.[8]

One additional study attempts to extend Guttentag and Secord's ideas but relies heavily on inference. The uneven gender ratios that have emerged in many Asian nations in the last few decades sparked this study, which predicts devastating consequences such as war and social disorder, as restless male adolescents fail to find wives.[9] This is a particularly grim view of imbalanced populations in which men outnumber women, but it does not focus on migration. The view that immigration threatens national security was codified in the United States as early as 1798 with the passage of the U.S. Alien and Sedition Act that defined foreigners as potential security threats. It continues today, as many believe that immigration is related to rising crime rates despite substantial evidence to the contrary,[10] and secondarily, as the deportations of immigrants rise despite the fact that most are related to misdemeanor offenses.[11]

Finally, we would be remiss if we did not mention contemporary discussions about the consequences of predominantly male populations. Although these studies do not focus on migration, they are part of ongoing debates about the problem of men outnumbering women in Asian populations. Many noted how the problem of missing women, who died from infanticide, neglect, or abuse related to boy preference, reflected much higher rates of female mortality in Asia and in North Africa than comparable rates observed in Europe and North America.[12] About India and China, where cultural preferences for male offspring are strong, debates have been especially intense. Yi Zeng and colleagues suggest that male majorities result from the underreporting of female births, greater use of prenatal identification, and a rise in abortion of female fetuses, rather than from female infanticide, which is relatively rare.[13] More recently, Yong Cai argues that, although low fertility resulted from China's restrictive one-child policy, changes related to socioeconomic development and to ideas related to globalization have also been important.[14] Our point here is that variations in gender ratios are viewed as significant when their consequences are either assumed or understood to be troublesome. Moreover, most scholarly studies of gender imbalance focus on the negative consequences of male-, not female-, predominant populations. → *Because pred. male pop seen as potentially problematic*

Data and Analytical Plan

As in chapter 6, we use census data to examine variation in the gender composition of U.S. immigrant populations.[15] These data yield estimates of migrant gender composition while considering the age structure of these populations. Because our focus is on the United States, we use individual-level census data from the Integrated Public Use Micro Data Series (IPUMS-USA). In addition, as in chapter 6, the analysis relies mostly on adult samples, either immigrants who are eighteen years and older, or subsets who are of working ages or who are married in their twenties. The only exception is when we describe the age distribution of the U.S. foreign-born population; here we parse all migrants across the full range of age groups to examine shifts over time.

The analysis relies on the variables defined in chapter 6 (age, gender, nativity, and national origin) as well as measures of labor force participation and intermarriage, which are the key effects we consider. We define labor force participation as persons who are employed or unemployed out of the total civilian noninstitutionalized population eligible to work. We define intermarriage as a cross-nativity marriage, whereby someone who is foreign born is married to a person born in the United States and vice versa.[16] We also examine cross-nativity intermarriage among Latinos and Asians.

Our analytic strategy is to map broad shifts and variations in the gender composition of U.S. immigrant populations.[17]

Variation and Shifts in the U.S. Immigrant Population

Based mainly on flow data, our earlier chapters establish that women's and men's representation among migrants has changed across the nineteenth and twentieth centuries. Here, we use U.S. Census data to describe how the gender composition of U.S. adult immigrants has shifted between 1850 and 2010. Figure 7.1 presents two lines that summarize age-standardized estimates of migrant gender composition: the first is for all adult foreign born and the second describes the adult foreign-born population excluding those born in Mexico. We remove Mexican-born immigrants for the second set of estimates because Mexican men outnumber women among unauthorized migrants and because Mexico-U.S. unauthorized migration grew dramatically since

Figure 7.1   Gender Composition of U.S. Foreign Born, Including and Excluding Mexican Born, 1850–2010

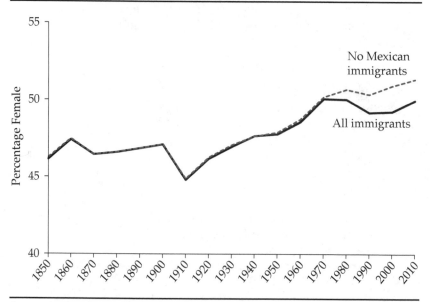

Source: Authors' compilation based on Minnesota Population Center 2010.

the 1970s.[18] Therefore, by excluding the Mexican born, we observe how gender variation varies independent from the male-predominant, unauthorized Mexico-U.S. migration, which rose for several decades before declining after 2007.

The first finding of note is the variation in age-standardized estimates of the gender composition of all foreign-born persons. Figure 7.1 presents estimates that range from a low of 45 percent in 1910 to a high of 50 percent in 1970 and 1980. Between 1850 and 1930, the pattern was one of ups and downs. For example, between 1870 and 1900, women made up approximately 46 percent of U.S. immigrants, but by 1910, their share dropped slightly to 45 percent. For the next twenty years, women's share increased again, to 47 percent.

Since 1930, we see a gradual rise in women's representation among immigrants, also suggested by the flow data that Marion Houstoun and her colleagues analyze.[19] In 1940, both sets of estimates converged to describe an immigrant population that was close to 48 percent female. Over the next thirty years, women's share among total U.S. immigrants and among those excluding the Mexican born continued to rise. What is striking is how close the two estimates are until 1970. Since then, the proportion of women among the total foreign-born population declined but among the foreign born without those born in Mexico, women's share continued to grow.[20] However, by the end of the first decade of the twenty-first century, both sets of estimates suggest gender balance even though without the Mexican born, the percentage female (51 percent) is only slightly higher than that for the total U.S. born (50 percent).

On the whole, figure 7.1 underscores two important findings. First, it demonstrates shifts in the sex composition of U.S. immigrant populations across a long period, complementing our flow data analysis, which always shows more variability in migrant sex composition than stock data do. Second, it suggests that gender dynamics in immigration were more complex before 1930 than afterward, a finding consistent with Donna Gabaccia's analysis of nineteenth-century flow data.[21] Third, it may suggest how women's increasing share among the U.S. migrant population in the twentieth century was associated with shifts in the absolute numbers of foreign-born persons, though other explanations—such as shifts in labor demand and immigrant composition related to emigration and admission policies—may also operate.[22] Prior to 1960, for example, women's share rose even as the numbers of immigrants fell; afterward, women's representation rose even as the number of U.S. immigrants also increased. After 1970, however, shifts in women's share were small and fell largely within our category of gender balance, despite a substantial rise in the overall number of immigrants, an increase that continued into the twenty-first century and was related to the growing significance of Mexican male-predominant migration.[23]

A Story of Moderation and Convergence

We now tackle the question that has generally remained unstated and unexamined in recent analyses of the feminization of migration. Few scholars have presented empirical evidence that shifts in migrant women's representation have had any demographic, social, or political consequences, whether in rates of marriage, female or male wage-earning, female emancipation, or the building or collapse of feminist movements. Why should we care about how many women or how many men move about, leave one region, or work or settle in another if we do not consider their consequences? Although the analysis that follows suggests some effects, these are in fact limited and temporary rather than widespread and stable. Moreover, as we will see, the main consequence of gender balance among U.S. migrants has been a pronounced convergence between natives and foreigners in many outcomes.

We begin by providing an overview of the demographic attributes of the U.S. foreign-born population since 1910. Table 7.1 compares age, marital status, education, and labor force participation of foreign-born and U.S.-born populations for three distinct periods, each characterized

Table 7.1   Demographics of U.S. Foreign Born, 1910–2010

	Male Predominant 1910–1920				Gender Balance: Increasing Female Migration 1930–1960				Gender Balance 1970–2010			
	Foreign Born		U.S. Born		Foreign Born		U.S. Born		Foreign Born		U.S. Born	
	W	M	W	M	W	M	W	M	W	M	W	M
Age (total)												
Mean (years)	39.9	40.0	24.8	24.9	48.0	48.8	28.0	27.4	43.0	40.7	35.6	33.4
Less than 18	8.2	6.7	42.9	43.6	5.6	5.6	35.6	37.5	11.6	13.2	28.4	31.4
25–54	58.0	62.1	34.3	34.3	47.6	46.6	38.6	38.0	48.9	49.9	38.0	38.3
65 and older	10.1	8.7	3.8	3.7	21.0	21.1	6.4	5.8	18.1	14.9	12.7	9.8
Marital status												
Married	78.7	69.0	69.4	63.8	81.1	79.5	77.8	76.2	68.8	65.2	61.7	60.9
Married spouse	76.6	62.4	66.9	61.7	78.6	76.1	75.4	74.0	65.4	59.8	60.1	59.7
Present Education[a]												
Mean (years)	–	–	–	–	7.1	7.3	7.7	7.4	10.2	10.4	10.3	10.2
Less than high school	–	–	–	–	55.0	54.3	42.8	45.6	31.5	33.0	15.8	17.1
High school	–	–	–	–	15.5	11.3	23.3	17.9	30.7	26.2	39.7	37.5
More than high school	–	–	–	–	29.5	34.4	33.9	36.5	37.8	40.9	44.5	45.4

Labor force participation[b]

In labor force	21.0	97.8	25.9	95.9	30.8	95.6	34.5	94.5	58.9	90.3	63.4	91.7
Employed	22.0	92.7	25.5	91.8	28.8	88.5	32.4	88.4	56.3	82.8	64.4	84.1
Unemployed	0.8	5.6	1.4	4.6	2.0	7.0	2.1	6.0	5.0	5.5	4.4	5.8
Weighted N (millions)	11.9	14.3	83.1	83.4	12.7	14.6	97.9	97.8	12.2	13.5	110.9	109.6
Unweighted N (thousand)	118.2	142.0	826.3	829.2	125.2	145.0	970.1	969.7	122.5	136.0	1126.6	1115.0

Source: Authors' compilation based on Minnesota Population Center 2010.

[a]Education not included in Census from 1910–1930.

[b]Labor force excludes members of the armed forces, except for 1920 when persons in the armed forces were included.

All numbers except means are in percentages. W is women; M is men. Marital status, education, and labor force all for ages twenty-five through fifty-four.

by a somewhat different gender composition. Between 1910 and 1920, the foreign-born population was male predominant, that is, less than 47 percent female. The years between 1970 and 2010 were characterized by gender balance, with women's share among immigrants between 47 and 53 percent. Table 7.1 also describes the period between 1930 and 1960 as one of rising percentage female. Already gender balanced in 1930, the percentage female rose modestly during the period without becoming female predominant.

In all three broad groups, we see that in every period, foreign-born women and men were considerably older than their U.S.-born counterparts. From 1910 to 1920, these differences (between immigrant and U.S.-born women, and immigrant and U.S.-born men) were approximately fifteen years. The differences grew to about twenty years between 1930 and 1960, a period of gender balance when women's presence among immigrants increased, but thereafter narrowed substantially as the foreign born became younger and the U.S. born older.

The age breakdowns also show convergence between foreign-born and U.S.-born women and men. For example, among children, the gaps between immigrants and the U.S. born for women and men were fairly large during the male-predominant period, at 34.7 and 36.9 percent. From 1930 to 1960, when the immigration population first achieved gender balance, these gaps ranged between 30 and 31 percent. However, from 1970 to 2010, when gender balance among immigrants was clearly established, children as a share of immigrants and the U.S. born grew so that the gap for women and men narrowed substantially to 16.8 and 18.3 percent, respectively. Among those of working ages, from twenty-five to fifty-four, a dramatic convergence also occurred across the first two periods, from 1910 to 1920 and from 1930 to 1960. Gender differences between the foreign and U.S. born were very large in the first period, 23.7 and 27.8 percent respectively, reflecting the much larger shares of the foreign born who were of working age. By later periods of gender balance, the gaps grew smaller: 9 versus 8.6 percent from 1930 to 1960, and 10.9 versus 11.3 percent from 1970 to 2010. During the later periods, the share of working-age immigrants remained higher than that for their U.S.-born counterparts. In contrast, the gender differences between the foreign and U.S. born for those sixty-five and older reveal a different pattern. From 1910 to 1920, the difference for women was 6.3 percent and for men 4 percent, with shares among the foreign born higher than the U.S. born. Between 1930 and 1960, the gaps grew considerably, to 14.7 and 15.3 percent, respectively. However, from 1970 to 2010, they narrowed again to 5.4 years and 5.1 years as the share of those sixty-five and older declined among the foreign born but grew among the U.S. born. We suspect that the large difference between immigrants and the U.S. born among those sixty-five and older results from the many who arrived early in the twentieth century, a period of male-predominant and large-scale immigration to the United States.

Table 7.1 presents two indicators of marital status: whether someone is currently married and whether someone who is currently married has a spouse present in the household. Across the groups and years, we see that the percentages for foreign-born women were always highest; in the first two periods, at least three-quarters of immigrant women were currently married and had a spouse present. From 1970 to 2010, the percentages dropped back to 68.8 and 65.4 percent, respectively, but were still larger among U.S.-born women or either group of men. In addition, gender differences between the foreign and U.S. born conformed to the model of convergence we saw with age. Early in the twentieth century, gaps for currently married were 9.3 for women and 5.2 percent for men, and for currently married with spouse present were 9.7 and 0.7 percent, respectively. By the 1970 to 2010 period, the gaps narrowed to 7.1 and 4.3 versus 5.3 and 0.1, respectively. Pointing toward more convergence than divergence across this hundred year period, these trends suggest that gender balance among U.S. immigrants is linked to a growing presence of migrant women living in families, as is also the case for U.S.-born natives.

With respect to the educational attributes of those age twenty-five to fifty-four, more complexity in the story about convergence emerges. Although small gender differences between the foreign and U.S. born in average education suggest some convergence between the 1930 to 1960 and the 1970 to 2010 periods, the foreign-born versus U.S.-born gaps for women and men grew for those with less than a high school degree, those with only high school, and those with at least some college or more. In addition, for all comparisons involving the foreign and U.S. born, immigrants had higher shares of lower levels of schooling, and lower shares of higher levels, than their U.S.-born counterparts.

Finally, we examine labor force participation differences between the foreign and U.S. born by gender. Here we also see some converging trends, though the story is again somewhat more mixed. For example, among women, the gap between the foreign born and U.S. born was 4.9 percent between 1910 and 1920, declined to 3.7 percent between 1930 and 1960, but then grew slightly to 4.5 percent between 1970 and 2010. In addition, across all three periods, immigrant women were less likely to be in the labor force than U.S.-born women. Among men, gaps between the foreign and U.S. born were much smaller—1.9, 1.1, and 1.4, respectively—and immigrant men were more likely than their U.S.-born counterparts to be in the labor force. However, the big story was the dramatic growth in all women's labor force participation over time. Among immigrant women, rates of labor force participation rose from 21 to 30.8 to 58.9 percent across the three periods. Among U.S.-born women, shares also rose, but at slightly higher levels in the three periods, from 25.9 to

34.5 to 63.4 percent. In contrast, the overwhelming majority of men were in the labor force in all three periods, though shares for both immigrants and the U.S. born were lowest between 1970 and 2010.

As they increasingly came to resemble the U.S. born in their gender composition—which likely occurred as a response to immigration policy restrictions in the 1920s—immigrants also began to resemble the U.S. born on a number of demographic attributes, such as age, marital status, and labor force participation. Exactly how this convergence emerged depends on the demographic attribute. At times, the convergence resulted from both immigrants and natives becoming more like the other. At other times, one group moved more significantly in the direction of the other. Education is the one exception: here we see divergence in the nativity groups of women and men over time. Although growing education gaps between immigrants and the U.S. born could significantly affect the life chances of women and men in these groups, foreign-born and U.S.-born differences in labor force participation were much smaller and, especially among women, growth in activity was impressive.

We now shift to a different analysis that focuses only on labor force participation of those between twenty-five and fifty-four, offering a then-and-now comparison of women's labor market activity in the early twentieth century and the current period (late twentieth and early twenty-first centuries). As Nancy Foner says, this approach can improve understanding about "what really happened then and what is happening today."[24] Our then-and-now analysis compares labor force participation rates among U.S.-born, Italian-born, and Irish-born women a hundred years ago to U.S.-born, Mexican-born, and Filipina-born women in the current period. Our focus is on immigrants from Italy and Ireland at the turn of the twentieth century because they had quite different gender compositions, the Italians predominantly male and the Irish predominantly female. For example, Irish immigrants in the United States were 56 percent female in 1900, 58.5 percent in 1920, but then 57.3 percent in 1930. Among the Italian born, 34 percent were women in 1900, 41.1 percent in 1920, and 42.3 percent in 1930. In contrast, for the recent period from 1980 to 2010, we focus on Mexican and Filipina immigrants because, again, like the Italian and Irish, they were predominantly male and predominantly female immigrant groups, respectively. Between 1980 and 2010, the gender composition of Mexicans ranged from 43 to 45 percent female, and of Filipinos 51.8 to 57.4 percent.[25]

Figure 7.2 compares the labor market activity of these three groups of women in the 1910 to 1930 period. Panel A refers to unmarried women and the bottom to current married women. Unmarried women's labor force participation rates were highest among the Irish born. Their labor force activity rates were also remarkable because they remained stable across the three years at approximately 72 percent. Unmarried U.S.-born women had the next highest rates, and their activity shifted upward across

Figure 7.2   Labor Force Participation of Women, 1910–1930

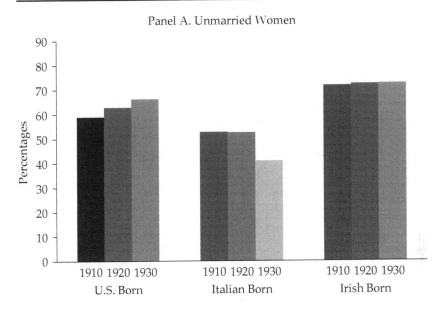

Panel A. Unmarried Women

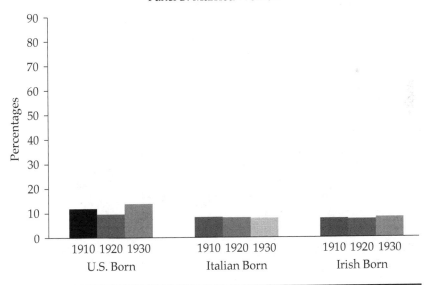

Panel B. Married Women

Source: Authors' compilation based on Minnesota Population Center 2010.

the three years, from 59 to 62.9 to 66.3 percent, respectively. Italian-born unmarried women had the lowest rates, and these declined from approximately 52 to 41 percent between 1910 and 1930. By contrast, labor market participation among married women at this period was relatively rare. Although U.S.-born married women's activity ranged from 9.6 in 1920 to 13.8 in 1930, both Irish- and Italian-born married women had rates of less than 10 percent in all years.

Figure 7.3 describes the labor market participation of U.S.-born, Mexican-born, and Filipina-born women between 1980 and 2010. As expected, unmarried women had much higher rates of labor activity than unmarried women between 1910 and 1930 (compare panel A of figure 7.3 with panel A of figure 7.2). However, once again, we see that women immigrants from the Philippines, a nation that sends predominantly women as migrants, had the highest labor market activity. In most years, approximately 90 percent participated; the exception was 2000, when participation dropped to 78.6 percent. Rates for unmarried U.S.-born women were the next highest, from 76.6 to 79.8 percent across the four years. Moreover, among the Mexican born, who are predominantly male immigrants, women's labor market activity shifted from year to year: from 69.1 percent in 1980 to 70.9 percent in 1990, dropping to 61.1 percent in 2000 and rising again to 71.4 percent in 2010. Also noteworthy are the findings for married women in the contemporary period. Compared with early in the twentieth century, married women's labor force participation rates for all three groups are much higher after 1980. But again, we see that rates for Mexican-born married women were lowest, between 43.7 and 54 percent, followed by the U.S. born, between 58.4 and 76.3 percent, and Filipinas, between 74.9 and 84.3 percent.

Together, these numbers tell us that a century ago unmarried Irish immigrants, who were heavily female predominant, typically single young women searching for work,[26] were much more likely to be in the labor force than immigrants from Italy, who were predominantly male. U.S.-born women's activity fell in between these two groups. By comparison, the 1980 to 2010 period shows a similar pattern for both unmarried and married women: Filipinas were much more likely than Mexican women to participate in the labor force, and U.S.-born women once again fell in between these two groups. On the whole, these numbers suggest a relationship between migrant gender composition of immigrants from specific national origins and labor market activity in a host society. Immigrants from national origins with relatively more (or fewer) women migrants were less likely to participate in the labor force. Moreover, the gaps between those with the highest activity rates and the U.S. born were roughly comparable to gaps between those with the lowest activity rates and the U.S. born. These findings are consistent with the expectations of Guttentag and Secord.[27] Compared with the U.S. born, the relative

Figure 7.3   Labor Force Participation of Women, 1980–2010

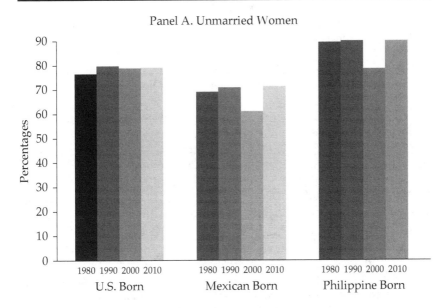

Panel A. Unmarried Women

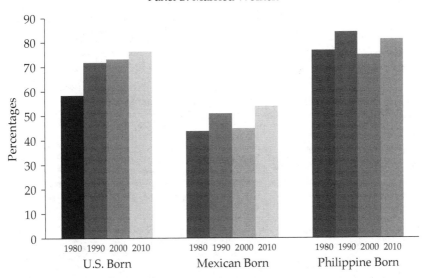

Panel B. Married Women

Source: Authors' compilation based on Minnesota Population Center 2010.

numbers of men and women in migrant populations intersect in ways that affect the labor market activity of different foreign-born groups, reflecting either supply and demand issues or segmented labor market processes.

To further unpack the convergence we have observed in our descriptive results so far, we now examine shifts since 1960 using results generated from a logistic regression model that predicts the likelihood of being in the labor force versus being out of it. In this analysis, we ask whether, during a period of gender balance among U.S. immigrants, the foreign-born and U.S.-born populations converge after we control for relevant characteristics such as gender, age, age squared, education, marital status, and number of children less than six years of age in households. We also control for year using 1960 as the reference group, and the interaction between marital status and year. These permit us to consider how the chances of being in the labor force shift over time while controlling for the changing impact of marriage on women's labor force participation. To do so, we pool six years of IPUMS-USA data (1960 as the reference category, 1970, 1980, 1990, 2000, and 2010) and focus only on those twenty-five to fifty-four years old.[28]

Figure 7.4 presents predicted probabilities of labor force activity estimated from the multivariate model described earlier. Panel A refers to women and panel B to men. The black lines (whether perforated or not) refer to the U.S. born and gray lines the foreign born. Overall, the most noteworthy finding—for both women and men—is convergence in the labor force activity between foreign-born and U.S.-born populations since 1960. Among women, the convergence occurred as more and more married women (both foreign- and U.S.-born) participated in the labor force after 1960. The probabilities that foreign- and U.S.-born women were in the labor force almost doubled between 1960 and 2010, from 38.8 and 43.4 percent to 64 and 76.4 percent, respectively. Despite declines in foreign-born women's probabilities of being in the labor force in 2000, which are consistent with slower growth described for the entire U.S. population in the 1990s,[29] in 2010 the labor force activity of both native and foreign-born unmarried women were at their highest and comparable to that for U.S.-born married women. The chances that these three groups were in the labor force ranged between 76 and 80 percent in 2010. Only one group, married foreign-born women, had lower chances, yet even among these women, almost two-thirds—64 percent—were in the labor force.

Men's labor force activity among the foreign born and U.S. born converged in a different direction: downward. As for women, the difference between foreign-born and U.S.-born married men is small. In 1960, the chances that married men, whether foreign or U.S. born, were in the labor force were very high—approximately 98 percent. In the same year, 91.6 and 93.1 percent of unmarried foreign-born and U.S.-born men, respectively, were likely to participate in the labor force. Thereafter, the probabilities of being in the labor force declined for the four groups of men

Figure 7.4   Predicted Probabilities of Being in Labor Force by Nativity and Gender, 1960–2010

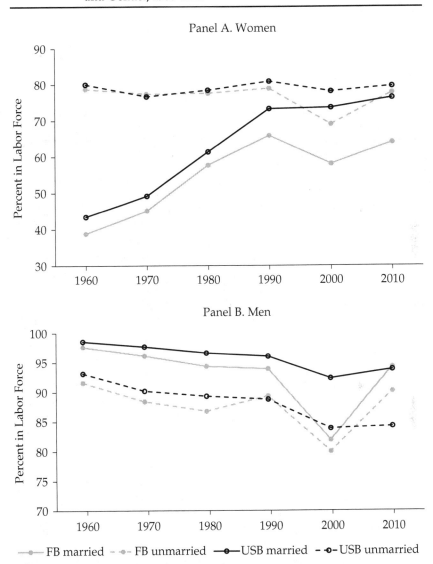

Panel A. Women

Panel B. Men

——◆—— FB married   - -◆- - FB unmarried   ——●—— USB married   - -○- - USB unmarried

Source: Authors' compilation based on Minnesota Population Center 2010.
Note: Analysis restricted to those aged twenty-five to fifty-four; FB is foreign born; USB is U.S. born.

and, as for women, were the lowest in 2000, from 80 percent for married foreign-born men to 92.3 percent for married U.S.-born men. However, by 2010, predicted probabilities for both foreign-born groups as well as for married U.S.-born men rose again. Approximately 93.9 percent of married U.S.-born and foreign-born men participated in the labor force in 2010, followed by 90 percent of unmarried foreign-born and 84.3 percent of unmarried U.S.-born men.

These findings illustrate the convergence that has occurred in the labor force activity of foreign- and U.S.-born women and men.[30] For women, the direction is upward and largely due to growth in married women's activity. Among men, the direction is downward among all four groups, married and unmarried foreign and U.S. born—although foreign-born married and unmarried men exhibited the most dramatic shifts, whether downward in 2000 or upward in 2010.

In our final consideration of consequences, we shift gears to consider cross-nativity marriage. If the United States has witnessed the emergence of gender balance among immigrants in the twentieth century, then we can ask what impact this has had on marriage formation and, more specifically, on marital exogamy, which many assume increases in gender-imbalanced populations. This is an important question for scholars who study immigrant integration. As Gillian Stevens and her colleagues argue, marriages between U.S.-born and foreign-born immigrants are "marked by (or a marker of) rapid political, economic, social, and cultural integration."[31] This aspect of cross-nativity marriages makes them important for social scientists to study, even though studies of assimilation "often" neglect them.[32]

As Albert Esteve and his colleagues note, worldwide marriage migration is on the rise as the costs of travel and communication have decline.[33] Many studies describe how women from poor Asian countries marry Asian men from wealthier nations[34] because of unbalanced sex ratios in populations and cultural preferences for submissive women.[35] Constable's edited volume is especially important because it questions assumptions "about the passivity or desperation of foreign brides," describes the enormous heterogeneity in contemporary cross-border marriages, and gives voice to the many types of women who migrate for marriage.[36]

For this analysis, we use same IPUMS-USA data to identify the nativity of household heads and their spouses.[37] We focus only on married persons, ages twenty to twenty-nine, because this means that each married person is counted only once and not included in the subsequent census year or decade. With this information, we calculate several percentages for each census year: U.S.-born men married to foreign-born women; U.S.-born women married to foreign-born men; foreign-born men married to U.S.-born women; foreign-born women married to U.S.-born men.

Figure 7.5 describes the percentages of U.S.-born women or men who were married to foreign-born men or women between 1910 and 2010.[38]

Figure 7.5   U.S.-Born Household Heads Married to Foreign Born

Panel A. Descriptive Analysis

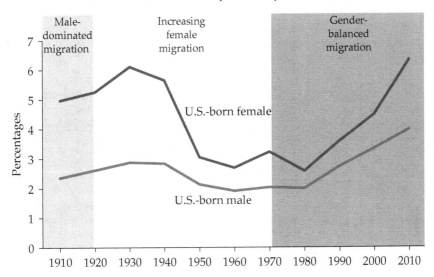

Panel B. Predicted Probabilities

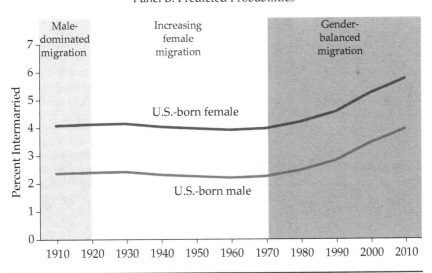

Source: Authors' compilation based on Minnesota Population Center 2010.
Note: Analysis restricted to those aged twenty to twenty-nine.

Panel A presents descriptive trends in these types of cross-nativity marriage for women and men. Panel B presents predicted probabilities for women and men generated from a straightforward regression model that includes only one variable: the size of the foreign-born population in each year. Whereas results in panel A describe general trends, those in panel B describe the probabilities of being intermarried controlling for or net of the size of the foreign-born population. Before describing our results, we remind readers that from 1910 until 1920 the U.S. foreign-born population was male predominant, or less than 47 percent female. The period between 1930 and 1960 witnessed modest increases in the percentage female in a context of gender balance among U.S. immigrants. The years between 1970 and 2010 were characterized by gender balance in the immigrant population, without becoming female predominant.

Figure 7.5 documents three general findings during the last hundred years. First, U.S.-born women were consistently more likely than men to be married to someone who was foreign born. This finding supports Albert Esteve and his colleagues, who also document U.S. native women's greater chance to marry foreign-born husbands than U.S.-born men marrying foreign-born wives.[39] Second, the percentage of all married U.S.-born persons who were married to foreign-born immigrants is rather small. In no year did it exceed 6.4 percent, which corresponded to U.S.-born women having foreign-born husbands in 2010. Third, the percentages of married U.S.-born persons with foreign-born spouses shifted over the century. For both native U.S. women and men, the tendency to marry out—that is, marry someone who is foreign born—rose from approximately 5 percent for women and 2 percent for men in 1910 to 6.1 and 2.9 percent, respectively, by 1930. Afterward, however, both declined as all immigrants achieved gender balance between 1930 and 1960. That decline was especially steep for U.S.-born women married to foreign-born men; in 1960, the figure was 2.7 percent against the 1.9 percent of U.S.-born men married to foreign-born women. After 1970, as gender balance of the U.S. immigrant population persisted, the percentage of U.S.-born women and men married to foreign-born spouses rose modestly again. By 2010, 6.3 percent of U.S.-born women were married to foreign-born men and 4 percent of U.S.-born men were married to foreign-born women.

After controlling for shifts in the size of the foreign-born population (see figure 7.5, panel B), we see fewer shifts in U.S.-born women's and men's intermarriage. In fact, removing the effect for changes in the size of the immigrant population, there is stability between 1910 and 1970 at approximately 4 and 2 percent, respectively. However, after 1970, the predicted probabilities rose equally in a monotonic fashion for both women and men. By 2010, 5.7 percent of U.S.-born women were married to foreign-born husbands and 3.9 percent of U.S.-born men were married to foreign-born wives. Not surprisingly, these findings suggest that intermarriage is a consequence of the size of immigrant populations. In addition, recent shifts are consistent with the greater acceptance of intermarriage occurring in the United States.

Figure 7.6 describes a different gender story among foreign born marrying U.S. born between 1910 and 1920, when foreign-born men were more likely than foreign-born women to have U.S.-born spouses. However, during the 1930 to 1960 period, the gender shift occurred and foreign-born women became more likely than their male counterparts to have U.S-born spouses. The difference was largest in 1960, although the chance of this type of cross-nativity marriage was still quite small. Eventually, after 1970, the percentages of foreign-born-to-U.S.-born marriages rose, but only to 3 percent for women and 2 percent for men. Once again, panel B shows that controlling for the size of the foreign-born population flattened the tendencies of foreign-born women's and men's intermarriage until after 1970, when the predicted probabilities rose but, again, only modestly. By 2010, 2.6 percent of foreign-born women and 2.2 percent of foreign-born men were married to U.S.-born spouses.

Perhaps more significant are trends in inter-foreign-born marriage, that is, intermarriage that occurs between U.S.- and foreign-born Hispanics, Latinos, and Asians. For the period from 1910 to 2010, we show four figures. The first two (figures 7.7 and 7.8) describe the percentages of U.S.-born Hispanics or Latinos married to foreign-born Hispanics or Latinos, and the percentages of foreign-born Hispanics or Latinos married to U.S.-born Hispanics or Latinos. The second two figures (figures 7.9 and 7.10) present comparable percentages for Asian U.S.-born and foreign-born household heads. Once again, each figure contains descriptive trends (panel A) and predicted probabilities (panel B) for women and men generated from a regression model that includes only one variable: the size of the Hispanic, Latino, or Asian foreign-born population in each year.

These figures show that U.S.-born Hispanic or Latino women were consistently more likely than men of their group to be married to someone who was foreign born and Hispanic or Latino. However, this tendency to marry out (someone ethnically similar but foreign born) shifted across the century; among Hispanics and Latinos, the chances that U.S.-born Hispanic or Latino women marry an immigrant of Hispanic origin began to decline after 1970, a period when cross-nativity interethnic marriage dropped from approximately 12 to 6 percent by 2010. Among Asians, the chances that U.S.-born women married an Asian immigrant also declined such that by 2000, women and men's chances of cross-nativity interethnic marriage were no longer different. Moreover, for both women and men, intermarriage chances became quite small.

Note that similar to our estimates of all cross-nativity intermarriage, we see fewer shifts in U.S.-born women's and men's cross-nativity

(*Text continues on p. 175.*)

Figure 7.6   Foreign-Born Household Heads Married to U.S. Born

Panel A. Descriptive Analysis

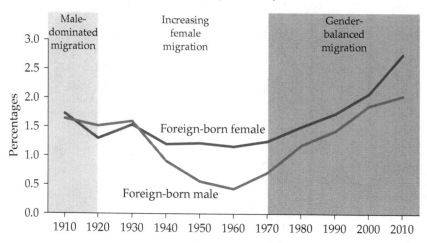

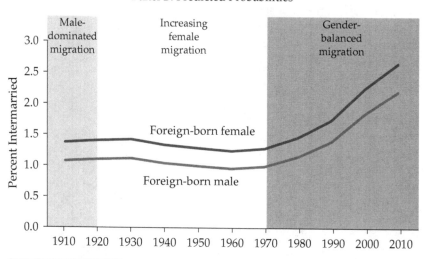

Source: Authors' compilation based on Minnesota Population Center 2010.
Note: Analysis restricted to those aged twenty to twenty-nine.

**Figure 7.7   U.S.-Born Hispanic-Latino Household Heads Married
to Foreign-Born Hispanics-Latinos**

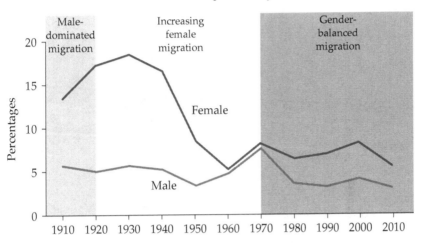

Panel A. Descriptive Analysis

Panel B. Predicted Probabilities

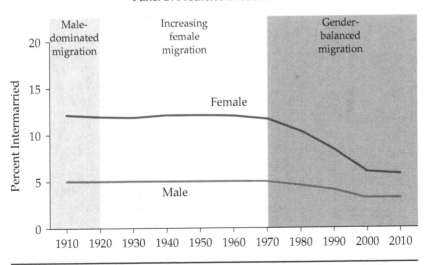

Source: Authors' compilation based on Minnesota Population Center 2010.
Note: Analysis restricted to those aged twenty to twenty-nine.

Figure 7.8   Foreign-Born Hispanic-Latino Household Heads Married to U.S.-Born Hispanics-Latinos

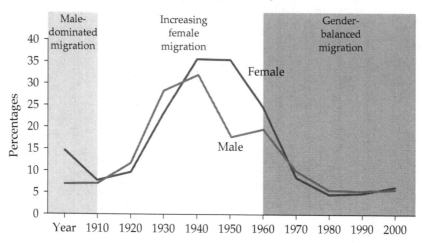

Panel A. Descriptive Analysis

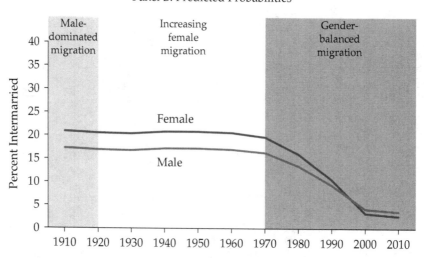

Panel B. Predicted Probabilities

Source: Authors' compilation based on Minnesota Population Center 2010.
Note: Analysis restricted to those aged twenty to twenty-nine.

Figure 7.9   U.S.-Born Asian Household Heads Married
to Foreign-Born Asians

Panel A. Descriptive Analysis

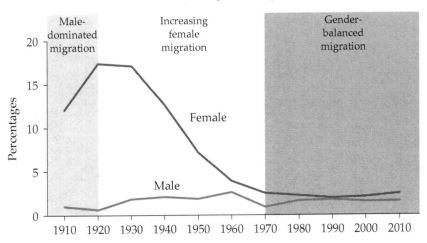

Panel B. Predicted Probabilities

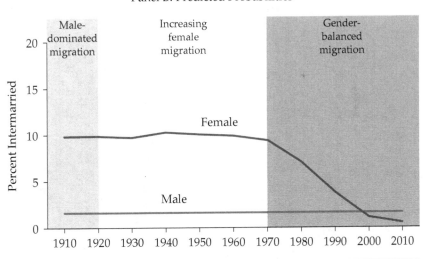

Source: Authors' compilation based on Minnesota Population Center 2010.
Note: Analysis restricted to those aged twenty to twenty-nine.

**Figure 7.10   Foreign-Born Asian Household Heads Married
to U.S.-Born Asians**

Panel A. Descriptive Analysis

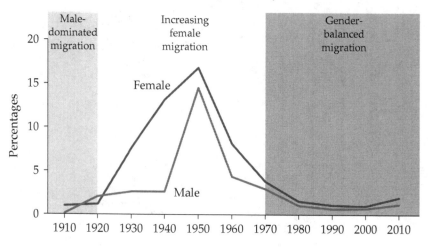

Panel B. Predicted Probabilities

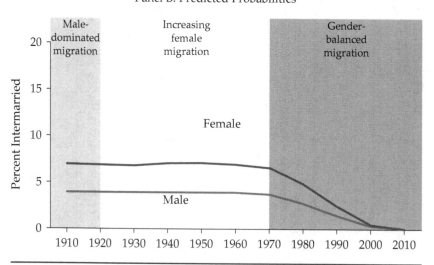

Source: Authors' compilation based on Minnesota Population Center 2010.
Note: Analysis restricted to those aged twenty to twenty-nine.

interethnic marriage after controlling for shifts in the size of the corresponding Hispanic, Latino, or Asian foreign-born population. In fact, like the earlier results, after removing the effect for changes in the size of the immigrant ethnic population, stability is considerable between 1910 and 1970 in all forms of cross-nativity interethnic marriage. However, unlike earlier results, after 1970 the predicted probabilities declined for both women and men. The only exception was for male U.S.-born Asian household heads who married foreign-born Asian women. The probabilities for this type of cross-nativity interethnic marriage hovered around 2.5 percent between 1910 and 2010.

Conclusion

We have covered considerable ground in this chapter, yet our findings suggest modest, at best, consequences of changing migrant gender composition among immigrants in the United States. We see clear signs of convergence between U.S.-born women and men and their foreign-born counterparts since 1910, whether we consider broad demographic attributes or labor force activity. We also see persistent differences that, on the whole, are fairly small in findings that link labor force participation rates to specific national-origin immigrant groups with relatively more migrant women or men. Gaps between women with the highest activity rates—Irish in 1910 and the Filipinas in 2010—and the U.S. born were roughly comparable to gaps between those with the lowest activity rates—Italians in 1910 and Mexicans in 2010—and the U.S. born.

Signs of convergence in labor market activity were especially clear after 1960. Although shifts were upward for women and downward for men, both groups converged toward the rates of the U.S. born. Finally, our findings on cross-nativity marriage suggests that marriages between U.S.- and foreign-born persons (and vice versa) were not common. Although they increased modestly during the 1970 to 2010 period of gender balance, they were related to changes in the size of the total foreign-born population across the twentieth century. With respect to cross-nativity interethnic marriages, we found evidence suggesting that these marriages declined after 1970.

Our findings suggest that gender balance among an immigrant population may have some but, if they exist, fairly modest consequences. We found repeatedly that outcomes for the foreign- and U.S.-born populations were converging, especially since the mid-twentieth century. Although we present and describe these findings in this chapter, we remind readers that the analyses here were designed mainly to open a conversation about possible impacts of gender presence among migrant populations, whether male predominant, female predominant, or gender balanced. These are preliminary findings, and we hope that future scholars will build on what we present by using different data and methods for a variety of populations outside the United States, taking into account changes in gender composition over time. One straightforward and logical extension of our work would be to consider the consequences for women and families of being left behind when husbands, brothers, and fathers participate in migration flows that are male or heavily male predominant.[40] Far fewer studies have considered the impacts of being left behind for men and families, whose wives, sisters, and mothers participate in out-migration.[41] Integrating both into a comparative study design would be fascinating because it would help us understand the consequences of the left-behind experience related to migrant gender composition.[42]

A second extension is to interrogate how gender migrant composition is related to skill and other resources. Hamilton suggests that the gender disparity in Mexico-U.S. migration varies by class.[43] At high levels of education, that is, at least a college degree, and occupational status, the gender disparity is smallest. For Mexico, Jenna Nobles and Christopher McKelvey show that who controls these resources matters; when women control more resources in their households, their spouses are less likely to migrate. Therefore, resources and who controls them may affect migrant gender composition in different nations in different ways.[44] These are just two of many approaches that we hope scholars will embrace in their future work.

$=$ Conclusion $=$

In this book, we analyze the gender composition of immigrant populations across time and space. We also emphasize how, why, and in what
form data are created, showing that using different types of data and
measurements may make women and feminization visible or invisible.
In this way, we seek to "learn the language of statistics" by understanding the perspectives that underlie different data sets and their measurements and showing how they render (or do not render) gender invisible.
In addition, we conceptualize feminization as a temporal process made
up of significant variations in migrant gender composition defined as
male- and female-predominant, heavily male- and female-predominant,
and gender-balanced migration. As migration scholars, we hope that our
work will help experts and nonexperts alike to appreciate the extent to
which they, through their decisions to collect, use, and interpret data,
may limit what we know about migrant gender composition and thus
about gender and migration.

Explaining Migrant Gender Composition

Our analyses rely on flow and stock data to examine variation in migrant
gender composition during the early modern era (1492–1867), the proletarian mass migrations (1800–1924), and the twentieth and twenty-first centuries. Across four centuries, our findings indicate that gender ideology
and gender relations are central to explanations of variation in the gender
composition of immigrant populations. For example, during the early
modern era, when global efforts at colonization led to large-scale coerced
migrations, our data from the Trans-Atlantic Slave Database reveal that
the earliest forced migrants from Africa were not the most heavily male.
In contrast to prior studies, we found substantial variation in the gender
composition of coerced African migrants. This finding requires understanding how gender organized sending and receiving societies, and the
interactions in gender beliefs and relations between Europe and Africa.
After slavery was abolished, most migrations were voluntary and made

up of new settler colonizers and laborers. Interestingly, although initially heavily male predominant, after 1830 and the elimination of European indentured servitude, these migrations to North America became more female (40 percent female toward the middle of the nineteenth century) because settler colonizers often traveled in families. At the same time, migrations to Oceania became more feminized (and for a short time, gender balanced) as Britain implemented various strategies to increase women's migration and marriage in an attempt to govern the heavily male ex-prisoner populations in Australia.

After 1860, gender composition among both immigrants and emigrants becomes more complex. On the one hand, emigration trends suggest heavily male flows, especially from China, Japan, and eastern and southern Europe. However, by the early decades of the twentieth century, immigration to the United States, South America, Oceania, and northwest Europe had feminized and women's presence was increasing across almost all migration streams. This convergence toward gender balance was global, and it continued as volumes of male labor migrations fell sharply, often in response to the onset of immigration restrictions in the late nineteenth century. Moreover, after 1920, migration control regimes enhanced permanent settlement by family groups, which thereafter appears to have facilitated gender balance as smaller and more selective groups of immigrants became eligible in the twentieth and twenty-first centuries. One consequence was that since the 1960s, marriage migrations and those related to unifying families became the largest source of visas for women in Europe and the United States. However, as migration restriction regimes allocated fewer visas for other types of migrants, all continents witnessed a rise in an unauthorized and mostly male migration.

Our examination of recent global variation in migrant gender composition analyzes stock data, takes into account the age structure of migrant populations, and yields three findings. First, nations attracting many immigrants, such as the United States, Canada, Israel, and others, have not witnessed a substantial upward trend toward higher shares of women since 1970. Rather, their immigrant populations have been gender balanced, reflecting a complex set of processes related in part to shifts in labor demand, civil strife, increased refugee movements, a gendered normalization of international moves, and increased state investment in regulating migrations of all types. Second, among destination nations with small immigrant populations, such as South Africa, the Philippines, Costa Rica, Argentina, Uruguay, and Chile, women's presence among immigrants has grown substantially, suggesting that in nations that have only recently attracted immigrants, gender dynamics have become more complex since 1970. Third, today's international migrations are still gender selective. Different from the selectivity observed a century ago, today's migrant gender composition reflects a much stronger demand for female labor in a variety of occupations, such as domestic service, other care work, and factory assembly work. In addition, migration restrictions that privilege marital and family unification and that treat refugees differently from labor migrants also contribute to gender balance.

Consequences of Migrant Gender Composition

Our analysis also considers the consequences of feminization and focuses only on the United States. The findings suggest modest, if any, effects of a growing female presence among U.S. immigrants. Labor market participation rates of natives and foreigners have converged since 1970, especially for women, and trends in intermarriage suggest a small increase in cross-nativity marriages but declines in cross-nativity interethnic marriages. On the whole, these findings offer some evidence to suggest that gender balance among U.S. immigrants is related to assimilation as a two-way process with immigrants and natives playing salient roles. Indeed, we find that the gap between immigrants and natives remained quite small among unmarried women between 1960 and 2012, but among married women, it widened. In contrast, among married men, the small nativity gap in 1960 to 1990 disappeared by 2012; among unmarried men, it widened by 2012, with immigrant men's labor force participation exceeding U.S.-born men's. Although preliminary, we hope these findings spur future scholarship that evaluates the effects of migrant gender composition and its variations.

Policy Effects and Gendered Migration

We now move, with some trepidation, beyond our findings to consider policy effects. We begin by stating the obvious: the data sources we use in our analysis do not permit us to directly assess the policy consequences related to our findings. For example, none of the data we use include information on legal status that is salient to understanding contemporary policies worldwide. Despite this limitation, we think about possible links between migrant gender composition and some specific policies and practices in countries that receive immigrants and others that send them. We differentiate how migrant gender composition may be related to policies of the past and how contemporary policy responses may encourage or limit the global migration of women or men. Our goal is to spark a dialogue about whether and how policies may affect the gender composition of immigrant populations.

Although human mobility has been linked to the policies of nation-states for centuries, early modern era policies and practices did not explicitly address immigration or out-migration. Most often state policies promoted economic development strategies that had straightforward and observable effects on global migration. Thus, well before the immigration policies that emerged late in the nineteenth century in many wealthy nations, such as the United States, economic development policies and practices facilitated migration in ways that were often gendered. For example, as we discussed in chapter 3, colonization led to large-scale coerced African out-migration, which varied in its gender composition because of localized gender beliefs and interactions. Subsequently, after 1830 when European policies terminated indentured servitude, mass migrations to the United States and elsewhere became more female. Furthermore, because of Britain's policy to feminize the largely male ex-prisoner migrant populations in Australia, Britain encouraged more women to migrate to this and other countries in Oceania.

However, just as the gender composition of both immigrants and emigrants became more complex after 1860 (see chapters 4 and 5), so too did the policies that propelled these gendered populations and their consequences. As we describe in chapter 5, by the end of the nineteenth century, nations receiving many immigrants began to implement restrictions, many of them racially or xenophobically motivated. Gradually, throughout the twentieth century, complex and more restrictive immigrant policy regimes emerged in many nations worldwide, creating more gender variation and selectivity among global migrants than in the past. In most of Europe and the United States, one consequence was that marriage migrations and those related to unifying families became the largest source of visas for immigrant women. Yet, as migration restriction regimes allocated fewer visas for other types of migrants, all continents witnessed a rise in an unauthorized and mostly male migration.

Policies in Host Societies

In this section, we consider contemporary immigration policies in the United States and Canada—two nations to which many have migrated since the early twentieth century. The United States, for example, is currently the largest receiver of immigrants worldwide. What U.S. immigration policies have encouraged or limited the migration of women and men and to what extent might these help us explain different migrant gender compositions? We begin by thinking about the 1965 amendments to the Immigration and Nationality Act (INA); these privileged family unification which, since then, has favored women. But linking immigration visas to family members is a vestige of earlier immigration policy, thus also contributing to the rising share of women among U.S. immigrants that was obvious already in the late 1920s. The 1924 Immigration Act exempted some wives and dependent children of U.S. citizens from the restrictive national origin quotas it implemented. However, exemptions were not the same for U.S. citizen women as for U.S. citizen men. In 1928, the U.S. Congress exempted husbands and children of U.S. women citizens only if their marriages had occurred before that year. Male U.S. citizens faced no year restriction related to when they had married. As a result, for several decades, more wives than husbands were able to enter as immigrants to the United States. As David Reimers reports, approximately 231,000 exempted wives and 13,000 husbands arrived between 1925 and 1948.[1] This inequality remained in place until 1952, when the INA was passed and spouses and children of all U.S. citizens became exempt from visa quotas. Passage of the 1945 War Brides Act and related legislation, as well as the 1952 INA, made it possible for U.S. military men to bring in spouses and biological and adopted children.

More recent policies have also affected the gender composition of U.S. immigrants, but in paradoxical ways. On the one hand, the amnesty provision of the 1986 Immigration Reform and Control Act led to approximately three million formerly undocumented immigrants having legal status. Most were men, in part because undocumented migrations had been heavily male but also because men were more likely than women to be able to document formal employment.[2] In contrast, other policies related to amnesty recipients largely benefited women. For example, in 1990, visas were set aside for relatives of amnesty recipients, of whom many were women. Moreover, by 2010, approximately one-third of those who received amnesty had become U.S. naturalized citizens, making it possible for their immediate family relatives to enter exempt from visa quotas. Currently, nearly half of all U.S. immigrants are U.S. citizen immediate family members, who are largely women.

Another dominant feature of contemporary U.S. policy is enforcement. Since the 1990s, increased border and internal enforcement has led to more unauthorized migrants and more deportations, men being the overwhelming majority of both populations. In addition, however, and influenced by the 1986 amnesty program, more women began to migrate without documents.[3] Yet, because more unauthorized immigrants have been men than women, U.S. migrant gender composition has not exceeded gender balance since 1970s (see figure 6.1). Therefore, as many before have noted, policy provisions may appear gender neutral but they often have gender-specific implications.[4]

Other studies describe how gender intersects with illegality and immigration policies, producing gendered consequences for U.S. immigrants. These studies argue that unauthorized status prevents women and men from fulfilling their gendered expectations and, as a result, they experience and navigate gendered expectations differently from those authorized. For example, Leisy Abrego finds that migrant El Salvadoran women in the United States send larger percentages of their earnings as remittances than men because women have to live up to gendered ideals as selfless mothers.[5] More recently, Abrego reports that, because these women are mothers migrating alone, they have to prove that they are committed mothers by working and living in difficult conditions.[6] In contrast, men experience better conditions because their masculinity is not based on responsible parenting. Laura Enriquez shows that, because of immigration policies, Mexican unauthorized immigrant men and women have different family formation expectations, with men less likely than women to desire and form families.[7] To the extent that unauthorized status shifts expectations and creates more difficulty for incorporation, U.S. enforcement policies may elevate the chances of return.

Building on the ways that U.S. policies influence migrant gender composition, we now turn to Canada, an immigrant destination that relies on a visa system emphasizing skilled immigrants. Yet, similar to those entering the United States, more Canadian women immigrants enter as family members, including spouses, than men. Monica Boyd reports that women represented approximately 61 percent of "family class admissions" and 60 percent of "principal applicants in the family class."[8] However, Boyd also shows how gender is embedded in Canada's immigration system such that rules and procedures that seem gender neutral often have salient gendered implications. For example, admission criteria for economic migrants include years of work experience, which may disadvantage potential female migrants if family responsibilities interrupted their past labor force activity. Among those seeking refugee status from countries where educational achievement is stratified by gender and norms supporting marriage and childbearing at relatively young ages, women may be less able than men to demonstrate the ability to be economically independent, a necessary criterion for refugee applicants. Moreover, although no estimates of the gender composition of Canadian unauthorized migrants exist, data from those who applied for the 1983 to 1985 Canadian legalization program show that approximately half of its applicants were women and, from some nations, immigrant women represented considerably more than half.[9]

Thus, although policies in both nations are gender neutral, aspects of these policies have clear and observable gendered effects. One final example is the Canadian live-in caregiver program, which permits those who do not qualify for entry as other types of immigrants to work as live-in caregivers for two years and then apply for permanent residency. Because caregiving labor tends to be female, this program is likely to benefit more migrant women than men though the program is not explicitly written to benefit them.

Policies of Sending Nations

Since at least 1860, countries that send international migrants are relatively poorer than the nations who receive them. We limit our comments here to countries in contemporary Asia because it has seen the most uneven patterns of economic success and its labor migration sending policies have become more similar in recent decades.[10] Within this region, the Philippines stands out. It was the first nation to create a government agency designed to process migrant workers and regulate their recruiters in the early 1970s. Since then, its state apparatus has expanded to include welfare agencies designed to assist migrants and their families as well as permanent emigrants. Estimates suggests that more than half of Philippine emigrants are women; they migrate in very large numbers to meet the global demand for health and other care workers, including domestic laborers. Choy argues that the origins of Filipino nurse migration derives from early twentieth-century U.S. colonial rule of the Philippines, when it created a hospital training system comparable to that in the United States.[11] Current policies include the Republic Act 8042, also known as the Migrant Workers and Overseas Filipinos Act of 1995, which obligates the Filipino government to protect migrants abroad, and the Supermaid Program of 2006, which offers additional training to potential women geared to migrate as household service workers, and requires that these women receive no less than $400 (U.S.) a month and pay no recruitment fees.[12]

Other sending nations in South Asia have policies that influence migration and all have government agencies to promote and protect migrant workers. Interestingly, Nana Oishi argues that all Asian countries, even the Philippines, have restricted women's migration more than men's.[13] Generally speaking, policies relating to men originate in state economic concerns about men's labor, whereas those for women reflect a tension between economic interests and social or moral values related to a country's religion and nationalistic ideologies. The latter limit women's international mobility but not men's: when women depart, nations can no longer claim to protect them as future mothers of the national culture. For example, after the number of women migrants began to rise in the 1970s, the government of the Philippines banned female migration in response to growing concern about migrant abuses to women. Eventually, however, it shifted back to an open policy after women began to leave without authorization and other concerns about their protection, especially from traffickers, escalated.

In contrast, before 2005, Bangladesh—a majority Muslim country—had outright banned unskilled women's out-migration. After it formally recognized the equal rights of these women to migrate for employment, more women began to migrate. Between 2003 and 2009, women's labor out-migration as unskilled workers grew by 829 percent, rising from 2,393 to 22,224 women during the period.[14] Yet despite growing numbers, Bangladeshi women migrants continue to experience stigma and discrimination, mistreatment, and obstacles when accessing government services and the basic training necessary to prepare them to migrate and after migrating in countries of destination.[15]

Lessons Learned for Future Research

As migration scholars, we show how important it is for us to interrogate the data we use and question how they matter for studies related to gender and migration. Throughout this volume, we emphasize differences in flow versus stock data, their advantages and disadvantages, and illustrate what each offers to understanding migrant gender composition. We also note the important scholarly tradition established by early feminist demographers in the twentieth century, and how particular methodological approaches may be gendered as male and female and shift over time. In addition, we draw from many disciplines that facilitate an examination of shifts and variation in migrant gender composition across time and place, and understanding explanations for these patterns and shifts; sharpen our measure of migrant gender composition so that it is age-standardized; and initially examine the consequences of variations in gender composition. We suggest that all scholars—no matter their discipline and methodological expertise—query the underlying perspectives that data sets and their measurements produce to better appreciate the fluidity of gender composition without abandoning quantitative methods or empirical data. In the case of flow data about migration, although they existed for a long time, social scientists increasingly had concerns about the flaws inherent in these data, and historians were more likely to accept and use them, especially in interpreting the nineteenth-century migrations. Moreover, although individual-level stock data are now more readily available, they too—as we demonstrate—have their limits, especially for those interested migration as a process. This is why demographers have begun to change their minds about the value of flow data and to call again on the United Nations to focus more closely on the measurement of flows rather than immigrant stock. The result is that migration studies will have to rely on a mosaic or patchwork of data sources, of which each offers insights that may render some people, such as women and other empirical categories, invisible and thus mandate interpretation and debate.

= Notes =

Introduction

1. Zlotnik 1987, 943.
2. Sassen-Koob 1984.
3. Pear 1985, A15.
4. Castles and Miller 1993. Internal migration scholars also began to discuss feminization at this time, see Billsborrow and Zlotnik 1992.
5. See, as examples, Donato et al. 2006; Engle 2004; Piper 2005; Jolly and Reeves 2005; Fry 2006; Yinger 2006.
6. Zlotnik 2003; Alcalá 2006; Donato et al. 2006.
7. Oishi 2005.
8. On trafficking, Aronowitz 2009, 43; Kim and Fu 2008; on exploitation, Lutz 2002; Kaelin 2011.
9. "Feminization of migration," *Wikipedia,* http://en.wikipedia.org/wiki/Feminization_of_migration, accessed July 9, 2011.
10. Caldwell 2006.
11. Alcalá 2006.
12. The best estimate for the numbers of migrants worldwide in 1960 is 76 million and in 2000, 159 million (Özden et al. 2011). Çağlar Özden and his co-authors confirm that women's representation increased during the period studied but they conclude that worldwide, migrations were still slightly male predominant in 2000.
13. Migration data collected before the 1920s did not permit scholars to distinguish among different categories of migrants, such as refugees, those authorized and unauthorized, and labor versus family or marriage migrants. Gradually, after the 1920s, as these categories became more relevant, data sources incorporated such distinctions. Migration categories continue to change in our own times.
14. McKeown 2008.
15. Hollifield 2004.
16. ILO 1927.
17. Schrover and Moloney 2013. The UN's Declaration of Human Rights aims mainly to protect the right to exit. "The Universal Declaration of Human

Rights," Articles 13–14, http://www.un.org/en/documents/udhr/, accessed October 17, 2014.

18. *Trans-Atlantic Slave Trade Database*, http://www.slavevoyages.org/tast/index.faces, accessed October 17, 2014.
19. Solow 1999; Eltis and Richardson 2008, 2010.
20. Nwokeji and Eltis 2002.
21. Geggus 1989; Eltis and Engerman 1992, 1993; Morgan 2004; Nwokeji 2010.
22. Houstoun, Kramer, and Barrett 1984; Massey, Goldring, and Durand 1994; Donato, Alexander et al. 2011; Gabaccia and Zanoni 2012.
23. Lucassen 2005, 8–9; Gabaccia 2014.
24. See the definition for dominant as a political relation in the *Oxford English Dictionary* as "exercising chief authority or rule: ruling, governing, commanding; most influential."
25. The *Oxford English Dictionary* defines predominant as "constituting the main, most abundant, or strongest element; prevailing, prominent."
26. See, for example, Manning 2005, 124.
27. Guttentag and Secord 1983; Hesketh and Xing 2006.
28. On China, Hudson and Van den Boer 2004; on India, Larsen 2011.
29. Lorber and Farrell 1991.
30. Donato et al. 2006.
31. Heskith and Xing 2006.
32. Grosz 1987. First read by Lorde at a 1979 conference on Simone Beauvoir, later published as Lorde 1984.
33. Rosenau 1992; Gross and Levitt 1994.
34. Curran et al. 2006.
35. See Pessar and Mahler 2001.
36. Fonow and Cook 2005, 2226.
37. Manning 2005; Hoerder 2002.
38. Fonow and Cook 2005.
39. Ghosh 2007.
40. Boyd 1999.

Chapter 1

1. Koselleck 2004, 76.
2. Berger and Luckmann 1966.
3. Schiebinger 1989; Dzuback 2003.
4. Bosma, Kessler, and Lucassen 2013; Cerutti 2012.
5. Burchell, Gordon, and Miller 1991.
6. Drechsler 2001.
7. Hauser and Duncan 1959.
8. Manning 2005; Hoerder 2002; De Haan 2002.
9. Perdue 2009.
10. Ferris 2000; Di Cosmo 2002.
11. Harzig and Hoerder 2009, 20–25; Manning 2005.
12. In "Seditions and Troubles," Bacon urged rulers to guarantee that "the Population of a Kingdome (especially if it be not mowen downe by wars) does not exceed, the Stock of the Kingdome, which should maintaine them."

See the online version of the *Oxford English Dictionary* for etymology and early uses of the word *population,* including Bacon's.

13. Heilbron, Magnusson, and Wittrock 1999, 203.
14. Sussman 2004; Kreager 1993.
15. Harzig and Hoerder 2009, 54–55.
16. Compare Zelinsky (1971) and Lucassen and Lucassen (2009) with Hochstadt (1999) and Pooley and Turnbull (1998).
17. See, for example, Carnot 1856.
18. Baigent 2012; Ravenstein 1908.
19. Ravenstein 1889.
20. Poovey 1988.
21. Ravenstein 1885, 196.
22. Harzig and Hoerder 2009, 10.
23. Only in the late twentieth century would feminist scholars critique continued scholarly inattention to personal and familial motivations for moving (see Pessar 1982; Boyd 1989).
24. Ravenstein 1885, 196.
25. Lown 1983; Rose 1986.
26. Ravenstein 1885, 196.
27. Schwenken and Eberhardt 2008.
28. Brettell and de Berjeois 1992.
29. Rodgers 1998.
30. Gabaccia 2010.
31. Harzig and Hoerder 2009.
32. Willcox 1896, 728; Bailey 1906; 1913, 380.
33. Diner 2013; Conzen 1996. A new forthcoming book by Aldon Morris, 2015, shifts emphasis from the Chicago School to W. E. B. DuBois as founder of Science of Sociology.
34. Becker 1999.
35. The possible exception was the Polish scholar Florian Witold Znaniecki, who, with W. I. Thomas, published *The Polish Peasant in Europe and America* from 1918 to 1920. When the German invasion of Poland ended his career, Znaniecki found a position at the University of Illinois.
36. Although their research occurred during the onset of feminization in U.S. immigration, such change did not attract their attention.
37. Gordon 1964; Bulmer 1984; Turner 1988.
38. Handlin 1951.
39. Van Nederveen Meerker, Neusinger, and Hoerder forthcoming; Trolander 1991; Davis 1984; Lissak 1989; Carson 1990.
40. Deegan 1988.
41. Gabaccia forthcoming; Gjerde 1999.
42. Hesseltine and Kaplan 1943.
43. Kelly 1895.
44. Greenwald and Anderson 1996.
45. Crocker 2006.
46. Butler 1909; Byington 1910; More 1907; Van Kleeck 1913; Manning 1930.
47. Sicherman and Green 1980; Costin 1983, 159.
48. Willcox and Ferenczi 1929.

49. Although scholars today are sometimes reluctant to draw on the work of the first generation of U.S. demographers because of the role played by racists, eugenicists, immigration restrictionists, and social Darwinists in the founding of the Population Association of America (Greenhalgh 1996), no university-trained statisticians who helped to found the PAA were hostile to immigrants, eugenicists, or social Darwinists (Hodgson 1991).
50. Lazarsfeld 1961.
51. Bartlett 1928, 331.
52. Reinharz 1989; Thomas 1936, 1937, 1938.
53. Shryock and Eldridge 1947; Hauser and Eldridge 1947; Eldridge 1964, 1965.
54. Eldridge and Thomas 1964.
55. Taeuber and Taeuber 1938; Taeuber 1944; Pan and Taeuber 1952; Taeuber 1947, 1958, 1960, 1963.
56. Taeuber and Eldridge 1947; Hochschild 1973.
57. Eldridge and Siegel 1946.
58. Taeuber and Wang 1960.
59. Marshall 1994, 756.
60. Gabaccia 1989.
61. Beginning with Berger and Luckmann 1966.
62. Ortner 1972; Rosaldo and Lamphere 1974.
63. On immigrant women, Tilly and Scott 1978; Yans-McLaughlin 1977; Pleck 1978; Melville 1978; Diner 1983; Gabaccia 1984; Smith 1985; on boys and girls being socialized, Clausen 1968; on gender roles and employment, Powers and Holmberg 1978.
64. Peterson 1969; UN 1979.
65. Leeds 1976.
66. Dever 2003.
67. Bartlett 1928, 331.
68. Okin 2003.
69. Gonzales 1980; Tobe 1979.
70. Phizacklea 1983; Brettell and Simon 1986; Gabaccia 1992, 1994.
71. *Patriarchy* was feminists' preferred term for male domination cross-culturally at that time.
72. Guttentag and Secord 1983.
73. Ibid., 29–31.
74. Ibid., 72–76.
75. Ibid., 113–30.
76. Norton 1987; Smith 1989; Crane 1990.
77. Marcia Guttentag and Paul Secord (1983) believed that female predominance was a consequence of family patterns developed during slavery. In contrast, Herbert Gutman (1976) shows that family patterns had changed as the descendants of slaves moved to cities. Female majorities among Jewish Americans were due to practices that facilitated births of larger than average numbers of female babies.
78. Guttentag and Secord 1983, 9.
79. Bank, Delamont, and Marshall 2007, 373, 506.
80. Scott 1986; Butler 1909; Lorber and Farrell 1991.
81. Kosofsky-Sedgwick 1990.

82. For studies about the malleability of sex in the context of migration, see Manalansan 2006; Luibhéid 2008.
83. Donato et al. 2006.
84. Grosz 1987. First read by Lorde at a 1979 conference on Simone Beauvoir, later published as Lorde 1984.
85. Rosenau 1992; Gross and Levitt 1994.
86. Curran et al. 2006; Lutz 2010; Nawyn 2010; Hondagneu-Sotelo 1994.
87. Pessar and Grasmuck 1991.
88. For Europe, Kofman et al. 2000; for the United States, Hondagneu-Sotelo 1994, 2003.
89. Menard 1993, 357.
90. Mason 1987; Watkins 1993; Watkins and Danzi 1995; Riley and McCarthy 2003.
91. Raijman and Semyonov 1997; Humphreys 1999; Yeates 2004; Khalaf 2009; Bastia 2009; Schmalzbauer 2009; del Rio and Alonso-Villar 2012; Holst et al. 2012; Flippen 2012.
92. See Steven Ruggles, University of Minnesota, "The Decline of Quantitative History," Spring 2010, www.hist.umn.edu/~ruggles/hist5011/Decline.pptx, accessed October 17, 2014.
93. Katharine Donato, telephone interview, February 17, 2014.
94. Morokvasic 1984. For analysis about the women and feminists at the ILO who shared many of Zlotnik's and Morokvasic's concerns, see Boris and Jensen (2012).
95. Zlotnik 1987, 925.
96. UN 1977; UN Economic Commission for Europe 1982; UN Economic and Social Commission for Asia and the Pacific 1985.
97. Kelly 1987; Simmons 1987.
98. Houstoun et al. 1984.
99. UN 1995; Bilsborrow and Zlotnik 1992.
100. Klein 1971.
101. Pessar and Mahler 2001.
102. Parreñas 2001; Ehrenreich and Hochschild 2004; van Nederveen Meerkerk, Neunsinger, and Hoerder forthcoming.
103. Tyner 1999.
104. Pedraza 1991.
105. Houstoun et al. 1984.
106. Gabaccia 1996.
107. Donato 1992; see also Gordon 2005.
108. Floro and Schaefer 1998; Sassen-Koob 1984; Kofman 1998, 1999.
109. Hofman and Buckley 2013.
110. McMurray 1999; Aronowitz 2009; Kim and Fu 2008.
111. Lutz 2002; Kaelin 2011.
112. Parreñas 2011.
113. Jones 2008; Schwenken 2008. For example, Google NGram documents a sevenfold increase in discussions of sex trafficking found in the millions of texts it has digitized between 1990 and 2010.
114. Schrover 2013, 126.
115. Reeder 2003.
116. Guy 1991; Schrover 2014.
117. Labadie-Johnson 2008, 67.

118. E-mail to Donna Gabaccia from Black Alliance for Just Immigration, Priority Network, and Domestic Workers Union in New York and Women Watch America about a virtual briefing entitled, "Gender, Race, and Migration," March 8, 2010.
119. Green 1994.
120. Fonow and Cook 2005; Rosenberg and Howard 2008; Gabaccia and Maynes 2012.

Chapter 2

1. Dyson 2012.
2. Alterman 1969.
3. Daugherty and Kammeyer 1995.
4. Cunsolo 1993; Methorst 1936.
5. Ross 1827. Some historians of U.S. immigration used the term *stock* to make racialized distinctions between old and new Americans (see Kazal 2004).
6. See Nicholson 1891, 99.
7. Kreager 1991; Sussman 2004; Saeger 2008.
8. Williams 1964, 10.
9. Rogers 1990.
10. Grieco 2002.
11. Joppke 1996; Rubio-Marin 2000. One consequence is that Germany's foreigner population grew in the 1980s and 1990s, without significant new immigration. Through reproduction, foreigners gave birth to additional foreigners. In 1999, Germany passed a new law which allowed children born of foreign parents in Germany to acquire citizenship more easily than in the past.
12. One consequence is that noncitizen labor migrants are highly regulated, more so than Jewish foreign born citizens (Raijman and Kemp 2011). Zvi Eckstein (2010) estimates that noncitizen authorized and unauthorized labor migrants accounted for 12 percent of Israel's labor force in 2009.
13. Newbold 2001.
14. O'Reilly 2012.
15. Hoerder 1993.
16. Ravenstein 1889; Gregory 2004.
17. Filby 1988; Tepper 1988.
18. Hall and Ruggles 2004.
19. ILO 1922.
20. Preston 1795, 11.
21. Sutherland 1963.
22. Beniger and Robyn 1978.
23. Süssmilch 1741.
24. Sieff 1990.
25. Swanson, Shryock, and Siegel 2004.
26. Ibid., 129.
27. Brian and Jaisson 2007, 1–4.
28. Houstoun, Kramer, and Barrett 1984; Houstoun and Pooler 2002; Kandel and Massey 2002; Stecklov et al. 2010.
29. Donato and Armenta 2011.

30. Gabaccia and Zanoni 2012.
31. Zlotnik 2003.
32. Donato and Armenta 2011, figure 6.
33. Gabaccia and Zanoni 2012.
34. Stolnitz 1983, 429.
35. Swanson, Shryock, and Siegel 2004, 130.
36. See Taeuber and Taeuber 1964; see also Pryor and Long 1987; McDaniel and Preston 1994; Donato et al. 2011.
37. Alexander and Steidl 2012.
38. MacRaild 2011.
39. Donato 1993, 2010; Massey et al. 1994; Kanaiaupuni 2001; Cerrutti and Massey 2001; Curran and Rivero Fuentes 2003; Schrover 2013.
40. MacDonald and MacDonald 1964; Massey et al. 1993.
41. Bentley 1996.
42. Zlotnik 2003.
43. Foner 1999, 2000; Lucassen 2005.
44. These comparisons have been used in the social sciences, often to understand migrant minorities (for examples, see DuBois 1939; Wood 1955; Kindleberger 1965).
45. Foner 2006.
46. Hauser 1942; Eblen 1965.
47. Davis 1945; Dyson 2010
48. Heer 1968; Knodel 1977; Coale and Watkins 1986; Omran 1971; McKeown 2008; Haines 2001.
49. Van de Kaa 1987; Meyerson 2001; Laesthaege and Neels 2002; Van De Kaa 2004.
50. Ogden and Hall 2004; Perelli-Harris 2005.
51. Sassen-Koob 1984, 2008.
52. Lucassen 2005; Isaac and Lipold 2012; Gabaccia 2014.
53. Guttentag and Secord 1983.
54. Sophie Vause and Sorena Toma (forthcoming) address a similar concern using flow data about migration from Senegal and DR Congo to Europe.

Chapter 3

1. Hartley 1953, 1.
2. McNeill 1973; Hoerder 2002; O'Rourke and Williamson 1999; Manning 2005.
3. Elliott 2006, 2009.
4. Curtin 1990.
5. Bush 2000.
6. Palmer 1959.
7. On trade, DeVries 2010; on limits, Woodworth 2007.
8. Crosby 1972.
9. Curtin 1969; Thomas 1997; Klein 1999; Eltis and Richardson 2010.
10. Manning 1990; Savage 1992; Vink 2003; Wright 2007; Allen 2008.
11. Crosby 1991.
12. Indentured servants sold themselves into contractual servitude for two to seven years, usually in exchange for the price of their sea passage; they

received room and board from those owning their contracts and sometimes received a cash payment at the end of their term of service.

13. Ekirch 1987; Bullard 2000; Grubb 2000; Morgan and Rushton 2004.
14. Lucassen and Lucassen 2011.
15. McKeown 2004.
16. Hoerder 2002; Manning 2005.
17. O'Reilly 2012, 4.
18. Though counterintuitive, given early systems of communication and transportation, European migrants—and especially perhaps soldiers and missionaries—quite often returned to Europe (see Morner 1976).
19. Boyd-Bowman 1973, 1976; Morner 1976, 1995.
20. Boyd-Bowman 1973.
21. Altman 1989,191.
22. Boyd-Bowman 1976, 732.
23. Ibid.
24. Morner 1995.
25. Ibid. 1976, 756.
26. Ibid. 1995.
27. Ibid., 264.
28. Fogleman 1992.
29. Moller 1945.
30. Games 1999.
31. Anderson 1985, table 3.
32. Bailyn 1986a, 1986b.
33. Matt 2011, xx.
34. Salinger 1983.
35. Galenson 1981.
36. Grubb 1989.
37. Eltis and Jennings 1988; Inikori and Engerman 1992; Wright 1999; Davis 2000; Eltis 2002; Manning 2005; Harzig and Hoerder 2009; Eley 2007.
38. Hoerder 1999.
39. Fogleman 1998.
40. *Trans-Atlantic Slave Trade Database*, http://www.slavevoyages.org/tast/index.faces, accessed October 17, 2014.
41. Nwokeji and Eltis 2002.
42. Barbara Solow wisely but sadly concluded, "What we cannot get from these data is an understanding of the human experience of the Middle Passage" (1999, 10–11).
43. It is tempting to speculate that ship captains—who could and did directly easily observe the naked bodies or sex of slaves—avoided recording sex and other individual characteristics because it exacerbated the challenges they faced in dehumanizing living human beings and treating them as commodities.
44. The literature is rich on slave mortality both during and after Middle Passage. It is generally understood that male mortality surpassed female mortality during transport and adaptation to life in the Americas. This only modestly altered gender composition at the point of disembarkation, as discussed below (Galenson 1979; Klein et al. 2001) and in subsequent slave society (see, for example, Cushner 1975).

45. Blackburn 1988b; Davis 2006; Drescher 2009.
46. Klein 1986, 147.
47. Robertson and Klein 1983; Terborg-Penn, Hurley, and Rushing 1987; Gasper and Hine 1996; Campbell, Miers, and Miller 2007a.
48. Paton 2005; Robinson 2007.
49. Morgan 2004, 200.
50. Klein 1990.
51. Campbell, Miers, and Miller 2007b, 7–8.
52. Morgan 2004; Eltis and Engerman 1992, figure 2; Eltis 1982; Galenson 1984; Grubb 1989.
53. Morgan 2004, 3.
54. Blackburn 1988a; Smallwood 2007.
55. Hogerzeil and Richardson 2007.
56. Cited by Nwokeji 2010, 145.
57. Manning 1983.
58. Inikori 1992; Eltis and Engerman 1993; Freudenberger and Pritchett 1991, 452.
59. Lovejoy 1989; Campbell, Miers, and Miller 2007a.
60. Morgan 2004.
61. Ibid. 1997.
62. Morgan also notes that slave owners quickly recognized the ability of African women to perform hard labor in agricultural fields.
63. Morgan 1997.
64. Although Southeast Africa and the Indian Ocean Islands exported slaves with even lower percentages female, the numbers of slaves exported were much smaller than from other African regions, so we did not choose Southeast Africa for comparative case study.
65. Eltis 1995; Behrendt 1997; Klein 2002.
66. Walsh 2001; Burnard and Morgan 2001.
67. Nwokeji 2001, 2010.
68. Lancaster 1976; Carney and Watts 1990.
69. Nwokeji 2010.
70. Ibid., chapter 6.
71. Ibid.
72. Lovejoy and Richardson 1995.
73. Nwokeji 2010.
74. For Brazilian slaves, Miller 1989; for sugar plantations, Taylor 1970; Schwartz 1982; for mining, Ramos 1988.
75. Miller 1988.
76. Ibid., 105.
77. Heywood 2009.
78. Miller 1984.
79. Ibid.
80. Miller 1989.
81. Thornton 1982; Vansina 2005.
82. Nwokeji 2010.
83. Boyd-Bowman 1973, 1976.
84. Curtin 1975; Eltis 1987; Lovejoy 1989; Eltis 1990; Curto and Gervais 2001; Thornton 1980; Nwokeji 2000.

85. Nwokeji 2000; Lovejoy 1989, 387; Miller 1989.
86. Vansina 2005, 14; see also Thornton 1983.
87. Shammas 2012, 12.
88. Morgan 2004; Cushner 1975; Tadman 2000.
89. Guttentag and Secord 1983.
90. Broadhead 1983.
91. Thornton 2006.
92. Sturtz 2002, 5.
93. Crane 1990.
94. Guttentag and Secord 1983.
95. Boserup 1970.

Chapter 4

1. Marx and Engels 1888, 4.
2. Willcox and Ferenczi 1929.
3. Williamson 1996; O'Rourke and Williamson 1999; Robertson 2003.
4. Curtin 1990; Karras and McNeill 1992; Gabaccia 2004.
5. Guasco 2010.
6. Klooster 2009.
7. Gabaccia 2012.
8. Leonhard and von Hirschhausen 2010.
9. Tucker 2000; Lynch 2002.
10. Friedmann 1978.
11. Headrick 1981.
12. Pomeranz and Topik 2006.
13. Bodnar 1986.
14. Gabaccia and Hoerder 2011.
15. Tinker 1974; Northrup 1995.
16. Brass and van der Linden 1997.
17. Christiane Harzig and Dirk Hoerder call these the "body parts" migrations (2009, 4).
18. McKeown 2004.
19. Harzig and Hoerder 2009, 36.
20. McKeown 2004.
21. Ferenczi 1937.
22. McKeown 2004.
23. Willcox and Ferenczi 1929.
24. McKeown 2004.
25. See chapter 2 and the introduction for a definition of this and other categories of feminization.
26. In later data sources, Antipodean British settler colonies were in Oceania, and Hawaii became a U.S. territory after 1898.
27. McKeown 2001, 2004.
28. Friedman 1978.
29. These were documented in *International Migrations* only for Canada and the United States. Data for immigrants to South America are available in *International Migrations* only after 1857, so are not included here.

30. Lewis 1978; McKeown 2010; Rosenberg 2012.
31. Steinfeld 1991.
32. Grubb 1994.
33. On the Atlantic, Eltis 1982.
34. Atkinson 1994.
35. Robson 1994; Oxley 1996; Damousi 1997; Daniels 1998.
36. Many convicts transported to Australia were Irish but contrary to popular opinion the female Irish minority was composed of first-time petty thieves, not prostitutes (Robinson 1986).
37. Although imperial elites viewed these released prisoners as unruly and difficult-to-govern and they began to advocate for continued imprisonment in Britain rather transportation (Willis 2005), convict transport/release continued until the 1860s, especially in Western Australia.
38. Foner 1995.
39. Johnston 1972; Diner 1983; Ferrie 1999.
40. Gabaccia 1996.
41. Victorians generally viewed women as exercising a civilizing influence over men (Smithers 2009).
42. Gothard 2001; Diamond 1999.
43. Haines 1994; MacDonald and Richardson 1997; Hammerton 1979.
44. Rushen 2003.
45. Worsnop 1990.
46. Adele Perry (2001) and Janet Meyers (2001) suggest that the surplus had greater impact on settler migration in Canada.
47. On North America, see Hurtado 1999.
48. Blackburn and Ricards 1993.
49. For challenges, see Gabaccia 1997; Peck 2000; McKeown 2004. For the new slavery, see Tinker 1974.
50. Lee 1989; Jain and Reddock 1998.
51. Northrup 1995, table 3.1.
52. McKeown 2001.
53. C. Anderson 2000.
54. Northrup 1995, 74–77.
55. Campbell 1923; Stewart 1951; Hu-DeHart 1994; Meagher 2008.
56. Samaroo 2013.
57. We are grateful to Adam McKeown and Elizabeth Yuk Yee Sinn for giving us these data.
58. Data from *International Migrations* also document many other examples of very heavily male migrations from Bulgaria, Dalmatia, Rumania, Croatia, Greece, and Korea.
59. Again, data from *International Migrations* reveal gender-balanced and female-predominant emigrations from a diverse group of countries including Bulgaria, Hungary, Tasmania, New Zealand, the Azores, Madeira, Palestine, Martinique, and Madagascar.
60. Thomas 1954; Williamson 1996.
61. Gabaccia 1997; 2000; McKeown 2001.
62. Lee 2013.
63. Gabaccia 1997; Peck 2000.

64. Ramirez 1991; Hsu 2000; Gabaccia 2000, 2001.
65. Schrover 2013.
66. Fauve-Chamoux 2005; van Nederveen Merker, Neunsinger, and Hoerder forthcoming.
67. Leinonen and Gabaccia 2014.
68. On the Irish, see Miller 1988; on the Jews, see Lambroza 1987; Klier 2011.
69. Baum, Hyman, and Michel 1976; Weinberg 1988; Glenn 1990.
70. Diner 1983; Jackson 1984; Nolan 1989.
71. Lesser 2012.
72. Silberstein 2003, graph 1.
73. Gabaccia 1996.
74. Glenn 1986; Lee 2013.
75. Gabaccia 1996; Houstoun, Kramer, Barrett 1984.
76. Gabaccia and Zanoni 2012.
77. Schrover 2013; Silberstein 2003; Gabaccia 1996.
78. Jerome 1926.
79. Hsu 2000; Cinel 2002; Ramirez 1991; Gabaccia 2000.
80. Friedman 1982; Lopez 2013.
81. Reeder 2003.
82. Tirabassi 2002; Guttentag and Secord 1983.
83. Gabaccia 1997; Wyman 1993, 39.
84. Duggan 1990, 104; Lowrie 2013.
85. Lal 1985.
86. Modell and Hareven 1973; Zembrzycki 2007.
87. Kessner 1977; Kessler-Harris 1982; Gabaccia 1988; Foner 1999; Enstad 1999.
88. Angrist 2002, 997.
89. Panunzio 1942; Kennedy 1944.
90. Joel Perlmann and Mary Waters (2004) note that they were also sometimes from other immigrant groups.
91. Sinke 1999; Guttentag and Secord 1983.
92. Steidl and Fischer-Nebmaier 2014.
93. Leinonen and Gabaccia 2014.
94. Ibid.
95. Hareven and Langenbach 1978; Diner 1983; Jackson 1984; Nolan 1989; O'Sullivan 1995.
96. Harzig 2006.
97. Diner 1983. Leslie Page Moch (2012) also describes nineteenth-century Parisians as stereotyping of hardworking maids from Brittany as stupid and sluttish "Becassines."
98. Guttentag and Secord 1983.

Chapter 5

1. Hobsbawm 1994; Sluga 2013.
2. Hoerder 2002; Castles and Miller 1993; on the United States, Spickard 2007; on Canada, Avery 1995; on Australia, Jupp 2007.
3. Bashford 2007.

4. For Africa, data are available for Morocco, Cape Verde, Madagascar, Mauritius, Angola, Mozambique, Northern and Southern Rhodesia, Southwest Africa, Tanganyika, Uganda, and the Union of South Africa. For Asia, data are available for India, Indochina, Palestine and Israel, Japan, Malaya, the Philippines, and Thailand.

5. On the ILO, see Van Daele 2008, 2010; on the League of Nations, see Purseigle 2007.

6. ILO 1927.

7. Ferenczi 1937.

8. Kulischer 1943.

9. UN, Demographic Yearbooks, 1948, 31–35.

10. Permanent emigrants, departing temporary immigrants, residents or nationals departing temporarily and special classes such as refugees or deportees.

11. UN, Demographic Yearbooks, 1959, 30.

12. UN, Demographic Yearbooks, 1968.

13. UN, Demographic Yearbooks, 1977.

14. Ferenezi 1945; Fassman and Munz 1994; for Asian refugees, see Louis 1997.

15. UN, Demographic Yearbooks, 1953.

16. Much of the difference in the numbers of immigrants and emigrants internationally reflects the fact that *Demographic Yearbooks* after 1957 no longer included U.S. data on emigrants. It is likely that this change, plus the UN's efforts to remove short-term labor migrants from emigrant enumerations, explains the difference in immigration and emigration enumeration thereafter.

17. Abel 2013.

18. McKeown 2004.

19. Ibid. 2010. Asian emigrants also continued to figure prominently in global totals even after countries in the Americas had excluded them (see Lee 2007; Lee, Fojas, and Guevera 2012).

20. South America's limited importance as a generator of emigrants in this data may be explained by the fact that Mexico's migrants were classified as North Americans.

21. UN, Demographic Yearbooks, 1956.

22. Alcalá 2006.

23. But see Donato et al. 2011.

24. Steidl and Alexander 2012.

25. Schrover 2013.

26. Both countries included sizeable populations of German-speaking refugees born in parts of central and eastern Europe that, in the aftermath of World War II, were no longer German territories.

27. Alcalá 2006.

28. Torpey 2000; Robertson 2009.

29. Koslowski 2011.

30. McKeown 2008; Hatton and Williamson 2006; Bashford 2014.

31. Jerome 1926.

32. By contrast, the ILO—as critics later noted—largely ignored working women, and instead focused attention on the trafficking of women and children (Pliley 2010; Boris and Jensen 2012).

33. For example, Quack 1995.
34. Houstoun, Kramer, and Barrett 1984, appendix.
35. The heavily masculine Asian migrations largely explain the global masculinization among immigration and arrivals in the 1930s in figure 5.2, as immigration volumes to Europe and the Americas, but not to Asia, fell sharply (see Kaur 2009, 2011).
36. McKeown 2004.
37. Fitzgerald and Cook-Martin 2014.
38. Lee 2013.
39. LeMay and Barkan 1999.
40. Gabaccia 1996.
41. Perrings 1979; Van Onselen 1976.
42. Hahamovitch 2011.
43. King and Winter 2013.
44. Hahamovitch 1997, 2011.
45. Garcia y Griego 1981; Calavita 1992; Cohen 2006; Karjanen 2008.
46. Spoerer and Fleischhacker 2002.
47. Glenn 1986; Virden 1996; Yuh 2004; Wolgin and Bloemraad 2010; Zeiger 2010.
48. Leinonen and Gabaccia 2014.
49. Donato 1992.
50. Prashad 2007.
51. Gabaccia 2012.
52. Best et al. 2004.
53. In the United States beginning with Castles and Kosack (1973). See the extensive research program funded by the National Museum of American History, "Bittersweet Harvest: the Bracero Program 1942–1964," http://american history.si.edu/exhibitions/bittersweet-harvest-bracero-program-1942-1964, accessed October 17, 2014.
54. Morokvasic 1984.
55. Calliste 1991, 1995.
56. Although renewed labor migrations of Europe and North America are well understood, the importance of Asia's immigrants and their feminization to almost 40 percent female (see table 5.2) are not.
57. UNHCR 2013, 36.
58. Houstoun et al. 1984.
59. Schrover et al. 2008.
60. Passell, Cohn, and Gonzalez-Barrera 2013; Bacon 2008.
61. Fry 2006; Passell and Cohn 2009; Donato and Armenta 2011.
62. Sassen-Koob 1984.
63. Chiu and Lee 1997.
64. Giles and Arat-Koc 1994; Raijman, Schammah-Gesser, and Kemp 2003; Chang and Groves 2000; B. Anderson 2000; Ehrenreich and Hochschild 2002; Kofman 1999.
65. Korany 1994; Parreñas 2000; Lan 2008; Sassen-Koob 2008; Cerrutti 2009; Kushnirovich and Raijman 2014.
66. Kofman 1999.
67. UNODC 2009.
68. Agustín 2007; Fitzgerald 2010.

69. Ibid. Yet sex trafficking remains a central focus of many studies of feminization, suggesting the emergence of a new round of moral panic about female mobility, as discussed in chapter 1.

70. Population Association of America 2013.

71. UNData, Statistics, "Outbound Mobility Ratio," http://data.un.org/Data.asp x?q=mobility+&d=UNESCO&f=series%3aED_FSOPTE, accessed October 17, 2014.

72. United Nations Population Division, "The International Migrant Stock: A Global View," http://www.iom.int/jahia/webdav/site/myjahiasite/shared/ shared/mainsite/microsites/IDM/workshops/Data_Collection_08090903/ conf_osaki.pdf, accessed July 19, 2013.

73. International Migrant Stock, 2, https://www.iom.int/jahia/webdav/site/ myjahiasite/shared/shared/mainsite/microsites/IDM/workshops/Data_ Collection_08090903/conf_osaki.pdf, accessed December 3, 2014.

74. The Migratory Observatory, "UNPD International Migrant Stock Data," http://migrationobservatory.ox.ac.uk/data-and-resources/data-sources-and-limitations/unpd-international-migrant-stock-data, accessed July 18, 2013.

75. Tomas, Summers, and Santos 2009.

76. Migration Policy Institute, "International Migrants by Country of Destination 1960–2013," http://www.migrationpolicy.org/programs/data-hub/inter national-migration-statistics, accessed October 17, 2014.

Chapter 6

1. Minnesota Population Center, IPUMS USA, https://usa.ipums.org/usa, accessed October 17, 2014; Minnesota Population Center, North Atlantic Population Project, https://www.nappdata.org/napp, accessed October 17, 2014.

2. Donato et al. 2011.

3. The bureau continued to use cutting-edge technology to analyze data throughout the twentieth century, in the form of film optical sensing devices that read in answers from the 1960 surveys and transferred them onto magnetic tapes, or optical character scanners that created images and translated them into standard code for the 2000 census.

4. https://international.ipums.org/international/, accessed January 15, 2015.

5. McCaa and Jaspers-Faijer 2000, 287.

6. Bob McCaa, interview with the author, February 19, 2014.

7. Steven Ruggles, interview with the author, February 17, 2014.

8. UN 2013.

9. See PAA Statement to the United Nations, July 2013, http://www.population association.org/2013/07/21/paa-statement-to-united-nations-on-international-migration-and-development/, accessed October 6, 2014.

10. For India, for example, IPUMS data are available but do not include nativity.

11. Houstoun et al. 1984.

12. Guttentag and Secord 1983.

13. We count immigrants as persons entering a nation in a given year, and assume that observations are independent.

14. Borders of the countries in the data set have been stable over time.

15. Details about the weights used are available from authors on request.
16. Muus 2004; van Amersfoort 2011.
17. Fynn 2009, 153.
18. Tome and Vause 2014; Vause and Tome 2014.
19. Although the civil war may have killed more foreign born men than women, to our knowledge there is no empirical support for this idea.
20. Victor Agadjanian, Cecilia Menjívar, and Boaventura Cau (2013) consider the impact of men's labor migration on rural women's HIV risks in Mozambique.
21. The number of emigrants from the Philippines is much larger than the number of immigrants. The gender composition of emigrants favors women, who become domestic workers, nurses, and other care workers overseas. Men also migrate and work as seafarers, but in fewer numbers than women (Castles, de Haas, and Miller 2013). For other studies related to the gender composition of those who leave, see Choy 2003; Espiritu 2005.
22. Kaur 2004.
23. Kaur 2009, 290.
24. Pearson and Kusakabe 2012.
25. Song 2013.
26. Tsogtsaikhan 2008.
27. Most immigrants in Puerto Rico were born on the U.S. mainland, in the Dominican Republic, or in Cuba.
28. Mahler and Ugrina 2006.
29. The nations we include in Europe are those in our sample that are in the European Union and those officially recognized for full membership for which negotiations are officially underway.
30. Bassel 2012.
31. Malheiros 2002.
32. Ruhs and Quinn 2009.
33. Kirisci 2003.
34. Ibid.
35. Cerrutti and Gaudio 2010.
36. Jachimowicz 2006. Unfortunately, we do not know what percentage of women are involved in sex trafficking. Recent estimates suggest earnings of $6.6 billion each year by criminal groups engaged in sex trafficking in Argentina (Fox 2012). Lydia Cacho (2011) argues that, since 2006, two large drug cartels from Mexico have expanded into Argentina and the business of sex trafficking.
37. Amaral and Fusco 2005. We are unsure whether Japanese Brazilians who return from visits to Japan are counted as foreigners.
38. Gabaccia and Zanoni 2012.
39. Drumtra 2003, 1.
40. Despite the substantial decline in traditional mining labor in South Africa since 1990 because of industry restructuring and declining reserves, the nation was the largest African employer of contract labor miners in 2000 (Crush and Williams 2005).
41. Daley 1991.
42. Omondi 2013.

43. Recently, Bangladesh rescinded restrictions that were placed on the migration of unskilled and semi-skilled women workers. Although the first of several bans against the migration of less-skilled women was a 1981 presidential order, after 2003 all restrictions were lifted for this group of women (Siddiqui 2008).
44. Kansakar 2001.
45. Chandler 1993.
46. Walton 2011.
47. Suryadinata 2008.
48. McGann 2013.
49. Pitea 2010.
50. Werner 2014.
51. Parrenas 2001; Donato and Tyree 1986; Ehrenreich and Hochschild 2004; Choy 2003; Massey and Taylor 2004; Oishi 2005.
52. For Mexico, see Donato 1993, 2010.
53. See Cerrutti and Gaudio 2010.
54. Amaral and Fusco 2005.
55. Amemiya 1998.
56. Filipino men predominate among migrants to the oil-producing nations in the Middle East (Tyree and Donato 1986; Semyonov and Gorodzeisky 2004), but unfortunately, most countries in the Middle East are not included in the IPUMS-International data set.

Chapter 7

1. Guttentag and Secord 1983.
2. Ibid.
3. South and Trent 1988.
4. Larsen and Kaur 2013.
5. Hofmann and Buckley 2013.
6. Angrist 2002.
7. Krohnert and Vollmer 2012.
8. Angrist 2002; Krohnert and Vollmer 2012; Guttentag and Secord 1983.
9. Hudson and Van den Boer 2004.
10. Hagan and Palloni 1999; Rumbaut and Ewing 2007; Feldmeyer 2009.
11. Donato and Rodriguez 2014.
12. Sen 1990 and others.
13. Zeng et al. 1993.
14. Cai 2010.
15. Ruggles et al. 2009. The data source for all analyses in this chapter is IPUMS-USA, 1910–2010.
16. This definition only includes cross-nativity marriages: when a U.S.-born person marries a foreign-born person, or when a foreign-born person marries a U.S. born person.
17. This updates work published elsewhere (see Donato et al. 2011).
18. On gender balance, Fry 2006; on migration increase, Massey et al. 2002; Donato and Armenta 2011.

19. Houstoun, Kramer, and Barrett 1984.
20. Donato et al. (2011) suggest that this finding may derive from a variety of factors, including a shift toward more women in the Mexican unauthorized migrant population.
21. Gabaccia 1996.
22. Counts of U.S. foreign-born persons in each year are not shown but available on request.
23. We thank one reviewer who asked us to note other explanations unrelated to the size of the migration pool affecting gender selectivity in migration.
24. Foner 2006, 34.
25. Available from authors on request.
26. Diner 1983.
27. Guttentag and Secord 1983.
28. Regression results are available on request.
29. Juhn and Potter 2006.
30. Findings in figure 7.4 reveal gender and marital status differences in labor force activity, a topic investigated further by Katharine Donato, Bhumika Piya, and Anna Jacobs (2014).
31. Stevens, Ishizawa, and Escandell 2012, 740.
32. Qian and Lichter 2001, 289.
33. Esteve, Garcia, and McCaa 2012.
34. Wang and Chang 2002; Chen 2007; Belanger, Lee, and Wang 2010.
35. Piper 1999.
36. Constable 1997, 3.
37. IPUMS permits attaching the attributes of respondents' spouses to the respondent's record. We therefore created a variable that provided the birthplace of each respondent's spouse (see https://usa.ipums.org/usa-action/faq#ques38, accessed October 17, 2014). The unit of analysis is the census year. More details about the analysis are available from the authors on request.
38. For estimates on intramarriage, see Wang 2012, appendix 2.
39. Esteve, Garcia, and McCaa 2012.
40. Kanaiaupuni 2001; Roy and Nangia 2005; Kuhn 2006; Dreby 2010; Sevoyan and Agadjanian 2010; Donato and Duncan 2011; Nobles 2011, 2013; Poeze and Mazzucato 2014.
41. Battistella and Conaco 1998; Asis 2006; Fresnoza-Flot 2014.
42. Andrews 2014 examines how gender operates in the politics of one Mexia community as men and women participate in migration and their origins.
43. Hamilton 2009.
44. Nobles and McKelvey 2013.

Conclusion

1. Reimers 2013.
2. Hagan 1994; Hagan and Gonzalez Baker 1993; Gonzalez Baker 1990.
3. Durand, Massey, and Parrado, 1999; Donato 1993.

4. Banerjee, Pearce, Clifford, and Tandon 2015; Donato, Wagner, and Patterson 2008; Mahler and Pessar 2006; Piper 2005; Boyd and Grieco 2003; Fitzpatrick 1997.
5. Abrego 2009.
6. Ibid. 2014.
7. Enriquez 2014.
8. Boyd 2006, 2.
9. Boyd 1989.
10. Martin 2008.
11. Choy 2003.
12. Migration News 2014.
13. Oishi 2005.
14. Migrant Forum Asia, no date.
15. Siddiqui 2003.

═ References ═

Abel, Guy J. 2013. "Estimating Global Migration Flow Tables using Place of Birth Data." *Demographic Research* 28(18): 505–46.

Abrego, Leisy. 2009. "Economic Well-Being in Salvadoran Transnational Families: How Gender Affects Remittance Practices." *Journal of Marriage and Family* 71:1070–85.

———. 2014. *Sacrificing Families: Navigating Laws, Labor, and Love Across Borders.* Stanford, Calif.: Stanford University Press.

Agadjanian, Victor, Cecilia Menjívar, and Boaventura Cau. 2013. "Economic Uncertainties, Social Strains, and HIV Risks: The Effects of Male Labor Migration on Rural Women in Mozambique." In *How Immigrants Impact their Homelands,* edited by Susan Eckstein and Adil Najam, 234–52. Durham, N.C.: Duke University Press.

Agustín, Laura María. 2007. *Sex at the Margins: Migration, Labour Markets and the Rescue Industry.* London: Zed Books.

Alcalá, María José. 2006. *State of World Population 2006: A Passage to Hope, Women and International Migration.* Policy Analysis and Research Branch of UNODC. Geneva: United Nations Population Fund. Accessed September 19, 2014. http://www.unfpa.org/swp/2006/pdf/en_sowp06.pdf.

Alexander, J. Trent, and Annemarie Steidl. 2012. "Gender and the Laws of Migration: A Reconsideration of Nineteenth-Century Patterns." *Social Science History* 36(2): 223–41.

Allen, Richard B. 2008. "The Constant Demand of the French: The Mascarene Slave Trade and the Worlds of the Indian Ocean and Atlantic During the Eighteenth and Nineteenth Centuries." *Journal of African History* 49(1): 43–72.

Alterman, Hyman. 1969. *Counting People: The Census in History.* New York: Harcourt, Brace & World.

Altman, Ida. 1989. *Emigrants and Society: Extremadura and America in the Sixteenth Century.* Berkeley: University of California Press.

Amaral, Ernesto Friedrich, and Wilson Fusco. 2005. *Shaping Brazil: The Role of International Migration.* Washington, D.C.: Migration Information Source. http://www.migrationpolicy.org/article/shaping-brazil-role-international-migration. Accessed October 17, 2014.

Amemiya, Kozy K. 1998. *Being "Japanese" in Brazil and Okinawa.* Tokyo: Japan Policy Institute.

Anderson, Clare. 2000. *Convicts in the Indian Ocean: Transportation from South Asia to Mauritius, 1815–1853*. New York: St. Martin's Press.

Anderson, Virginia DeJohn. 1985. "Migrants and Motives: Religion and the Settlement of New England, 1630–1640." *New England Quarterly* 58(3): 339–83.

Anderson, Bridget. 2000. *Doing the Dirty Work? The Global Politics of Domestic Labour*. London, England: Zed Books.

Andrews, Abigail. 2014. "Women's Political Engagement in a Mexican Sending Community: Migration as Crisis and the Struggle to Sustain an Alternative." *Gender & Society* 28(4): 583–608.

Angrist, Josh. 2002. "How Do Sex Ratios Affect Marriage and Labor Markets? Evidence from America's Second Generation." *Quarterly Journal of Economics* 117(3): 997–1038.

Aronowitz, Alexis A. 2009. *Human Trafficking, Human Misery: The Global Trade in Human Beings*. Westport, Conn.: Praeger.

Asis, Maruja M. B. 2006. "Living with Migration: Experiences of Children Left Behind in the Philippines." *Asian Population Studies* 2(1): 45–67.

Atkinson, Alan. 1994. "The Free-Born Englishman Transported: Convict Rights as a Measure of Eighteenth-Century Empire." *Past & Present* 144 (August): 88–115.

Avery, Donald H. 1995. *Canada's Response to Immigrant Workers, 1896–1994*. Toronto: McClelland & Stewart.

Bacon, David. 2008. *Illegal People: How Globalization Creates Migration and Criminalizes Immigrants*. Boston, Mass.: Beacon Press.

Bade, Klaus. 2003. *Migration in European History*. Malden, Mass.: Wiley-Blackwell.

Baigent, Elizabeth. 2012. "Ravenstein, Ernst Georg (1834–1913)." *Oxford Dictionary of National Biography*. Online edition. Accessed December 3, 2014. http://dx.doi.org/10.1093/ref:odnb/41114.

Bailey, William B. 1906. *Modern Social Conditions: A Statistical Study of Birth, Marriage, Divorce, Death, Disease, Suicide, Immigration, Etc., with Special Reference to the United States*. New York: The Century Company.

———. 1913. "Some Recent Changes in the Composition of the Population of the United States." *Publications of the American Statistical Association* 13(101): 379–92.

Bailyn, Bernard. 1986a. *The Peopling of British North America: An Introduction*. New York: Alfred A. Knopf.

———. 1986b. *Voyagers to the West: A Passage in the Peopling of America on the Eve of the Revolution*. New York: Alfred A. Knopf.

Banerjee, Pallavi. 2015. "When Men Stay Home: Household Labor and Parenthood in Female-Led Families of Indian Migrant Nurses." In *Families as They Really Are*. Vol. 2., edited by B. J. Risman and V. Rutter, New York: Norton.

Bank, Barbara J., Sara Delamont, and Catherine Marshall. 2007. *Gender and Education: Gendered Theories of Education*. Westport, Conn: Praeger.

Bartlett, Harriet M. 1928. "The Social Survey and the Charity Organization Movement." *American Journal of Sociology* 34(2): 330–46.

Bashford, Alison. 2007. "Nation, Empire, Globe: The Spaces of Population Debate in the Interwar Years." *Comparative Studies in Society and History* 49(1): 170–201.

———. 2014. *Global Population: History, Geopolitics, and Life on Earth*. New York: Columbia University Press.

Bassel, Leah. 2012. *Refugee Women: Beyond Gender Versus Culture*. New York: Routledge.

Bastia, Tanja. 2009. "Women's Migration and the Crisis of Care: Grandmothers Caring for Grandchildren in Urban Bolivia." *Gender and Development* 17(3): 389–401.

Battistella, Graziano, and Cecilia G. Conaco. 1998. "The Impact of Labour Migration on the Children Left Behind: A Study of Elementary School Children in the Philippines." *Journal of Social Issues in Southeast Asia* 13(2): 220–41.

Baum, Charlotte, Paula Hyman, and Sonya Michel. 1976. *The Jewish Woman in America*. New York: Dial Press.

Becker, Howard S. 1999. "The Chicago School, So-Called." *Qualitative Sociology* 22(1): 3–12.

Behrendt, Stephen D. 1997. "The Annual Volume and Regional Distribution of the British Slave Trade, 1780–1807." *Journal of African History* 38(2): 187–211.

Bélanger, Daniele, Hye-Kyung Lee, and Hong-zen Wang. 2010. "Ethnic Diversity and Statistics in East Asia: 'Foreign Brides' Surveys in Taiwan and South Korea." *Ethnic and Racial Studies* 33(6): 1108–30.

Beniger, James R., and Dorothy L. Robyn 1978. "Quantitative Graphics in Statistics: A Brief History." *American Statistician* 32(1): 1–11.

Bentley, Jerry H. 1996. "Cross-Cultural Interaction and Periodization in World History." *American Historical Review* 101(3):749–70.

Berger, Peter L., and Thomas Luckmann. 1966. *The Social Construction of Reality: A Treatise in the Sociology of Knowledge*. Garden City, N.Y.: Anchor Books.

Best, Antony, Jussi M. Hanhimäki, Joseph A. Maiolo, and Kristen Schulze. 2004. *International History of the Twentieth Century*. New York: Routledge, 2004.

Bilsborrow, Richard E., and Hania Zlotnik. 1992. "Preliminary Report of the United Nations Expert Group Meeting on the Feminization of Internal Migration." *International Migration Review* 26(1): 138–61.

Blackburn, George M., and Sherman L. Ricards. 1993. "Unequal Opportunity on a Mining Frontier: The Role of Gender, Race, and Birthplace." *Pacific Historical Review* 62(1): 19–38.

Blackburn, Robin. 1988a. *The Making of New World Slavery: From the Baroque to the Modern, 1492–1800*. London: Verso.

———. 1988b. *The Overthrow of Colonial Slavery, 1776–1848*. London: Verso.

Bodnar, John. 1986. *The Transplanted: A History of Immigrants in Urban America*. Bloomington, Ind.: Indiana University Press.

Boris, Eileen, and Jill Jensen. 2012. "The ILO: Women's Networks and the Making of the Women Worker." In *Women and Social Movements International, 1840-Present*, edited by Thomas Dublin and Kathryn Kish Sklar. Alexandria, Va.: Alexander Street Press. Accessed February 28, 2014. http://wasi.alexander street.com/help/view/the_ilo_womens_networks_and_the_making_of_the_ women_worker.

Boserup, Ester. 1970. *Women's Role in Economic Development*. London: Allen & Unwin.

Bosma, Ulbe, Gijs Kessler, and Leo Lucassen, eds. 2013. *Migration and Membership Regimes in Global and Historical Perspective*. Leiden: Brill Publishers.

Boyd, Monica. 1989. "Family and Personal Networks in International Migration: Recent Developments and New Agendas." *International Migration Review* 23(3): 638–70.

———. 1999. "Gender, Refugee Status, and Permanent Settlement." *Gender Issues* 17(1): 5–25.

———. 2006. "Gender Aspects of International Migration to Canada and the United States." Paper presented at the International Symposium on International Migration and Development. Turin, Italy (June 28–30, 2006).

Boyd, Monica, and Elizabeth Grieco. 2003. "Women and Migration: Incorporating Gender into International Migration Theory." Migration Information Source. Washington, D.C.: Migration Policy Institute. Accessed September 19, 2014. http://www.migrationpolicy.org/article/women-and-migration-incorporating-gender-international-migration-theory.

Boyd-Bowman, Peter. 1973. "Spanish Emigrants to the Indies, 1595–98: A Profile." In *First Images of America: the Impact of the New World on the Old*, vol. II, edited by Fredi Chiappelli. Berkeley: University of California Press.

———. 1976. "Patterns of Spanish Emigration to the Indies 1579–1600." *The Americas* 33(1): 78–95.

Brass, Tom, and Marcel van der Linden, eds. 1997. *Free and Unfree Labour: The Debate Continues*. New York: Peter Lang.

Brettell, Caroline B., and Patricia A. de Berjeois. 1992. "Anthropology and the Study of Immigrant Women." In *Seeking Common Ground: Female Immigration to the United States*, edited by Donna Gabaccia. Westport, Conn: Praeger.

Brettell, Caroline B., and Rita James Simon, eds. 1986. *International Migration: The Female Experience*. Totowa, N.J.: Rowman & Allanheld.

Brian, Éric, and Marie Jaisson. 2007. *The Descent of Human Sex Ratio at Birth: A Dialogue Between Mathematics, Biology and Sociology*. New York: Springer.

Broadhead, Susan Herlin. 1983. "Slave Wives, Free Sisters: Bakongo Women and Slavery, c. 1700–1850." In *Women and Slavery in Africa*, edited by Claire C. Robertson and Martin Klein. Madison: University of Wisconsin Press.

Bullard, Alice. 2000. *Exile to Paradise: Savagery and Civilization in Paris and the South Pacific, 1790–1900*. Stanford, Calif.: Stanford University Press.

Bulmer, Martin. 1984. *The Chicago School of Sociology: Institutionalization, Diversity, and the Rise of Sociological Research*. Chicago: University of Chicago Press.

Burchell, Graham, Colin Gordon, and Peter Miller 1991. *The Foucault Effect: Studies in Governmentality*. Chicago: University of Chicago Press.

Burnard, Trevor, and Kenneth Morgan. 2001. "The Dynamics of the Slave Market and Slave Purchasing Patterns in Jamaica, 1655–1788." *William and Mary Quarterly*, 3rd ser., 58(1): 205–28.

Bush, Michael L. 2000. *Servitude in Modern Times*. Malden, Mass.: Blackwell Publishers.

Butler, Elizabeth Beardsley. 1909. *Women and the Trades: Pittsburgh, 1907–1908*. New York: Russell Sage Foundation.

Byington, Margaret Frances. 1910. *Homestead: The Households of a Mill Town*. New York: Russell Sage Foundation.

Cacho, Lydia. 2011. *Esclavas del Poder: Un Viaje al Corazon de la Trata Sexual de Mujeres y Ninas en el Mundo*. Mexico City: Grijalbo Publishers.

Cai, Yong. 2010. "China's Below-Replacement Fertility: Government Policy or Socioeconomic Development?" *Population and Development Review* 36(3): 419–40.

Calavita, Kitty. 1992. *Inside the State: The Bracero Program, Immigration, and the I.N.S.* New York: Routledge.

Caldwell, John C. 2006. *Demographic Transition Theory*. Dordrecht, The Netherlands: Springer.

Calliste, Agnes. 1991. "Canada's Immigration Policy and Domestics from the Caribbean: The Second Domestic Scheme." In *Race, Class, Gender: Bonds and Barriers*, 2nd rev. ed., edited by Jesse Vorst. Toronto: Between the Lines.

———. 1995. "Gender and Immigration Law: The Recruitment of Domestic Workers to Canada, 1867–1940." *Indian Journal of Gender Studies* 2 (March): 25–43.

Campbell, Gwyn, Suzanne Miers, and Joseph C. Miller, eds. 2007a. *Women and Slavery*, vol. 1: *Africa, the Indian Ocean World and the Medieval North Atlantic*. Athens: Ohio University Press.

———. 2007b. *Women and Slavery*, vol. 2: *The Modern Atlantic*. Athens: Ohio University Press.

Campbell, Persia Crawford. 1923. *Chinese Coolie Emigration to Countries within the British Empire*. London: P. S. King and Son.

Carney, Judith, and Michael Watts. 1990. "Manufacturing Dissent: Work, Gender, and the Politics of Meaning in a Peasant Society." *Africa* 60(2): 207–41.

Carnot, M. 1856. "La Population Feminine de 1835 à 1855 dans la Ville de Paris." *Review Medicale* (15 Fevrier).

Carson, Mina. 1990. *Settlement Folk: Social Thought and the American Settlement Movement, 1885–1930*. Chicago: University of Chicago.

Castles, Stephen, Hein de Haas, and Mark J. Miller. 2013. *The Age of Migration: International Population Movements in the Modern World*. New York: Guilford Press.

Castles, Stephen, and Godula Kosack. 1973. *Immigrant Workers and Class Structure in Western Europe*. London: Oxford University Press.

Castles, Stephen, and Mark J. Miller. 1993. *The Age of Migration: International Population Movements in the Modern World*. New York: Guilford Press.

Cerutti, Simona. 2012. *Étrangers: Étude d'une condition d'incertitudes dans une société d'Ancien Régime*. Montrouge, France: Bayard.

Cerrutti, Marcela. 2009. "Gender and Intra-Regional Migration in South America." Human Development Research Paper Series no. 12. New York: United Nations Development Programme. Accessed September 19, 2014. http://hdr.undp.org/sites/default/files/hdrp_2009_12_rev.pdf.

Cerrutti, Marcela, and Magali Gaudio. 2010. "Gender Differences Between Mexican Migration to the United States and Paraguayan Migration to Argentina." *Annals of the American Academy of Political and Social Science* 630(1): 93–113.

Cerrutti, Marcela, and Douglas S. Massey. 2001. "On the Auspices of Female Migration from Mexico to the United States." *Demography* 38(2): 187–200.

Chandler, David P. 1993. *The Tragedy of Cambodian History: Politics, War, and Revolution Since 1945*. New Haven, Conn: Yale University Press.

Chang, Kimberly A., and Julian McAllister Groves. 2000. "Neither 'Saints' nor 'Prostitutes': Sexual Discourse in the Filipina Domestic Worker Community in Hong Kong." *Women Studies International Forum* 23(1): 73–87.

Chiu, Stephen W. K., and Chig Kwan Lee. 1997. "After the Hong Kong Miracle: Women Workers under Industrial Restructuring." *Asian Survey* 37(8): 752–70.

Choy, Catherine Ceniza. 2003. *Empire of Care: Nursing and Migration in Filipino American History*. Durham, N.C.: Duke University Press.

Cinel, Dino. 2002. *The National Integration of Italian Return Migration, 1870–1929*. New York: Cambridge University Press.

Clausen, John A. 1968. "Recent Developments in Socialization Theory and Research." *Annals of the American Academy of Political and Social Science* 377: 139–55.

Coale, Ansley J., and Susan Cott Watkins. 1986. *The Decline of Fertility in Europe.* Princeton, N.J.: Princeton University Press.

Cohen, Deborah. 2006. "From Peasant to Worker: Migration, Masculinity, and the Making of Mexican Workers in the U.S." *International Labor and Working-Class History* 69(1): 81–103.

Constable, Nicole. 1997. *Maid to Order in Hong Kong: Stories of Filipina Workers.* Reprint. Ithaca, N.Y.: Cornell University Press, 2005.

Conzen, Kathleen Neils. 1996. "Thomas and Znaniecki and the Historiography of American Immigration." *Journal of American Ethnic History* 16(1): 16–25.

Costin, Lela B. 1983. *Two Sisters for Social Justice: A Biography of Grace and Edith Abbott.* Champaign: University of Illinois Press.

Crane, Elaine Forman. 1990. "The Socioeconomics of a Female Majority in Eighteenth-Century Bermuda." *Signs* 15(2): 231–58.

Crocker, Ruth. 2006. *Mrs. Russell Sage: Women's Activism and Philanthropy in the Gilded Age and Progressive Era.* Bloomington: Indiana University Press.

Crosby, Alfred W. 1972. *The Columbian Exchange: Biological and Cultural Consequences of 1492.* Westport, Conn: Greenwood Press.

———. 1991. "Infectious Disease and the Demography of the Atlantic Peoples." *Journal of World History* 2(2): 119–33.

Crush, Jonathan, and Vincent Williams. 2005. "International Migration and Development: Dynamics and Challenges in South and Southern Africa." Paper presented at the United Nations Expert Group Meeting on International Migration and Development. New York (July 6–8, 2005). Accessed October 17, 2014. http://www.un.org/esa/population/migration/turin/Symposium_Turin_files/P05_Crush&Williams.pdf.

Cunsolo, Ronald S. 1993. "Nationalists and Catholics in Giolittian Italy: An Uneasy Collaboration." *Catholic Historical Review* 79(1): 22–53.

Curran, Sara R., and Estela Rivero-Fuentes. 2003. "Engendering Migrant Networks: The Case of Mexican Migration." *Demography* 40(2): 289–307.

Curran, Sara R., Steven Shafer, Katharine M. Donato, and Filiz Garip. 2006. "Mapping Gender and Migration in Sociological Scholarship: Is It Segregation or Integration?" *International Migration Review* 40(1): 199–223.

Curtin, Philip D. 1969. *The Atlantic Slave Trade: A Census.* Madison: University of Wisconsin Press.

———. 1975. *Economic Change in Precolonial Africa: Senegambia in the Era of the Slave Trade.* Madison: University of Wisconsin Press.

———. 1990. *The Rise and Fall of the Plantation Complex: Essays in Atlantic History.* Cambridge: Cambridge University Press.

Curto, José C., and Raymond R. Gervais. 2001. "The Population History of Luanda during the Late Atlantic Slave Trade, 1781–1844." *African Economic History* 29(1): 1–59.

Cushner, Nicholas P. 1975. "Slave Mortality and Reproduction on Jesuit Haciendas in Colonial Peru." *Hispanic American Historical Review* 55(2): 177–99.

Daley, Patricia. 1991. "Gender, Displacement, and Social Reproduction: Settling Burundi Refugees in Western Tanzania." *Journal of Refugee Studies* 4(3): 248–66.

Damousi, Joy. 1997. *Depraved and Disorderly: Female Convicts, Sexuality and Gender in Colonial Australia.* Cambridge: Cambridge University Press.

Daniels, Kay. 1998. *Convict Women*. Sydney: Allen & Unwin.

Daugherty, Helen Ginn, and Kenneth C. W. Kammeyer. 1995. *An Introduction to Population*. 2nd ed. New York: Guildford Press.

Davis, Allen F. 1984. *Spearheads for Reform: The Social Settlements and the Progressive Movement, 1890 to 1914*. New Brunswick, N.J.: Rutgers University Press.

Davis, David Brion. 2000. "Looking at Slavery from Broader Perspectives." *The American Historical Review* 105(2): 452–66.

———. 2006. *Inhuman Bondage: The Rise and Fall of Slavery in the New World*. New York: Oxford University Press.

Davis, Kingsley. 1945. "The World Demographic Transition." *Annals of the American Academy of Political and Social Science* 237: 1–11.

De Haan, Arjan. 2002. "Migration and Livelihoods in Historical Perspective: A Case Study of Bihar, India." *Journal of Development Studies* 38(5): 115–42.

Deegan, Mary Jo. 1988 *Jane Addams and the Men of the Chicago School, 1892–1918*. New Brunswick, N.J.: Transaction Publishers.

del Río, Coral, and Olga Alonso-Villar. 2012. "Occupational Segregation of Immigrant Women in Spain." *Feminist Economics* 18(2): 91–123.

Dever, Carolyn. 2003. *Skeptical Feminism: Activist Theory, Activist Practice*. Minneapolis: University of Minnesota Press.

DeVries, Jan. 2010. "The Limits of Globalization in the Early Modern World." *The Economic History Review* 63(3): 710–733.

Diamond, Marion. 1999. *Emigration and Empire: The Life of Maria S. Rye*. New York: Garland Press.

Di Cosmo, Nicola. 2002. *Ancient China and Its Enemies: The Rise of Nomadic Power in East Asian History*. Cambridge: Cambridge University Press.

Diner, Hasia. 1983. *Erin's Daughters in America: Irish Immigrant Women in the Nineteenth Century*. Baltimore, Md.: Johns Hopkins University Press.

———. 2013. "Oscar Handlin: A Jewish Historian." *Journal of American Ethnic History* 32(3): 53–61.

Donato, Katharine M. 1992. "Understanding U.S. Immigration: Why Some Countries Send Women and Others Send Men." In *Seeking Common Ground: Female Immigration to the United States,* edited by Donna Gabaccia. Westport, Conn: Praeger.

———. 1993. "Current Trends and Patterns of Female Migration: Evidence from Mexico." *International Migration Review* 27(4): 748–71.

———. 2010. "U.S. Migration from Latin America: Gendered Patterns and Shifts." *Annals of the American Academy of Political and Social Science* 630(1): 78–92.

Donato, Katharine M., J. Trent Alexander, Donna Gabaccia, and Johanna Leinonen. 2011. "Variations in the Gender Composition of Immigrant Populations: How and Why They Matter." *International Migration Review* 45(3): 495–525.

Donato, Katharine M., and Amada Armenta. 2011. "What Do We Know About Undocumented Migration." *Annual Review of Sociology* 37: 529–43.

Donato, Katharine M., and Ebony Duncan. 2011. "Migration, Social Networks and Children's Health in Mexican Families." *Journal of Marriage and the Family* 73(4): 713–28.

Donato, Katharine M., Donna Gabaccia, Jennifer Holdaway, Martin Manalansan IV, and Patricia R. Pessar. 2006. "A Glass Half Full? Gender in Migration Studies." *International Migration Review* 40(1): 3–26.

Donato, Katharine M., Bhumika Piya, and Anna Jacobs. 2014. "The Double Disadvantage Reconsidered: Gender, Immigration, Marital Status, and Global Labor Force Participation in the 21st Century." *International Migration Review* S1(Fall): S335–76.

Donato, Katharine M., and Leslie Rodriguez. 2014. "Police Arrests in a Time of Uncertainty: The Impact of 287(g) on Arrests in a New Immigrant Gateway." *American Behavioral Scientist.* First published online June 11, 2014. doi:10.1177/0002764214537265.

Donato, Katharine M., and Andrea Tyree. 1986. "Family Reunification, Health Professionals, and the Sex Composition of Migrants to the United States." *Sociology and Social Research* 70:226–30.

Donato, Katharine M., Brandon Wagner, and Evelyn Patterson. 2008. "The Cat and Mouse Game at the México-U.S. Border: Gendered Patterns and Recent Shifts." *International Migration Review* 42(2): 330–59.

Dreby, Joanna. 2010. *Divided by Borders: Mexican Migrants and Their Children.* Berkeley: University of California Press.

Drescher, Seymour. 2009. *Abolition: A History of Slavery and Antislavery.* Cambridge: Cambridge University Press.

Drechsler, Wolfgang. 2001. "On the Viability of the Concept of the *Staatswissenschaften.*" *European Journal of Law and Economics* 12(2): 105–11.

Drumtra, Jeff. 2003. "West Africa's Refugee Crisis Spills Across Many Borders." Washington, D.C.: Migration Information Source. Accessed September 19, 2014. http://www.migrationpolicy.org/article/west-africas-refugee-crisis-spills-across-many-borders.

DuBois, W. E. B. 1939. *Black Folk Then and Now: An Essay in the History of the Sociology of the Negro Race.* New York: Henry Holt.

Duggan, Lisa. 1990. "From Instincts to Politics: Writing the History of Sexuality in the U.S." *Journal of Sex Research* 27(1): 95–109.

Durand, Jorge, Douglas S. Massey, and Emilio A. Parrado. 1999. "The New Era of Mexican Migration to the United States." *Journal of American History* 86(2): 518–36.

Dyson, Tim. 2012. "Causes and Consequences of Skewed Sex Ratios." *Annual Review of Sociology* 38: 443–61.

Dzuback, Mary Ann. 2003. "Gender and the Politics of Knowledge." *History of Education Quarterly* 43(2): 171–95.

Eblen, Jack E. 1965. "An Analysis of Nineteenth-Century Frontier Populations." *Demography* 2: 399–413.

Eckstein, Zvi. 2010. *Labour Migrants Employment.* The Israel Democracy Institute. Tel Aviv: Forum Cesarea.

Ehrenreich, Barbara, and Arlie Russell Hochschild. 2004. *Global Woman: Nannies, Maids and Sex Workers in the New Economy.* New York: Macmillan.

Ekirch, A. Roger. 1987. *The Transportation of British Convicts to the Colonies, 1718–1775.* New York: Oxford University Press.

Eldridge, Hope Tisdale. 1964. "A Cohort Approach to the Analysis of Migration Differentials." *Demography* 1(1): 212–19.

———. 1965. "Net Intercensal Migration for States and Geographic Division of the United States, 1950–1960: Methodological and Substantive Aspects." Analytical and Technical Report no. 5. Philadelphia: Population Studies Center, University of Pennsylvania.

Eldridge, Hope Tisdale, and Jacob S. Siegel. 1946. "The Changing Sex Ratio in the United States." *American Journal of Sociology* 52(3): 224–34.

Eldridge, Hope Tisdale, and Dorothy Swaine Thomas. 1964. *Demographic Analysis and Interrelations*. Vol. 3, *Population Redistribution and Economic Growth, United States, 1870–1950*. Philadelphia: American Philosophical Society.

Eley, Geoff. 2007. "Historicizing the Global, Politicizing Capital: Giving the Present a Name." *History Workshop Journal* 63(1): 154–88.

Elliott, John H. 2006. *Empires of the Atlantic World. Britain and Spain in America, 1492–1830*. New Haven, Conn.: Yale University Press.

———. 2009. *Spain, Europe and the Wider World 1500–1800 2009*. New Haven, Conn.: Yale University Press.

Eltis, David. 1982. "Free and Coerced Transatlantic Migrations: Some Comparisons." *The American Historical Review* 88(2): 251–80.

———. 1987. *Economic Growth and the Ending of the Transatlantic Slave Trade*. New York: Oxford University Press.

———. 1990. "The Volume, Age/Sex Ratios, and African Impact of the Slave Trade: Some Refinements of Paul Lovejoy's Review of the Literature." *Journal of African History* 31(3): 485–92.

———. 1995. "The Volume and African Origins of the British Slave Trade Before 1714." *Cahiers D'Études Africaines* 35(138–39): 617–27.

———. 2002. *Coerced and Free Migration: Global Perspectives*. Stanford, Calif.: Stanford University Press.

Eltis, David, and Stanley L. Engerman. 1992. "Was the Slave Trade Dominated by Men?" *Journal of Interdisciplinary History* 23(1): 237–57.

———. 1993. "Fluctuations in Sex and Age Ratios in the Transatlantic Slave Trade, 1663–1864." *Economic History Review* 346(2): 308–23.

Eltis, David, and Lawrence C. Jennings. 1988. "Trade Between Western Africa and the Atlantic World in the Pre-Colonial Era." *American Historical Review* 93(4): 936–59.

Eltis, David, and David Richardson. 2008. *Extending the Frontiers: Essays on the New Transatlantic Slave Trade Database*. New Haven, Conn.: Yale University Press.

———. 2010. *Atlas of the Transatlantic Slave Trade*. New Haven, Conn.: Yale University Press.

Engle, Lauren B. 2004. *The World In Motion: Short Essays on Migration and Gender*. Geneva: International Organization for Migration.

Enriquez, Laura. 2014. "Gendering 'Illegality': The Family Formation Experiences of Undocumented Immigrant Young Adults." Unpublished manuscript, University of California, Irvine.

Enstad, Nan. 1999. *Ladies of Labor, Girls of Adventure: Working Women, Popular Culture and Labor Politics at the Turn of the Twentieth Century*. New York: Columbia University Press.

Espiritu, Yen Le. 2005. "Gender, Migration and Work: Filipina Health Care Professionals to the University States." *Revue Européenne des Migrations Internationales* 21(1): 55–75.

Esteve, Albert, Joan Garcia, and Robert McCaa. 2012. "Comparative Perspectives on Marriage and International Migration, 1970–2000: Findings from IPUMS-International Census Microdata Samples." In *Cross Border Marriage: Global Trends and Diversity*, edited by Doo-Sub Kim. Seoul: Korea Institute for Health and Social Affairs.

Fassmann, Heinz, and Rainer Munz. 1994. "European East-West Migration, 1945–1992." *International Migration Review* 28(3): 520–38.

Fauve-Chamoux, Antoinette. 2005. *Domestic Service and the Formation of European Identity: Understanding the Globalization of Domestic Work, 16th–21st Centuries.* Bern: Peter Lang.

Feldmeyer, Ben. 2009. "Immigration and Violence: The Offsetting Effects of Immigrant Concentration on Latino Violence." *Social Science Research* 38(3): 717–31.

Ferenczi, Imre. 1937. "Aliens in the World and Nationals Abroad." *Social Service Review* 11(4): 693–704.

———. 1945. "Relocation of Europeans." *Annals of the American Academy of Political and Social Science* 237:172–81.

Ferrie, Joseph P. 1999. *Yankeys Now: Immigrants in the Antebellum U.S., 1840–1860.* New York: Oxford University Press.

Ferris, Iain. 2000. *Enemies of Rome: Barbarians Through Roman Eyes.* Stroud, England: The History Press.

Filby, P. William, ed. 1988. *Passenger and Immigration Lists Bibliography, 1538–1900.* 2nd ed. Detroit, Mich.: Gale Research.

Fitzgerald, David Scott, and David Cook-Martin. 2014. *Culling the Masses: The Democratic Origins of Racist Immigration Policy.* Cambridge, Mass.: Harvard University Press.

Fitzgerald, Sharron A. 2010. "Biopolitics and the Regulation of Vulnerability: The Case of the Female Trafficked Migrant." *International Journal of Law in Context* 6(3): 227–94.

Fitzpatrick, Joan. 1997. "The Gender Dimension of U.S. Immigration Policy." *Yale Journal of Law and Feminism* 9(1): 23–49.

Flippen, Chenoa. 2014. "Intersectionality at Work: Determinants of Labor Supply Among Immigrant Latinas." *Gender & Society* 28(3): 404–34.

Floro, Maria Sagrario, and Kendall Schaefer. 1998. "Restructuring of Labor Markets in the Philippines and Zambia: The Gender Dimension." *Journal of Developing Areas* 33(1): 73–98.

Fogleman, Aaron. 1992. "Migrations to the Thirteen British North American Colonies, 1700–1775: New Estimates." *Journal of Interdisciplinary History* 22(4): 691–709.

———. 1998. "From Slaves, Convicts and Servants to Free Passengers: The Transformation of Immigration in the Era of the American Revolution." *The Journal of American History* 85(1): 43–76.

Foner, Eric. 1995. *Free Soil, Free Labor, Free Men: The Ideology of the Republican Party Before the Civil War.* New York: Oxford University Press.

Foner, Nancy. 1999. "Immigrant Women and Work in New York City, Then and Now." *Journal of American Ethnic History* 18(3): 95–113.

———. 2000. *From Ellis Island to J.F.K.: New York's Two Great Waves of Immigration.* New York and New Haven, Conn.: Russell Sage Foundation and Yale University Press.

———. 2006. "Then and Now or Then to Now: Immigration to New York in Contemporary and Historical Perspective." *Journal of American Ethnic History* 25(2/3): 33–47.

Fonow, Mary Margaret, and Judith A. Cook. 2005. "Feminist Methodology: New Applications in the Academy and Public Policy." *Signs* 30(4): 2211–36.

Fox, Edward. 2012. "Do Mexican Cartels Control Sex Trafficking in Argentina?" InSightCrime, April 20, 2013. Accessed October 17, 2014. http://www.insight crime.org/news-analysis/do-mexican-cartels-control-sex-trafficking-in-argentina.

Freudenberger, Herman, and Jonathan B. Pritchett. 1991. "The Domestic United States Slave Trade: New Evidence." *Journal of Interdisciplinary History* 21(3): 447–77.

Fresnoza-Flot, Asuncion. 2014. "Men's Caregiving Practices in Filipino Transnational Families: A Case Study of Left-Behind Fathers and Sons." In *Transnational Families, Migration and the Circulation: Understanding Mobility and Absence in Family Life,* edited by Loretta Baldassar and Laura Merla. New York: Routledge.

Friedman, Reena Sigman. 1982. "'Send Me My Husband Who Is in New York City': Husband Desertion in the American Jewish Immigrant Community 1900–1926." *Jewish Social Studies* 44(1): 1–18.

Friedmann, Harriet. 1978. "World Market, State, and Family Farm: Social Bases of Household Production in the Era of Wage Labor." *Comparative Studies in Society and History* 20(4): 545–86.

Fry, Richard. 2006. *Gender and Migration.* Washington, D.C.: Pew Hispanic Center.

Fynn, Veronica P. 2009. "Refugee Women & Children in Africa: Critique of International & Regional Refugee/Human Rights Instruments." In *Documenting the Undocumented: Redefining Refugee Status,* edited by Veronica P. Fynn, 151–76. Boca Raton, Fl.: Universal-Publishers.

Gabaccia, Donna R. 1988. "'The Transplanted': Women and Family in Immigrant America." *Social Science History* 12(3): 243–53.

———. 1989. *Immigrant Women in the United States: A Selectively Annotated Bibliography.* Westport, Conn: Greenwood Press.

———. 1991. "Immigrant Women: Nowhere at Home?" *Journal of American Ethnic History* 10(4): 61–87.

———, ed. 1992. *Seeking Common Ground: Female Immigration to the United States.* Westport, Conn: Greenwood Press.

———. 1996. "Women of the Mass Migrations: From Minority to Majority, 1820–1930." In *European Migrants: Global and Local Perspectives,* edited by David Hoerder and L. Moch. Boston, Mass.: Northeastern University Press.

———. 1997. "The 'Yellow Peril' and the 'Chinese of Europe': Global Perspectives on Race and Labor, 1815–1930." In *Migrations, Migration History, History: Old Paradigms and New Perspectives,* edited by Jan Lucassen and Leo Lucassen. Berlin: Peter Lang.

———. 2000. *Italy's Many Diasporas: Elites, Exiles and Workers of the World.* London: University College of London Press.

———. 2001. "When the Migrants Are Men: Women, Transnationalism, and Italian Family Economies." In *Women, Gender, and Labor Migration: Global and Historical Perspectives,* edited by Pamela Sharpe. London: Routledge Press.

———. 2004. "A Longer Atlantic in a Wider World," *Atlantic Studies* 1(1): 1–27.

———. 2010. "Nations of Immigrants: Do Words Matter?" *The Pluralist* 5(3): 5–31.

———. 2012. *Foreign Relations: Global Perspectives on American Immigration.* Princeton, N.J.: Princeton University Press.

————. 2014. "Time and Temporality in Migration Studies." In *Migration Theory: Talking Across Disciplines*, 3rd ed., edited by Caroline Brettell and James Hollifield. New York: Routledge.

————. Forthcoming. "The Minnesota School and Immigration History at Midwestern Land Grant Universities, 1890–2005."

Gabaccia, Donna R., and Dirk Hoerder. 2011. *Connecting Seas and Connected Ocean Rims: Indian, Atlantic, and Pacific Oceans and China Seas Migrations from the 1830s to the 1930s.* Amsterdam: Brill.

Gabaccia, Donna R., and M.J. Maynes. 2012. "Introduction: Gender History Across Epistemologies." *Gender and History* 24(3): 521–39.

Gabaccia, Donna R., and Elizabeth Zanoni. 2012. "Transition in Gender Ratios Among International Migrants, 1820–1930." *Social Science History* 36(2): 197–222.

Galenson, David W. 1979. "The Slave Trade to the English West Indies, 1673–1724." *Economic History Review* 32(2): 241–49.

————. 1981. *White Servitude in Colonial America: An Economic Analysis.* New York: Cambridge University Press.

————. 1984. "The Rise and Fall of Indentured Servitude in the Americas: An Economic Analysis." *Journal of Economic History* 44(1): 1–26.

Games, Alison. 1999. *Migration and the Origins of the English Atlantic World.* Cambridge, Mass.: Harvard University Press.

Garcia y Griego, Manuel. 1981. *The Importation of Mexican Contract Laborers to the United States, 1942–1964: Antecedents, Operation and Legacy.* La Jolla: Program in United States-Mexican Studies, University of California, San Diego.

Gasper, David Barry, and Darlene Clark Hine, eds. 1996. *More than Chattel: Black Women and Slavery in the Americas.* Bloomington: Indiana University Press.

Geggus, David. 1989. "Sex Ratio, Age and Ethnicity in the Atlantic Slave Trade: Data from French Shipping and Plantation Records." *Journal of African History* 30(1): 23–44.

Ghosh, Jayati. 2007. "Informalization, Migration, and Women: Recent Trends in Asia." In *Labor, Globalization and the State: Workers, Women and Migrants Confront Neoliberalism*, edited by Debdas Benerjee and Michael Goldfield, 97–120. New York: Routledge.

Giles, Winona, and Sedef Arat-Koc. 1994. *Maid in the Market: Women's Paid Domestic Labour.* Halifax, NS: Fernwood Publishing.

Gjerde, Jon. 1999. "New Growth on Old Vines: The State of the Field: The Social History of Immigration to and Ethnicity in the United States." *Journal of American Ethnic History* 18(4): 40–65.

Glenn, Evelyn Nakano. 1986. *Issei, Nisei, War Bride: Three Generations of Japanese American Women in Domestic Service.* Philadelphia, Pa.: Temple University Press.

Glenn, Susan Anita. 1990. *Daughters of the Shtetl: Life and Labor in the Immigrant Generation.* Ithaca, N.Y.: Cornell University Press.

Gonzales, Sylvia. 1980. "Toward a Feminist Pedagogy for Chicana Self-Actualization." *Frontiers: A Journal of Women Studies* 5(2): 48–51.

Gonzalez Baker, Susan. 1990. *The Cautious Welcome: The Legalization Programs of the Immigration Reform and Control Act.* Washington, D.C.: The Urban Institute.

Gordon, Linda W. 2005. "Trends in the Gender Ratio of Immigrants to the United States." *International Migration Review* 39(4): 796–818.

Gordon, Milton. 1964. *Assimilation in American Life.* New York: Oxford University Press.

Gothard, Jan. 2001. *Blue China: Single Female Migration to Colonial Australia.* Melbourne: Melbourne University Press.

Green, Nancy. 1994. "The Comparative Method and Poststructural Structuralism: New Perspectives for Migration Studies." *Journal of American Ethnic History* 13(4): 3–22.

Greenhalgh, Susan. 1996. "The Social Construction of Population Science: An Intellectual, Institutional, and Political History of Twentieth-Century Demography." *Comparative Studies in Society and History* 38(1): 26–66.

Greenwald, Maurine W., and Margo Anderson. 1996. *Pittsburgh Surveyed: Social Science and Social Reform in the Early Twentieth Century.* Pittsburgh, Pa.: University of Pittsburgh Press.

Gregory, James N. 2004. "The Southern Diaspora: 20th Century America's Great Migrations." In *Repositioning North American Migration History: New Directions in Modern Continental Migration and Citizenship,* edited by Marc S. Rodriguez. Rochester, N.Y.: University of Rochester Press.

Grieco, Elizabeth. 2002. "Defining 'Foreign Born' and 'Foreigner' in International Migration Statistics." *Migration Information Source.* Washington, D.C.: Migration Policy Institute. Accessed February 28, 2014. http://www.migrationpolicy.org/article/defining-foreign-born-and-foreigner-international-migration-statistics.

Grosz, Elizabeth A. 1987. "Feminist Theory and the Challenge to Knowledges." *Women's Studies International Forum* 10(5): 475–80.

Gross, Paul R., and Norman Levitt. 1994. *Higher Superstition: The Academic Left and Its Quarrels with Science.* Baltimore, Md.: Johns Hopkins University Press.

Grubb, Farley. 1989. "Servant Auction Records and Immigration into the Delaware Valley, 1745–1831: The Proportion of Females Among Immigrant Servants." *Proceedings of the American Philosophical Society* 133(2): 154–69.

———. 1994. "The End of European Immigrant Servitude in the United States: An Economic Analysis of Market Collapse, 1772–1835." *Journal of Economic History* 54(4): 794–824.

———. 2000. "The Transatlantic Market for British Convict Labor." *Journal of Economic History* 60(1): 94–122.

Guasco, Michael. 2010. *Abolition of Slavery.* New York: Oxford University Press.

Gutman, Herbert G. 1976. *The Black Family in Slavery and Freedom, 1750–1925.* New York: Pantheon Books.

Guttentag, Marcia, and Paul F. Secord. 1983. *Too Many Women?: The Sex Ratio Question.* Beverly Hills, Calif.: Sage Publications.

Guy, Donna J. 1991. *Sex and Danger in Buenos Aires: Prostitution, Family, and Nation in Argentina.* Lincoln: University of Nebraska Press.

Hagan, Jacqueline Maria. 1994. *Deciding to be Legal: A Maya Community in Houston.* Philadelphia, Pa.: Temple University Press.

Hagan, Jacqueline Maria, and Susan Gonzalez Baker. 1993. "Implementing the U.S. Legalization Program: The Influence of Immigrant Communities and Local Agencies on Immigration Policy Reform." *International Migration Review* 27(3): 513–36.

Hagan, John, and Alberto Palloni. 1999. "Sociological Criminology and the Mythology of Hispanic Immigrant Crime." *Social Problems* 4: 617–32.

Hahamovitch, Cindy. 1997. *The Fruits of Their Labor: Atlantic Coast Farmworkers and the Making of Migrant Poverty, 1870–1945*. Chapel Hill: University of North Carolina Press.

———. 2011. *No Man's Land: Jamaican Guestworkers in America and the Global History of Deportable Labor*. Princeton, N.J.: Princeton University Press.

Haines, Michael R. 2001. "The Urban Mortality Transition in the United States, 1800–1940." *NBER* Historical Working Paper no. 134. Cambridge, Mass.: National Bureau of Economic Research.

Haines, Robert F. 1994. "Indigent Misfits or Shrewd Operators? Government-Assisted Emigrants from the United Kingdom to Australia, 1831–1860." *Population Studies* 48(2): 223–47.

Hamilton, Erin. 2009. "The Sources of Recent Mexico-U.S. Migration: Geography, Domestic Migration, and Gender." Ph.D. diss., University of Texas, Austin.

Hammerton, James. 1979. *Emigrant Gentlewomen: Genteel Poverty and Female Emigration, 1830–1914*. Totowa, N.J. and London: Rowman and Littlefield and Croom Helm.

Handlin, Oscar. 1951. *The Uprooted: The Epic Story of the Great Migrations*. Boston: Little, Brown.

Hareven, Tamara, and Randolph Langenbach. 1978. *Amoskeag: Life and Work in an American Factory City*. New York: Pantheon.

Hartley, Leslie Poles. 1953. *The Go-Between*. New York: New York Review of Books Classics.

Harzig, Christiane. 2006. "Domestics of the World (Unite?): Labor Migration Systems and Personal Trajectories of Household Workers in Historical and Global Perspective." *Journal of American Ethnic History* 25(2): 48–73.

Harzig, Christiane, and Dirk Hoerder. 2009. *What Is Migration History?* Cambridge, Mass.: Polity Press.

Hatton, Timothy J., and Jeffrey G. Williamson. 2006. "A Dual Policy Paradox: Why Have Trade and Immigration Policies Aways Differed in Labor-Scarce Economics," NBER Working Paper No. 11866. Accessed November 15, 2014. http://www.nber.org/papers/w11866.

Hauser, Philip M. 1942. "Population and Vital Phenomena." *American Journal of Sociology* 48(3): 309–22.

Hauser, Philip M., and Otis Dudley Duncan. 1959. *The Study of Population: An Inventory and Appraisal*. Chicago: University of Chicago Press.

Hauser, Philip M., and Hope Tisdale Eldridge. 1947. "Projection of Urban Growth and Migration to Cities in the United States." *Milbank Memorial Fund Quarterly* 25(3): 293–307.

Headrick, Daniel R. 1981. *The Tools of Empire: Technology and European Imperialism in the Nineteenth Century*. Oxford: Oxford University Press.

Heer, David M. 1968. "Economic Development and the Fertility Transition." *Daedalus* 97(2): 447–62.

Heilbron, Johan, Lars Magnusson, and Björn Wittrock, eds. 1999. *The Rise of the Social Sciences and the Formation of Modernity: Conceptual Change in Context, 1750–1850*. Reprint. New York: Springer, 2001.

Hesketh, Therese, and Zhu Wei Xing. 2006. "Abnormal Sex Ratios in Human Populations: Causes and Consequences." *Proceedings of the National Academy of Sciences* 103(36): 13271–75.

Hesseltine, William B., and Louis Kaplan. 1943. "Women Doctors of Philosophy in History." *Journal of Higher Education* 14(5): 254–99.

Heywood, Linda M. 2009. "Slavery and Its Transformation in the Kingdom of Kongo: 1491–1800." *Journal of African History* 50(1): 1–22.

Hobsbawm, Eric. 1994. *The Age of Extremes: The Short Twentieth Century, 1914–1991.* New York: Vintage.

Hochschild, Arlie Russell. 1973. "A Review of Sex Role Research." *American Journal of Sociology* 78(4): 1011–29.

Hochstadt, Steve. 1999. *Mobility and Modernity: Migration in Germany, 1820–1989.* Ann Arbor: University of Michigan Press.

Hodgson, Dorothy. 1991. "The Ideological Origins of the PAA." *Population and Development Review* 17(1): 1–34.

Hoerder, Dirk. 1993. "[European Ports of Emigration]: Introduction." *Journal of American Ethnic History* 13(1): 3–5.

———. 1999. "From Immigration to Migration Systems: New Concepts in Migration History." *OAH Magazine of History* 14(1): 5–11.

———. 2002. *Cultures in Contact: World Migrations in the Second Millennium.* Durham, N.C.: Duke University Press.

Hofmann, Erin Trouth, and Cynthia J. Buckley. 2012. "Cultural Response to Changing Gender Patterns of Migration in Georgia." *International Migration* 50(5): 77–94.

Hofmann, Erin Trouth, and Cynthia J. Buckley. 2013. "Global Changes and Gendered Responses: The Feminization of Migration From Georgia." *International Migration Review* 47(3): 508–38.

Hogerzeil, Simon J., and David Richardson. 2007. "Slave Purchasing Strategies and Shipboard Mortality: Day-to-Day Evidence from the Dutch African Trade, 1751–1797." *Journal of Economic History* 67(1): 160–90.

Hollifield, James F. 2004. "The Emerging Migration State." *International Migration Review* 38(3): 885–912.

Holst, Elke, Andrea Schafer, and Mechthild Schrooten. 2012. "Gender and Remittances: Evidence from Germany." *Feminist Economics* 18(2): 201–29.

Hondagneu-Sotelo, Pierrette. 1994. *Gendered Transitions: Mexican Experiences of Immigration.* Berkeley: University of California Press.

———. 2003. *Gender and U.S. Immigration: Contemporary Trends.* Berkeley: University of California Press.

Houstoun, Marion F., Roger J. Kramer, and Joan Mackin Barrett. 1984. "Female Predominance of Immigration to the U.S." *International Migration Review* 18(4): 908–63.

Hsu, Madeline Yuan-yin. 2000. *Dreaming of Gold, Dreaming of Home: Transnationalism and Migration Between the United States and South China, 1882–1943.* Stanford, Calif.: Stanford University Press.

Hu-Dehart, Evelyn. 1994. "Chinese Coolie Labor in Cuba in the Nineteenth Century: Free Labor or Neoslavery?" *Contributions in Black Studies* 12(1994): 5. Accessed September 19, 2014. http://scholarworks.umass.edu/cibs/vol12/iss1/5.

Hudson, Valerie M., and Andrea M. Van den Boer. 2004. *Bare Branches: The Security Implications of Asia's Surplus Male Population.* Cambridge, Mass.: MIT Press.

Humphreys, Rachel. 1999. "Skilled Craftswomen or Cheap Labour? Craft-Based NGO Projects as an Alternative to Female Urban Migration in Northern Thailand." *Gender and Development* 7(2): 56–63.

Hurtado, Albert L. 1999. "Sex, Gender, Culture, and a Great Event: The California Gold Rush." *Pacific Historical Review* 68(1): 1–19.

Inikori, Joseph E. 1992. "Export Versus Domestic Demand: The Determinants of Sex Ratios in the Transatlantic Slave Trade." *Research in Economic History* 14: 117–66.

Inikori, Joseph E., and Stanley L. Engerman, eds. 1992. *The Atlantic Slave Trade: Effects on Economies, Societies, and Peoples in Africa, the Americas and Europe.* Durham, N.C.: Duke University Press.

International Labour Organization (ILO). 1922. *Recommendation Concerning Communication to the International Labour Office of Statistical and Other Information Regarding Emigration, Immigration and the Repatriation and Transit of Emigrants.* Geneva: ILO.

———. 1927. "Migration in Its Various Forms." From World Economic Conference. International Labour Organization, League of Nations (May 1927).

Isaac, Larry W., and Paul F. Lipold. 2012. "Toward Bridging Analytics and Dialectics: Nonergodic Processes and Turning Points in Dynamic Models of Social Change with Illustrations from Labor Movement History." In *Theorizing Modern Society as a Dynamic Process, Current Perspectives in Social Theory* 30(1): 3–33.

Jachimowicz, Maia. 2006. *Argentina: A New Era of Migration and Migration Policy. Migration Information Source.* Washington, D.C.: Migration Policy Institute.

Jackson, Pauline. 1984. "Women in 18th Century Irish Emigration." *International Migration Review* 18(4): 1004–20.

Jain, Shobhirta, and Rhonda Reddock (eds). 1998. *Women Plantation Workers: International Experiences.* New York: Bloomsburg Academic.

Jerome, Harry. 1926. *Migration and Business Cycles.* New York: National Bureau of Economic Research.

Johnston, Hugh J.M. 1972. *British Emigration Policy, 1815–1830: 'Shoveling out Paupers.'* Oxford: Clarendon Press.

Jolly, Susie, and Hazel Reeves. 2005. *Gender and Migration: Overview Report.* Brighton, England: BRIDGE, Institute of Development Studies.

Jones, Adele. 2008. "A Silent but Mighty River: The Costs of Women's Economic Migration." *Signs: Journal of Women in Culture and Society* 33(4): 761–69.

Joppke, Christian. 1996. "Multiculturalism and Immigration: A Comparison of the United States, Germany, and Great Britain." *Theory and Society* 25(4): 449–500.

Juhn, Chinkui, and Simon Potter. 2006. "Changes in Labor Force Participation in the United States." *Journal of Economic Perspectives* 20(3); 27–41.

Jupp, James. 2007. *From White Australia to Woomera.* Melbourne: Cambridge University Press.

Kaelin, Lukas. 2011. "Care Drain: The Political Making of Health Worker Migration." *Journal of Public Health Policy* 32(4): 489–98.

Kanaiaupuni, Shawn M. 2001. "Reframing the Migration Question: Men, Women, and Gender in Mexico." *Social Forces* 78(4): 1311–48.

Kandel, William, and Douglas S. Massey. 2002. "The Culture of Mexican Migration: A Theoretical and Empirical Analysis." *Social Forces* 80(3): 981–1004.

Kansakar, Vidya Bir Sirgh. 2001. *Nepal-India Border: Prospects, Problems and Challenges. Discussion Report.* Kathmandu: Institute of Foreign Affairs.

Karjanen, David. 2008. "Gender, Race, and Nationality in the Making of Mexican Migrant Labor in the United States." *Latin American Perspectives* 35(1): 51–63.

Karras, Alan L., and J.R. McNeill, eds. 1992. *Atlantic American Societies: From Columbus Through Abolition, 1492–1888.* London: Routledge.

Kaur, Amarjit, ed. 2004. *Women Workers in Industrialising Asia: Costed, Not Valued.* Basingstoke: Palgrave Macmillan.

Kaur, Amarjit. 2009. "Shifting Geographies of Migration in Southeast Asia: Continuity and Change in Proletarian and Gendered Migrations." In *Proletarian and Gendered Mass Migrations: A Global Perspective on Continuities and Discontinuities from the 19th to the 21st Centuries,* edited by Dirk Hoerder and Amarjit Kaur. Leiden: Brill.

———. 2011. "Indian Ocean Crossings: Indian Labor Migration and Settlement in Southeast Asia, 1870 to 1940." In *Connecting Seas and Connected Ocean Rims: Indian, Atlantic, and Pacific Oceans and China Seas Migrations from the 1830s to the 1930s,* edited by Donna R. Gabaccia and Dirk Hoerder. Leiden: Brill.

Kazal, Russell A. 2004. *Becoming Old Stock: The Paradox of German-American Identity.* Princeton, N.J.: Princeton University Press.

Kelly, Florence, ed. 1895. *Hull House Maps and Papers.* New York: Thomas Y. Crowell. Accessed December 3, 2014. https://homicide.northwestern.edu/pubs/hullhouse/.

Kelly, John J. 1987. "Improving the Comparability of International Migration Statistics: Contributions by the Conference of European Statisticians from 1971 to Date." *International Migration Review* 23(3): 1017–37.

Kennedy, Ruby Jo Reeves. 1944. "Single or Triple Melting-Pot? Intermarriage Trends in New Haven, 1870–1940." *Journal of Sociology* 49(4): 331–39.

Kessler-Harris, Alice. 1982. *Out to Work: The History of Wage-Earning Women in the United States.* New York: Oxford University Press.

Kessner, Thomas. 1977. *The Golden Door: Italian and Jewish Immigrant Mobility in New York City, 1980–1915.* New York: Oxford University Press.

Khalaf, Mona Chemali. 2009. "Male Migration and the Lebanese Family: The Impact on the Wife Left Behind" *Journal of Middle East Women's Studies* 5(3): 102–19.

Kim, Joon K., and May Fu. 2008. "International Women in South Korea's Sex Industry: A New Commodity Frontier." *Asian Survey* 48(3): 492–513.

Kindleberger, C.P. 1965. "Mass Migration, Then and Now." *Foreign Affairs* 43(4): 647–58.

King, Steven, and Anne Winter, eds., 2013. *Migration, Settlement and Belonging in Europe, 1500s–1930s.* New York: Berghahn.

Kirisci, Kemal. 2003. "Turkey: A Transformation from Emigration to Immigration." Washington, D.C.: Migration Policy Institute.

Klein, Herbert S. 1971. "The Internal Slave Trade in Nineteenth-Century Brazil: A Study of Slave Importations into Rio de Janeiro in 1852." *The Hispanic American Historical Review* 51(4): 567–85.

———. 1986. *African Slavery in Latin America and the Caribbean.* New York: Cambridge.

———. 1990. "Economic Dimensions of the Eighteenth-Century Atlantic Slave Trade." In *The Rise of Merchant Empires: Long Distance Trade in the Early Modern World, 1350–1750*, edited by James D. Tracey. Cambridge: Cambridge University Press.

———. 1999. *The Atlantic Slave Trade: New Approaches to the Americas*. Cambridge: Cambridge University Press.

———. 2002. "The Slave Trade and Decentralized Societies." *Journal of African History* 42(1): 49–65.

Klein, Herbert, Stanley L. Engerman, Robin Haines, and Ralph Shlomowitz. 2001. "Transoceanic Mortality: The Slave Trade in Comparative Perspective." *William and Mary Quarterly*, 3rd ser., 58(1): 93–118.

Klier, John Doyle. 2011. *Russians, Jews, and the Pogroms of 1881–1882*. Cambridge: Cambridge University Press.

Klooster, Wim. 2009. *Revolutions in the Atlantic World: A Comparative History*. New York: New York University Press.

Knodel, John. 1977. "Family Limitation and the Fertility Transition: Evidence from the Age Patterns of Fertility in Europe and Asia." *Population Studies* 31(2): 219–49.

Kofman, Eleonore. 1998. "Migrant Women and Exclusion in European Union." *European Journal of Women's Studies* 5(3/4): 381.

———. 1999. "Female 'Birds of Passage' a Decade Later: Gender and Immigration in the European Union." *International Migration Review* 33(2): 269–99.

Kofman, Eleonore, Annie Phizacklea, Parvati Raghuram, and Rosemary Sales. 2000. *Gender and International Migration in Europe: Employment, Welfare, and Politics*. New York: Routledge.

Korany, Bahgat. 1994. "End of History, or Its Continuation and Accentuation? The Global South and the 'New Transformation' Literature." *Third World Quarterly* 15(1): 7–15.

Koselleck, Reinhart. 2004. "Begriffsgeschichte and Social History." In *Futures Past: On the Semantics of Historical Time*. New York: Columbia University Press.

Koslowski, Rey. 2011. *Global Mobility Regimes*. Basingstoke: Palgrave-Macmillan.

Kosofsky-Sedgwick, Eve. 1990. *Epistemology of the Closet*. Berkeley: University of California Press.

Kreager, Philip. 1991. "Early Modern Population Theory: A Reassessment." *Population and Development Review* 17(2): 207–27.

———. 1993. "Histories of Demography: A Review Article." *Population Studies* 47(3): 519–39.

Krohnert, Steffen, and Sebastian Vollmer. 2012. "Where Have All the Young Women Gone? Gender-Specific Migration from East to West Germany." *International Migration* 50(5): 95–112.

Kuhn, Randall. 2006. "The Effects of Fathers' and Siblings' Migration on Children's Pace of Schooling in Rural Bangladesh." *Asian Population Studies* 2(1): 69–92.

Kulischer, Eugene M. 1943. *The Displacement of Population in Europe*. Montreal: International Labour Office.

Kushnirovich, N., and Rebeca Raijman. 2014. "Recruitment Practices of Labour Migrants in Israel: The Case of the Domestic Care Sector" in *Work and the Challenges of Belonging: Migrants in Globalizing Economies*, edited by Mojca Pajnik and Floya Anthias. England: Cambridge Scholars Publishing.

Labadie-Johnson, Glenda. 2008. "Reflections on Domestic Work and the Feminization of Migration." *Campbell Law Review* 31(2008): 67–90.

Laestaeghe, Ron, and Karel Neels. 2002. "From the First to the Second Demographic Transition: An Interpretation of the Spatial Continuity of Demographic Innovation in France, Belgium, and Switzerland." *European Journal of Population* 18(4): 325–60.

Lal, Brij V. 1985. "Veil of Dishonour: Sexual Jealousy and Suicide on Fiji Plantations." *Journal of Pacific History* 20(3): 135–55.

Lambroza, Shlomo. 1987. "The Tsarist Government and the Pogroms of 1903–06." *Modern Judaism* 7(3): 287–96.

Lancaster, C. S. 1976. "Women, Horticulture, and Society in Sub-Saharan Africa." *American Anthropologist* 78(3): 539–64.

Larsen, Mattias. 2011. *Vulnerable Daughters in India: Culture, Development and Changing Contexts.* New Delhi: Routledge.

Larsen, Mattias, and Ravinder Kaur. 2013. "Signs of Change? Sex Ratio Imbalance and Shifting Social Practices in Northern India." *Economic and Political Weekly* 48(33): 45–52.

Lazarsfeld, Paul F. 1961. "Notes on the History of Quantification in Sociology, Trends, Sources and Problems." *Isis* 15(5): 277–335.

Lee, Catherine. 2013. *Fictive Kinship: Family Reunification and the Meaning of Race and Nation in American Immigration.* New York: Russell Sage Foundation.

Lee, Erika. 2007. "The 'Yellow Peril' and Asian Exclusion in the Americas." *Pacific Historical Review* 76(4): 537–62.

Lee, Erika, Camilla Fojas, and Rudy Guevera. 2012. *The "Yellow Peril" in the United States and Peru: A Transnational History of Japanese Exclusion, 1920s–World War II.* Lincoln: University of Nebraska Press.

Lee, Sharon M. 1989. "Female Immigrants and Labor in Colonial Malaya: 1860–1947." *International Migration Review* 23(2): 309–31.

Leeds, Anthony. 1976. "Women in the Migratory Process: A Reductionist Outlook." *Anthropological Quarterly* 49(1): 69–76.

Leinonen, Johanna, and Donna R. Gabaccia. 2014. "Migrant Gender Imbalance and Marriage Choices: Evidence from the United States, Canada, the United Kingdom, Sweden, and Norway, 1860–1910." Special Issue, "Heiraten nach Übersee." *L'Homme* 24(1): 31–50.

LeMay, Michael C., and Elliot R. Barkan. 1999. *U.S. Immigration and Naturalization Laws and Issues: A Documentary History.* Westport, Conn.: Greenwood Press.

Leonhard, Jorn, and Ulrike von Hirschhausen. 2010. *Comparing Empires: Encounters and Transfer in the Long Nineteenth Century.* Gottingen: Vandenhoeck & Ruprecht.

Lesser, Jeffrey. 2012. *Immigration, Ethnicity, and National Identity in Brazil.* New York: Cambridge University Press.

Lewis, W. Arthur. 1978. *The Evolution of the International Economic Order.* Princeton, N.J.: Princeton University Press.

Lissak, Rivka Shpak. 1989. *Pluralism & Progressives: Hull House and the New Immigrants, 1890–1919.* Chicago: University of Chicago Press.

Lopez, Kathleen. 2013. *Chinese Cubans: A Transnational History.* Chapel Hill: University of North Carolina Press.

Lorber, Judith, and Susan A. Farrell, eds. 1991. *The Social Construction of Gender.* Newbury Park, Calif.: Sage Publications.

Lorde, Audre. 1984. *Sister Outsider: Essays and Speeches.* Trumansburg, N.Y.: Cross Press.

Louis, Roger. 1997. "Hong Kong: The Critical Phase, 1945–1949." *American Historical Review* 102(4): 1052–84.

Lovejoy, Paul E. 1989. "The Impact of the Atlantic Slave Trade on Africa: A Review of the Literature." *Journal of African History* 30(3): 365–94.

Lovejoy, Paul E. and David Richardson. 1995. "Competing Markets for Male and Female Slaves: Prices in the Interior of West Africa, 1780–1850." *International Journal of African Historical Studies* 28(2): 261–93.

Lown, Judy. 1983. "Not So Much a Factory, More a Form of Patriarchy: Gender and Class During Industrialisation." In *Gender, Class and Work,* edited by Eva Garmarnikow et al. London: Heinemann.

Lowrie, Claire. 2013. "White 'Men' and Their Chinese 'Boys': Sexuality, Masculinity and Colonial Power in Darwin and Singapore, 1880s–1930s." *History Australia* 10(1): 35–57.

Lucassen, Jan, and Leo Lucassen. 2009. "The Mobility Transition Revisited, 1500–1900: What the Case of Europe Can Offer to Global History." *Journal of Global History* 4(3): 347–77.

———. 2011. "From Mobility Transition to Comparative Global Migration History." *Journal of Global History* 6(2): 299–307.

Lucassen, Leo. 2005. *The Immigrant Threat.* Champaign: University of Illinois Press.

Luibhéid, Eithne. 2008. *Queer/Migration.* Durham, N.C.: Duke University Press.

Lutz, Helma. 2002. "At Your Service Madam? The Globalization of Domestic Service." *Feminist Review* 70:89–104.

———. 2010. "Gender in the Migratory Process." *Journal of Ethnic and Migration Studies* 36(10): 1647–63.

Lynch, Martin. 2002. *Mining in World History.* London: Reaktion Books.

MacDonald, John S., and Leatrice D. MacDonald. 1964. "Chain Migration, Ethnic Neighborhood Formation, and Social Networks." *Millbank Memorial Fund Quarterly* 42(1): 82–97.

MacDonald, John, and Eric Richardson. 1997. "The Great Emigration of 1841: Recruitment for New South Wales in British Emigration Fields." *Population Studies* 51(3): 337–55.

MacRaild, Donald M. 2011. *The Irish Diaspora in Britain, 1750–1939.* New York: Palgrave Macmillan.

Mahler, Sarah J., and Patricia R. Pessar. 2006. "Gender Matters: Ethnographers Bring Gender from the Periphery Toward the Core of Migration Studies." *International Migration Review* 40(1): 27–63.

Mahler, Sarah J., and Dusan Ugrina. 2006. *Central America: Crossroads of the Americas.* Washington, D.C.: Migration Policy Institute.

Malheiros, Jorge. 2002. *Portugal Seeks Balance of Emigration, Immigration.* Washington, DC: Migration Information Source.

Manalansan, M. 2006. "Queer Intersections: Sexuality and Gender in Migration Studies." *International Migration Review* 40(1): 224–24.

Manning, Caroline. 1930. *The Immigrant Woman and Her Job.* Reprint. New York: Arno Press, 1970.

Manning, Patrick. 1983. "Contours of Slavery and Social Change in Africa." *American Historical Review* 88(4): 835–57.

———. 1990. *Slavery and African Life: Occidental, Oriental, and African Slave Trades.* Cambridge: Cambridge University Press.

———. 2005. *Migration in World History.* New York: Routledge.

Marshall, Gordon. 1994. "Irene B. Taeuber." In *A Dictionary of Sociology*, 1st ed., edited by Gordon Marshall. Oxford: Oxford University Press.

Martin, Phillip. 2008. "Another Miracle? Managing Labour Migration in Asia." Paper presented at United Nations Expert Group Meeting on International Migration and Development in Asia and the Pacific. Bangkok (September 20–21, 2008).

Marx, Karl, and Friedrich Engels. 1888. *Manifesto of the Communist Party.* London: William Reeves.

Mason, Karen Oppenheim. 1987. "The Impact of Women's Social Position on Fertility in Developing Countries." *Sociological Forum* 2(4): 718–45.

Massey, Douglas S., Joaquin Arango, Graeme Hugo, Ali Kouaouci, Adela Pellegrino, and J. Edward Taylor. 1993. "Theories of International Migration." *Population and Development Review* 19(3): 431–66.

Massey, Douglas S., Jorge Durand, and Nolan Malone. 2002. *Beyond Smoke and Mirrors: Mexican Immigration in an Age of Economic Integration.* New York: Russell Sage Foundation

Massey, Douglas S., Luin Goldring, and Jorge Durand. 1994. "Continuities in Transnational Migration: An Analysis of Nineteen Mexican Communities." *American Journal of Sociology* 99(6): 1492–533.

Massey, Douglas S., and J. Edward Taylor. 2004. *International Migration: Prospects and Policies in a Global Market.* England: Oxford University.

Matt, Susan J. 2011. *Homesickness: An American History.* New York: Oxford University Press.

McCaa, Robert, and Dirk J. Jaspers-Faijer. 2000. "The Standardized Census Sample Operation (OMUECE) of Latin America, 1959–1982: A Project of the Latin American Demographic Center (CELADE)." In *Handbook of International Historical Microdata for Population Research,* edited by Patricia Kelly Hall, Robert McCaa, and Gunnar Thorvaldsen. Minneapolis: Minnesota Population Center.

McDaniel, Antonio, and Samuel H. Preston. 1994. "Patterns of Mortality by Age and Cause of Death Among Nineteenth-Century Immigrants to Liberia." *Population Studies* 48(1): 99–115.

McGann, Nora. 2013. "The Opening of Burmese Borders: Impacts on Migration." Washington, D.C.: Migration Information Source.

McKeown, Adam. 2001. *Chinese Migrant Networks and Cultural Change: Peru, Chicago, Hawaii, 1900–1936.* Chicago: University of Chicago Press.

———. 2004. "Global Migration, 1846–1940." *Journal of World History* 15(2): 155–89.

———. 2008. *Melancholy Order: Asian Migration and the Globalization of Borders.* New York: Columbia University Press.

———. 2010. "Chinese Emigration in Global Context, 1850–1940." *Journal of Global History* 5(1): 95–124.

McMurray, David. 1999. "Trafficking and Transiting: New Perspectives on Labor Migration." *Middle East Report* 211 (Summer): 16–19.

McNeill, W. H. 1973. *The Ecumene: Story of Humanity.* New York: Harper and Row.

Meagher, Arnold J. 2008. *The Coolie Trade, the Traffic in Chinese Labourers to Latin America 1847–1874.* Bloomington, Ill.: Xlibris.

Melville, Margarita B. 1978. "Mexican Women Adapt to Migration." *International Migration Review* 12(2): 225–35.

Menard, Russell R. 1993. "Whatever Happened to Early American Population History?" *William and Mary Quarterly* 50(2): 356–66.

Methorst, H. W. 1936. "The New System of Population Accounting in the Netherlands." *Journal of the American Statistical Association* 31(196): 719–22.

Meyers, Janet C. 2001. "Performing the Voyage Out: Victorian Female Emigration and the Class Dynamics of Displacement." *Victorian Literature and Culture* 29(1): 129–46.

Meyerson, Frederick A. B. 2001. "Replacement Migration: A Questionable Tactic for Delaying the Inevitable Effects of Fertility Transition." *Population and Environment* 22(4): 401–09.

Migrant Forum Asia. n.d. "CEDAW and the Female Labour Migrants of Bangladesh." Quezon City, Philippines: Migrant Forum Asia.

Migration News. 2014. "Southeast Asia." *Migration News* 21(2). Accessed October 17, 2014. https://migration.ucdavis.edu/mn/more.php?id=3906_0_3_0.

Miller, Joseph C. 1984. "Capitalism and Slaving: The Financial and Commercial Organization of the Angolan Slave Trade, According to the Accounts of Antonio Coelho Guerreiro (1684–1692)." *International Journal of African Historical Studies* 17(1): 1–56.

———. 1988. *Way of Death: Merchant Capitalism and the Angolan Slave Trade, 1730–1830.* Madison: University of Wisconsin Press.

———. 1989. "The Numbers, Origins, and Destinations of Slaves in the Eighteenth-Century Angolan Slave Trade." *Social Science History* 13(4): 381–419.

Minnesota Population Center. 2010. *Integrated Public Use Microdata Series International: Version 5.0* [Machine-Readable Database]. Minneapolis: University of Minnesota.

Minnesota Population Center. 2014. *Integrated Public Use Microdata Series International: Version 6.3* [Machine-Readable Database]. Minneapolis: University of Minnesota.

Moch, Leslie Page. 1992. *Moving Europeans: Migration in Western Europe since 1650.* Bloomington, Ind.: Indiana University Press.

Moch, Leslie Page. 2012. *The Pariahs of Yesterday: Breton Migrants in Paris.* Durham, N.C.: Duke University Press.

Modell, John, and Tamara K. Hareven. 1973. "Urbanization and the Malleable Household: An Examination of Boarding and Lodging in American Families." *Journal of Marriage and Family* 35(5): 467–79.

Moller, Herbert. 1945. "Sex Composition and Correlated Culture Patterns of Colonial America." *William and Mary Quarterly,* 3rd ser., 2(2): 113–53.

More, L. B. 1907. *Wage-Earners' Budgets: A Study of Standards and Cost of Living in New York City.* New York: Henry Holt.

Morgan, Gwenda, and Peter Rushton. 2004. *Eighteenth-Century Criminal Transportation: The Formation of the Criminal Atlantic.* New York: Palgrave Macmillan.

Morgan, Jennifer L. 1997. " 'Some Could Suckle Over Their Shoulder': Male Travelers, Female Bodies, and the Gendering of Racial Ideology, 1500–1770." *William and Mary Quarterly,* 3rd ser., 54 (January): 167–92.

———. 2004. *Laboring Women: Reproduction and Gender in New World Slavery.* Philadelphia: University of Pennsylvania Press.

Morner, Magnus. 1976. "Spanish Migration to the New World Prior to 1800: A Report on the State of Research." In *First Images of America: the Impact of the New World on the Old,* vol. 2, edited by Fredi Chiappelli. Berkeley: University of California Press.

———. 1995. "Spanish Historians on Spanish Migration to America During the Colonial Period." *Latin American Research Review* 30(2): 251–67.

Morokvasic, Mirjana. 1984. "Birds of Passage Are Also Women." *International Migration Review* 18(4): 886–907.

Morris, Aldon. 2015. *The Scholar Denied: W. E. B. DuBois and the Birth of American Sociology*. Berkeley, Calif: University of California Press.

Muus, Philip. 2004. "The Netherlands: A Pragmatic Approach to Economic Needs and Humanitarian Considerations." In *Controlling Immigration: A Global Perspective*, edited by Wayne A. Cornelius. Stanford, Calif.: Stanford University Press.

Nawyn, Stephanie J. 2010. "Gender and Migration: Integrating Feminist Theory into Migration Studies." *Sociology Compass* 4(9): 749–65.

Newbold, Bruce K. 2001. "Counting Migrants and Migrations: Comparing Lifetime and Fixed-Interval Return and Onward Migration." *Economic Geography* 77(1): 23–40.

Nicholson, J.S. 1891. "The Living Capital of the United Kingdom." *Economic Journal* 1(1): 95–107.

Nobles, Jenna. 2011. "Parenting from Abroad: Migration, Nonresident Father Involvement and Children's Education in Mexico." *Journal of Marriage and the Family* 73(4): 729–46.

———. 2013. "Migration and Father Absence: Shifting Family Structure in Mexico." *Demography* 50(4): 1303–14.

Nobles, Jenna, and Christopher McKelvey. 2013. "Gender, Power, and Emigration from Mexico." Unpublished manuscript, University of Wisconsin, Madison.

Nolan, Janet. 1989. *Ourselves Alone: Women's Emigration from Ireland, 1885–1920*. Lexington, Ky.: The University Press of Kentucky.

Northrup, David. 1995. *Indentured Labor in the Age of Imperialism, 1834–1922*. New York: Cambridge University Press.

Norton, Mary Beth. 1987. "Gender and Defamation in Seventeenth-Century Maryland." *William and Mary Quarterly*, 3rd ser., 44(1): 3–39.

Nwokeji, G. Ugo. 2000. "The Atlantic Slave Trade and Population Density: A Historical Demography of the Biafran Hinterland." *Canadian Journal of African Studies* 34(3): 616–65.

———. 2001. "African Concepts of Gender and the Slave Traffic." *William and Mary Quarterly*, 3rd ser., 58(1): 47–68.

———. 2010. *The Slave Trade and Culture in the Bight of Biafra: An African Society in the Atlantic World*. New York: Cambridge University Press.

Nwokeji, G. Ugo, and David Eltis. 2002. "The Roots of the African Diaspora: Methodological Considerations in the Analysis of Names in the Liberated African Registers of Sierra Leone and Havana." *History in Africa* 29 (January): 365–79.

O'Reilly, William. 2012. "Movements of People in the Atlantic World, 1450–1850." In *The Oxford Handbook of the Atlantic World: 1450–1850*, edited by Nicholas Canny and Philip Morgan. Oxford Handbooks Online. doi: 10.1093/oxfordhb/9780199210879.001.0001.

O'Rourke, Kevin H., and Jeffrey G. Williamson. 1999. *Globalization and History: The Evolution of a Nineteenth-Century Atlantic Economy*. Cambridge, Mass.: MIT Press.

O'Sullivan, Patrick. 1995. *Irish Women and Irish Migration*. London: Leicester University Press.

Ogden, Philip E., and Ray Hall. 2004. "The Second Demographic Transition, New Household Forms and the Urban Population of France During the 1990s." *Transactions of the Institute of British Geographers* 29(1): 88–105.

Oishi, Nana. 2005. *Women in Motion: Globalization, State Policies and Labor Migration in Asia*. Stanford, Calif.: Stanford University Press.

Okin, Susan Moller. 2003. "Poverty, Well-Being, and Gender: What Counts, Who's Heard?" *Philosophy and Public Affairs* 31(3): 280–316.

Omondi, George. 2013. "10,000 Teaching Jobs on the Line as Dar Expels Aliens." *Business Daily Africa*, September 15, 2013. Accessed September 19, 2014. http://www.businessdailyafrica.com/teaching-jobs-on-the-line-as-Dar-expels-aliens/-/539546/1993924/-/1432a4ez/-/index.html.

Omran, Abdel R. 1971. "The Epidemiologic Transition: A Theory of the Epidemiology of Population Change." *Milbank Memorial Fund Quarterly* 49(4): 509–38.

Ortner, Sherry. 1972. "Is Female to Male as Nature Is to Culture?" *Feminist Studies* 1(2): 5–31.

Oxley, Deborah. 1996. *Convict Maids: The Forced Migration of Women to Australia*. Cambridge: Cambridge University Press.

Özden, Çağlar, Christopher Parsons, Maurice Schiff, and Terrie L. Walmsley. 2011. "Where on Earth Is Everybody? The Evolution of Global Bilateral Migration, 1960–2000." *World Bank Economic Review* 25(1): 12–56.

Palmer, Robert R. 1959. *The Age of Democratic Revolution: A Political History of Europe and America, 1760–1800*. Princeton, N.J.: Princeton University Press.

Pan, Chia-lin, and Irene Taeuber. 1952. "The Expansion of the Chinese: North and West." *Population Index* 18(2): 85–108.

Panunzio, Constantime. 1942. "Intermarriage in Los Angeles, 1924–33." *American Journal of Sociology* 47(5): 690–701.

Parreñas, Rhacel Salazar. 2000. "Migrant Filipina Domestic Workers and the International Division of Reproductive Labor." *Gender & Society* 14(4): 560–80.

———. 2001. *Servants of Globalization: Women, Migration, and Domestic Work*. Stanford, Calif.: Stanford University Press.

———. 2011. *Illicit Flirtations: Labor, Migration, and Sex Trafficking in Tokyo*. Stanford, Calif.: Stanford University Press.

Passel, Jeffrey S., and D'Vera Cohn. 2009. *A Portrait of Unauthorized Immigrants in the United States*. Washington, D.C.: Pew Research Center.

Passel, Jeffrey S., D'Vera Cohn, and Ana Gonzalez-Barrera. 2013. *New Estimate: 11.7 Million in 2012, Population Decline of Unauthorized Immigrants Stalls, May Have Reversed*. Washington, D.C.: Pew Research Center.

Paton, Diana. 2005. "Bibliographical Essay." In *Gender and Slave Emancipation in the Atlantic World*, edited by Pamela Scully and Diana Paton. Durham, N.C.: Duke University Press.

Pear, Robert. "Men Only a Third of U.S. Immigrants; Finding Upsets Conventional Wisdom, Suggesting Less Effect on Labor Market." *New York Times*, September 9, 1985.

Pearce, Susan C., Elizabeth J. Clifford, and Reena Tandon. 2011. *Immigration and Women: Understanding the American Experience*. New York: New York University Press.

Pearson, Ruth, and Kyoko Kusakabe. 2012. "Who Cares? Gender, Reproduction and Care Chains of Burmese Migrant Workers in Thailand." *Feminist Economics* 18(2): 149–75.

Peck, Gunther. 2000. *Reinventing Free Labor: Padrones and Immigrant Workers in the North American West, 1880–1930.* Cambridge: Cambridge University Press.

Pedraza, Silvia. 1991. "Women and Migration: The Social Consequences of Gender." *Annual Review of Sociology* 17: 303–25.

Perdue, Peter C. 2009. "Nature and Nurture on Imperial China's Frontiers." *Modern Asian Studies* 43(1): 245–67.

Perelli-Harris, Brienna. 2005. "The Path to Lowest-Low Fertility in Ukraine." *Population Studies* 59(1): 55–70.

Perlmann, Joel, and Mary C. Waters. 2004. "Intermarriage Then and Now: Race, Generation, and the Changing Meaning of Marriage." In *Not Just Black and White: Historical and Contemporary Perspectives on Immigration, Race, and Ethnicity in the United States,* edited by Nancy Foner and George Frederickson. New York: Russell Sage Foundation.

Perrings, Charles. 1979. *Black Mineworkers in Central Africa: Industrial Strategies and the Evolution of an African Proletariat in the Copperbelt, 1911–1941.* London: Heinemann.

Perry, Adele. 2001. *On the Edge of Empire: Gender, Race, and the Making of British Columbia, 1849–1871.* Toronto: University of Toronto Press.

Pessar, Patricia R. 1986. "The Role of Gender in Dominican Settlement in the United States." In *Women and Change in Latin America,* edited by J. Nash and H. Safa, 273–94. South Hadley, Mass.: Bergin and Garvey.

Pessar, Patricia R., and Sherri Grasmuck. 1991. *Between Two Islands: Dominican International Migration.* Berkeley: University of California Press.

Pessar, Patricia R., and Sarah J. Mahler. 2001. "Gendered Geographies of Power: Analyzing Gender Across Transnational Spaces." *Identities: Global Studies in Culture and Power* 7(4): 441–59.

Peterson, W. 1969. *Population.* 2nd ed. New York: Macmillan.

Phizacklea, Annie, ed. 1983. *One Way Ticket: Migration and Female Labour.* London: Routledge & Kegan.

Piper, Nicola. 1999. "Labor Migration, Trafficking and International Marriage: Female Cross-border Movements into Japan." *Asian Journal of Women Studies* 5(2): 69–99.

———. 2005. "Gender and Migration." Paper prepared for the Policy Analysis and Research Programme of the Global Commission on International Migration. Geneva (March 23–24, 2005).

Pitea, Roberto. 2010. "Transit Migration: Challenges in Egypt, Iraq, Jordan and Lebanon." *CARIM* Research Reports 2010/02. Florence: Institut Universitaire Européen, Robert Schuman Centre for Advanced Studies. Accessed September 19, 2014. http://cadmus.eui.eu/bitstream/handle/1814/15290/CARIM_RR_2010_02.pdf?sequence=1.

Pleck, Elizabeth H. 1978. "A Mother's Wages: Income Earning Among Married Italian and Black Women, 1896–1911." In *The American Family in Social-Historical Perspective,* 2nd ed., edited by Michael Gordon. New York: St. Martin's Press.

Pliley, Jessica. 2010. "Claims to Protection: The Rise and Fall of Feminist Abolitionism in the League of Nations' Committee on the Traffic in Women and Children, 1919–1936." *Journal of Women's History* 22(4): 90–113.

Poeze, Miranda, and Valentina Mazzucato. 2014. "Ghanaian Children in Transnational Families: A Case Understanding the Experiences of Left-Behind Children Through Local Parenting Norms." In *Transnational Families, Migration and the Circulation of Care: Understanding Mobility and Absence in Family Life,* edited by Loretta Baldassar and Laura Merla. New York: Routledge.

Pomeranz, Kenneth, and Steven Topik. 2006. *The World that Trade Created: Society, Culture, and the World Economy, 1400 to the Present,* 2nd ed. Armonk, N.Y.: M.E. Sharpe.

Pooley, Colin, and Jane Turnbull. 1998. *Migration and Mobility in Britain Since the Eighteenth Century.* London: UCL Press.

Poovey, Mary. 1988. *Uneven Developments: The Ideological Work of Gender in Mid-Victorian. England.* Chicago: University of Chicago Press.

Population Association of America. 2013. "Statement of the Population Association of America to the United Nations High-level Dialogue (HLD) on International Migration and Development." Accessed February 16, 2014. http://www.populationassociation.org/2013/07/21/paa-statement-to-united-nations-on-international-migration-and-development.

Powers, Mary G., and Joan J. Holmberg. 1978. "Occupational Status Scores: Changes Introduced by the Inclusion of Women." *Demography* 15(2): 183–204.

Prashad, Vijay. 2007. *The Darker Nations: A People's History of the Third World.* New York: The New Press.

Preston, William. 1795. *A Letter to Bryan Edwards: Esquire, Containing Observations on Some Passages of His History of the West Indies.* London: J. Johnson.

Pryor, Edward, and John F. Long. 1987. "The Canada-United States Joint Immigration Study: Issues in Data Comparability." *International Migration Review* 21(4): 1038–66.

Purseigle, Pierre. 2007. "'A Wave on to Our Shores': The Exile and Resettlement of Refugees from the Western Front, 1914–1918." *Contemporary European History* 16(4): 427–44.

Qian, Zhenchao, and Daniel T. Lichter. 2001. "Measuring Marital Assimilation: Intermarriage Among Natives and Immigrants." *Social Science Research* 30(2): 289–312.

Quack, Sibylle, ed. 1995. *Between Sorrow and Strength: Women Refugees of the Nazi Period.* New York: German Historical Institute and Cambridge University Press.

Quillian, Lincoln. 1995. "Prejudice as a Response to Perceived Group Threat: Population Composition and Anti-Immigrant and Racial Prejudice in Europe." *American Sociological Review* 60(4): 586–611.

Raijman, Rebecca, and Adriana Kemp. 2011. "Labor Migration in Israel: The Creation of a Non-Free Workforce." *Proto-Sociology* 27: 177–95.

Raijman, Rebecca, Silvina Schammah-Gesser, and Adriana Kemp. 2003. "International Migration, Domestic Work, and Care Work: Undocumented Latina Migrants in Israel." *Gender & Society* 17(5): 727–49.

Raijman, Rebecca, and Moshe Semyonov. 1997. "Gender, Ethnicity and Immigration: Double-Disadvantage and Triple-Disadvantage Among Recent Immigrant Women in the Israeli Labor Market." *Gender & Society* 11(1): 108–25.

Ramirez, Bruno. 1991. *On the Move: French-Canadian and Italian Migrants in the North Atlantic Economy, 1861–1914.* Toronto: McClelland and Stewart Publishing.

Ramos, Donald. 1988. "Slavery in Brazil: A Case Study of Diamantina, Minas Gerais." *The Americas* 45(15): 47–59.

Ravenstein, E. G. 1885. "The Laws of Migration." *Journal of the Statistical Society of London* 48(2): 167–235.

———. 1889. "The Laws of Migration." *Journal of the Royal Statistical Society* 52(2): 241–305.

———. 1908. *A Life's Work*. London: Hazell, Watson & Viney.

Reeder, Linda. 2003. *Widows in White: Migration and the Transformation of Rural Italian Women, Sicily, 1880–1920*. Toronto: University of Toronto Press.

Reimers, David. 2013. "More Liberal than We Thought: A Note on Immediate Family Member Immigrants of U.S. Citizens." *Journal of Policy History* 25(2): 289–98.

Reinharz, Shulamit. 1989. "Teaching the History of Women in Sociology: Dorothy Swaine Thomas, Wasn't She the Woman Married to William I?" *American Sociologist* 20(1): 87–94

Riley, Nancy E., and James McCarthy. 2003. *Demography in the Age of the Postmodern*. Cambridge: Cambridge University Press.

Robertson, Claire C., and Martin A. Klein, eds. 1983. *Women and Slavery in Africa*. Madison: University of Wisconsin Press.

Robertson, Craig. 2009. *Passport in America: The History of a Document*. New York: Oxford University Press.

Robertson, Robbie. 2003. *The Three Waves of Globalization: A History of a Developing Global Consciousness*. London: Zed Books.

Robinson, Marsha. 2007. "Re-modeling Slavery as if Women Mattered." In *Women and Slavery*, vols. 1 and 2, edited by Gwyn Campbell, Suzanne Miers, and Joseph C. Miller. Athens: Ohio University Press.

Robinson, Portia. 1986. "From Colleen to Matilda: Irish Women Convicts in Australia, 1788–1828." In *Australia and Ireland 1788–1988: Bicentenary Essays*, edited by Colm Kiernan. Dublin: Gill and Macmillan.

Robson, Leslie Lloyd. 1994. *The Convict Settlers of Australia*, 2nd ed. Melbourne: Melbourne University Press.

Rodgers, Daniel T. 1998. *Atlantic Crossings: Social Politics in a Progressive Age*. Cambridge, Mass.: Harvard University Press.

Rogers, Andrei. 1990. "Requiem for the Net Migrant." *Geographical Analysis* 22(4): 283–300.

Rosaldo, Michelle Zimbalist, and Lousie Lamphere. 1974. *Women, Culture, and Society*. Stanford, Calif.: Stanford University Press.

Rose, Sonya O. 1986. "'Gender at Work': Sex, Class and Industrial Capitalism." *History Workshop* 21(1): 113–31.

Rosenau, Pauline Marie. 1992. *Postmodernism and the Social Sciences*. Princeton, N.J.: Princeton University Press.

Rosenberg, Emily S. 2012. *A World Connecting, 1870–1945*. Cambridge, Mass.: Harvard University Press.

Rosenberg, Karen E., and Judith A. Howard. 2008. "Finding Feminist Sociology: A Review Essay." *Signs* 33(3): 675–96.

Ross, J. C. 1827. *An Examination of Opinions Maintained in the "Essay on the Principles of Population" by Malthus and in the "Elements of Political Economy" by David Ricardo*. London: J. M. Richardson.

Roy, Archana K., and Parveen Nangia. 2005. "Reproductive Health Status of Wives Left Behind by Male Out-migrants: A Study of Rural Bihar, India." In

Migration and Health in Asia, edited by Santosh Jantrana, Mika Toyota, and Brenda S. A. Yeoh. New York: Routledge.

Rubio-Marin, Ruth. 2000. *Immigration as a Democratic Challenge: Citizenship and Inclusion in Germany and the United States.* Cambridge: Cambridge University Press.

Ruggles, Steven, J. Trent Alexander, Katie Genadek, Ronald Goeker, Matthew B. Schroeder, and Matthew Sobek. *Integrated Public Use Microdata Series: Version5.0* [Machine-Readable database]. Minneapolis: University of Minnesota.

Ruhs, Martin, and Emma Quinn. 2009. *Ireland: From Rapid Immigration to Recession.* Migration Information Source. Washington, D.C.: Migration Policy Institute.

Rumbaut, Rubén G., and Walter A. Ewing. 2007. *The Myth of Immigrant Criminality and the Paradox of Assimilation: Incarceration Rates Among Native and Foreign-Born Men.* Houston: Texans for Sensible Immigration Policy.

Rushen, Elizabeth. 2003. *Single and Free: Female Migration to Australia, 1833–1837.* Melbourne: Australian Scholarly Publications.

Saeger, Nicholas. 2008. "Lies, Damned Lies, and Statistics: Epistemology and Fiction in Defoe's 'A Journal of the Plague Year'." *Modern Language Review* 103(3): 639–53.

Salinger, Sharon V. 1983. "Artisans, Journeymen and the Transformation of Labor in Late Eighteenth-Century Philadelphia." *William and Mary Quarterly* 40(1): 62–84.

Samaroo, Brinley. 2013. "Indian and Chinese Migration to the British Caribbean." *Encyclopedia of Global Human Migrations.* Basingstoke: Palgrave-Macmillan.

Sassen-Koob, Saskia. 1984. "Notes on the Incorporation of Third World Women into Wage Labor Through Offshore Production." *International Migration Review* 18(4): 1144–67.

———. 2008. "Two Stops in Today's New Global Geographies: Shaping Novel Labor Supplies and Employment Regimes." *American Behavioral Scientist* 52(3): 457–96.

Savage, Elizabeth, ed. 1992. *The Human Commodity: Perspectives on the Trans-Saharan Slave Trade.* London: Frank Cass.

Schiebinger, Londa. 1989. *The Mind Has No Sex? Women in the Origins of Modern Science.* Cambridge, Mass.: Harvard University Press.

Schmalzbauer, Leah. 2009. "Gender on a New Frontier: Mexican Migration in the Rural Mountain West." *Gender and Society* 23(6): 747–67.

Schrover, Marlou. 2013. "Feminization and Problematization of Migration: Europe in the Nineteenth and Twentieth Centuries." In *Proletarian and Gendered Mass Migrations: A Global Perspective on Continuities and Discontinuities from the 19th to the 21st Centuries,* edited by Dirk Hoerder and Amarjit Kaur. Leiden: Brill.

———. 2014. "No Longer a White Problem: The White Slavery Debate Moves from Europe to Asia." Paper presented at 2014 Berkshire Conference on the History of Women. Toronto (May 22–25, 2014).

Schrover, Marlou, and Deirdre M. Moloney, eds. 2013. *Gender, Migration and Categorisation: Making Distinctions Between Migrants in Western Countries, 1945–2010.* Amsterdam: Amsterdam University Press.

Schrover, Marlou, Joane van der Leun, Leo Lucassen, and Chris Quispel, eds. 2008. *Illegal Migration and Gender in a Global and Historical Perspective.* Amsterdam: Amsterdam University Press.

Schwartz, Stuart B. 1982. "The Plantations of St. Benedict: The Benedictine Sugar Mills of Colonial Brazil." *The Americas* 39(1): 1–22.

Schwenken, Helen. 2008. "Beautiful Victims and Sacrificing Heroines: Exploring the Role of Gender Knowledge in Migration Policies." *Signs* 33(4): 770–76.

Schwenken, Helen, and Pia Eberhardt. 2008. "Gender Knowledge in Economic Migration Theories and in Migration Practices." *GARNET* Working Paper no. 58/08. Warwick: University of Warwick, Centre for the Study of Globalisation and Regionalisation.

Scott, Joan. 1986. "Gender: A Useful Category of Historical Analysis." *American Historical Review* 91(5): 1053–75.

Semyonov, Moshe, and Anastasia Gordzeisky. 2004. "Occupational Destinations and Economic Mobility of Filipino Overseas Workers." *International Migration Review* 38(1): 5–25.

Sen, Amartya. 1990. "More Than 100 Million Women are Missing." *The New York Review of Books,* December 20.

Sevoyan, Arusyak, and Victor Agadjanian. 2010. "Male Migration, Women Left Behind, and Sexually Transmitted Diseases in Armenia." *International Migration Review* 44(2): 354–75.

Shammas, Carole. 2012. "Household Formation, Lineage, and Gender Relations in the Early Modern Atlantic World." In *The Oxford Handbook of the Atlantic World: 1450–1850,* edited by Nicholas Canny and Philip Morgan. Oxford: Oxford University Press. doi: 10.1093/oxfordhb/9780199210879.001.0001.

Shryock Jr., Henry S., and Hope Tisdale Eldridge. 1947. "Internal Migration in Peace and War." *American Sociological Review* 12(1): 27–39.

Sicherman, Barbara, and Carol Hurd Green, eds. 1980. *Notable American Women: The Modern Period: A Biographical Dictionary,* vol. 4. Cambridge, Mass.: Harvard University Press.

Siddiqui, Tasneem. 2003. "Migration as a Livelihood Strategy of the Poor: The Bangladesh Case." Paper presented at the Regional Conference on Migration, Development and Pro-Poor Policy Choices in Asia. Dhaka, Bangladesh (June 22–24, 2003). Accessed September 19, 2014. http://r4d.dfid.gov.uk/pdf/outputs/migrationglobpov/wp-c1.pdf.

———. 2008. "Migration and Gender in Asia." Paper presented at the United National Expert Group Meeting on International Migration and Development in Asia. Bangkok (September 20–21, 2008). Accessed September 19, 2014. http://www.un.org/esa/population/meetings/EGM_Ittmig_Asia/P06_Siddiqui.pdf.

Sieff, C. F. 1990. "Explaining Biased Sex Ratios in Human Populations: A Critique of Recent Studies." *Current Anthropology* 31(1): 25–48.

Silberstein, Carina Frid de. 2003. "Immigrants and Female Work in Argentina: Questioning Gender Stereotypes and Constructing Images—the Case of Italians, 1879–1900." In *Mass Migrations to Modern Latin America,* edited by Samuel L. Bailey and Eduardo J. Miguez. Wilmington, Del.: Scholarly Resources.

Simmons, Alan B. 1987. "The United Nations Recommendations and Data Efforts: International Migration Statistics." *International Migration Review* 21(4): 996–1016.

Sinke, Suzanne. 1999. "Migration for Labor, Migration for Love: Marriage and Family Formation across Borders." *OAH Magazine of History* 14(1): 17–21.

Sluga, Glenda. 2013. *Internationalism in the Age of Nationalism.* Philadelphia: University of Pennsylvania Press.

Smallwood, Stephanie E. 2007. *Saltwater Slavery: A Middle Passage from Africa to American Diaspora.* Cambridge, Mass.: Harvard University Press.

Smith, Daniel Scott. 1989. "'All in Some Degree Related to Each Other': A Demographic and Comparative Resolution of the Anomaly of New England Kinship." *American Historical Review* 94(1): 44–79.

Smith, Judith E. 1985. *Family Connections: A History of Italian and Jewish Immigrant Lives in Providence, Rhode Island, 1900–1940.* Albany, N.Y.: SUNY Press.

Smithers, Gregory D. 2009. "The 'Pursuits of the Civilized Man': Race and the Meaning of Civilization in the United States and Australia, 1790s–1850s." *Journal of World History* 20(2): 245–72.

Solow, Barbara. 1999. "The Transatlantic Slave Trade: A New Census." *William and Mary Quarterly,* 3rd ser., 58(1): 9–16.

Song, Jiyoung. 2013. "'Smuggled Refugees': The Social Construction of North Korean Migration." *International Migration* 51(4): 158–73.

South, Scott J., and Katherine Trent 1988. "Sex Ratios and Women's Roles: A Cross-National Analysis." *American Journal of Sociology* 93(5): 1096–115.

Spickard, Paul. 2007. *Almost All Aliens: Immigration, Race, and Colonialism in American History and Identity.* New York: Routledge.

Spoerer, Mark, and Jochen Fleischhacker. 2002. "Forced Laborers in Nazi Germany: Categories, Numbers and Survivors." *Journal of Interdisciplinary History* 33(2): 169–204.

Stecklov, Guy, Calogero Carletto, Carlo Azzarri, and Benjamin Davis. 2010. "Gender and Migration from Albania." *Demography* 47(4): 935–61.

Steidl, Annemarie, and Wladimir Fischer-Nebmaier. 2014. "Transatlantischer Heiratsmarkt und Heiratspolitik von MigrantInnen aus Österreich-Ungarn in den USA, 1870–1930." *L'Homme* 25(2): 51–68.

Steinfeld, Robert J. 1991. *The Invention of Free Labor: The Employment Relation in English and American Law and Culture, 1350–1870.* Chapel Hill: University of North Carolina Press.

Stevens, Gillian, Hiromi Ishizawa, and Xavier Escandell. 2012. "Marrying into the American Population: Pathways into Cross-Nativity Marriages." *International Migration Review* 46(3): 740–59.

Stewart, Watt. 1951. *Chinese Bondage in Peru: A History of the Chinese Coolie in Peru, 1849–1874.* Durham, N.C.: Duke University Press.

Stolnitz, George J. 1983. "Three to Five Main Challenges to Demographic Research." *Demography* 20(4): 415–32.

Sturtz, Linda. 2002. *Within Her Power: Propertied Women in Colonial Virginia.* New York: Routledge.

Suryadinata, Leo. 2008. *Ethnic Chinese in Contemporary Indonesia.* Singapore: Institute of Southeast Asian Studies.

Sussman, Charlotte. 2004. "The Colonial Afterlife of Political Arithmetic: Swift, Demography, and Mobile Populations." *Cultural Critique* 56 (Winter): 96–126.

Süssmilch, Johann Peter. 1741. "The Divine Order in the Circumstances of the Human Sex, Birth, Death and Reproduction." Berlin: Im Verlag des Buchladens der Realschule. Reprint 2008. Olms: Hildesheim.

Sutherland, Ian. 1963. "John Graunt: A Tercentenary Tribute." *Journal of the Royal Statistical Society Series A,* 126(4): 537–56.

Swanson, David, Henry S. Shryock, and Jacob S. Siegel. 2004. *Methods and Materials of Demography*, 2nd ed. New York: Academic Press.

Tadman, Michael. 2000. "The Demographic Cost of Sugar: Debates on Slave Societies and Natural Increase in the Americas." *American Historical Review* 105(5): 1534–75.

Taeuber, Conrad, and Irene B. Taeuber. 1938. "Short Distance Interstate Migrations." *Social Forces* 16(4): 503–06.

Taeuber, Irene B. 1944. "Population Displacements in Europe." *Annals of the American Academy of Political and Social Science* 234: 1–12.

———. 1947. "Migration and the Population Potential of Monsoon Asia." *Milbank Memorial Fund Quarterly* 25(1): 21–43.

———. 1958. *The Population of Japan*. Princeton, N.J.: Princeton University Press.

———. 1960. "Urbanization and Population Change in the Development of Modern Japan." *Economic Development and Cultural Change* 9(1): 1–28.

———. 1963. "Hong Kong: Migrants and Metropolis." *Population Index* 29(1): 3–25.

Taeuber, Irene B., and Hope T. Eldridge. 1947. "Some Demographic Aspects of the Changing Role of Women." *Annals of the American Academy of Political and Social Science* 251: 24–34.

Taeuber, Irene B., and Nai-Chi Wang. 1960. "Population Reports in the Qing Dynasty." *Journal of Asian Studies* 19(4): 403–17.

Taeuber, Karl E., and Alma F. Taeuber. 1964. "The Negro as an Immigrant Group: Recent Trends in Racial and Ethnic Segregation in Chicago." *American Journal of Sociology* 69(4): 374–82.

Taylor, Kit Sims. 1970. "The Economics of Sugar and Slavery in Northeastern Brazil." *Agricultural History* 44(3): 267–80.

Tepper, Michael. 1988. *American Passenger Arrival Records*. Baltimore, Md.: Genealogical Publishing.

Terborg-Penn, Rosalyn, Sharon Hurley, and Andrea Benton Rushing, eds. 1987. *Women in Africa and the African Diaspora*. Washington, D.C.: Howard University Press.

Thomas, Brinley. 1954. *Migration and Economic Growth: A Study of Great Britain and the Atlantic Economy*. Cambridge: Cambridge University Press.

Thomas, Dorothy Swaine. 1936. "Internal Migrations in Sweden: A Note on Their Extensiveness as Compared with Net Migration Gain or Loss." *American Journal of Sociology* 42(3): 345–57.

———. 1937. "The Analysis of Internal Migration in the Swedish Census of 1930." *Journal of the American Statistical Association* 32(197): 124–30.

———. 1938. "Research Memorandum on Migration Differentials." A Report of the Committee on Migration Differentials. Bulletin 43. New York: Social Science Research Council.

Thomas, Hugh. 1997. *The Slave Trade: The Story of the Atlantic Slave Trade, 1440–1870*. New York: Simon and Schuster.

Thornton, John K. 1980. "The Slave Trade in Eighteenth Century Angola: Effects on Demographic Structures." *Canadian Journal of African Studies* 14(3): 417–27.

———. 1982. "Kingdom of Kongo, ca. 1390–1678. The Development of an African Social Formation (Le royaume du Kongo, ca. 1390–1678. Développement d'une Formation Sociale Africaine)." *Cahiers D'Études Africaines* 22(Cahier 87/88): 325–42.

———. 1983. "Sexual Demography: The Impact of the Slave Trade on Family Structure." In *Women and Slavery in Africa,* edited by Claire Robertson and Martin Klein. Madison: University of Wisconsin Press.

———. 2006. "Elite Women in the Kingdom of Kongo: Historical Perspectives on Women's Political Power." *Journal of African History* 47(3): 437–60.

Tilly, Louise A., and Joan W. Scott. 1978. *Women, Work and Family.* New York: Holt, Rinehart and Winston.

Tinker, High. 1974. *A New System of Slavery: The Export of Indian Labour Overseas, 1830–1920.* London: Oxford University Press.

Tirabassi, Maddalena. 2002. "Bourgeois Men, Peasant Women: Rethinking Domestic Work and Morality in Italy." In *Women, Gender and Transnational Lives: Italian Workers of the World,* edited by Donna R. Gabaccia and Franca Iacovetta. Toronto: University of Toronto Press.

Tobe, Levin. 1979. "Women's Studies in West Germany: Community vs. Academy." *Women's Studies Newsletter* 7(1): 20–22.

Toma, Sorana, and Sophie Vause. 2014. "Gender Differences in the Role of Migrant Networks: Comparing Congolese and Senegalese Migration Flows." *International Migration Review* 48(8): Accessed December 4, 2014. http://www.imi.ox.ac.uk/people/sorana-toma#sthash.vCbSwrs3.dpuf.

Tomas, Patricia A. Santo, Lawrence H. Summers, and Patricia A. Santos. 2009. *Migrants Count: Five Steps Toward Better Migration Data.* Washington, D.C.: Center for Global Development.

Torpey, John. 2000. *The Invention of the Passport: Surveillance, Citizenship and the State.* Cambridge: Cambridge University Press, 2000.

Trolander, Judith Ann. 1991. "Hull-House and the Settlement House Movement." *Journal of Urban History* 17(4): 410–20.

Tsogtsaikhan, Bolormaa. 2008. "Mongolia." Presented at PECC-ABAC Conference "Demographic Change and International Labor Mobility in the Asia Pacific Region: Implications for Business and Cooperation." Seoul, Korea (March 25–26, 2008).

Tucker, Richard P. 2000. *Insatiable Appetite: The United States and the Ecological Degradation of the Tropical World.* Berkeley: University of California Press.

Turner, Johnathan. 1988. "The Mixed Legacy of the Chicago School of Sociology." *Sociological Perspectives* 31(3): 325–38.

Tyner, J. A. 1999. "The Global Context of Gendered Labor Migration from the Philippines to the United States." *American Behavioral Scientist* 42(4): 671–89.

Tyree, Andrea, and Katharine M. Donato. 1986. "A Demographic Overview of the International Migration of Women." In *International Migration: The Female Experience,* edited by Rita James Simon and Caroline B. Brettell, 21–41. Totowa, N.J.: Rowman & Allanheld.

United Nations (UN). 1977. "Recommendations on Statistics of International Migration." Statistical Papers Series M, no. 58, rev. 1. New York: United Nations Statistical Office.

———. 1979. "Trends and Characteristics of International Migration Since 1950." *Demographic Studies* 64. New York: United Nations Press.

———. 1995. "Measuring the Extent of Female International Migration." In *International Migration Policies and the Status of Female Migrants.* Proceedings of the United Nations Expert Group Meeting on International Migration Policies and the Status of Female Migrants. New York: United Nations.

———. 2013. "Secretary-General's Message for 2013." International Migrants Day, December 18. Accessed September 19, 2014. http://www.un.org/en/events/migrantsday/2013/sgmessage.shtml.

United Nations (UN). Department of Economic and Social Affairs. *Demographic Yearbooks 1948–1985.* Accessed December 15, 2014. http://unstats.un.org/unsd/demographic/products/dyb/dyb2.htm.

———. Department of Social Affairs, Population Division. 1953. *Sex and Age of International Migrants: Statistics for 1918–1947, Population Studies #11.* New York: United Nations.

———. Economic and Social Commission for Asia and the Pacific. 1985. Expert Group Meeting on International Migration in Asia and the Pacific. Manila (November 6–12, 1985).

United Nations Economic Commission for Europe. 1982. "Questionnaire on Statistics of International Migration." New York: Conference of European Statisticians.

United Nations High Commissioner on Refugees (UNHCR). 2013. *UNHCR'S Dialogues with Refugee Women: Progress Report on Implementation of Recommendations.* Geneva: UNHCR.

United Nations Office on Drugs and Crime (UNODC). 2009. *Global Report on Trafficking in Persons: Human Trafficking, A Crime that Shames Us All.* New York: UNODC. Accessed October 17, 2014. http://www.unodc.org/documents/Global_Report_on_TIP.pdf.

van Amersfoort, Hans. 2011. "How the Dutch Government Stimulated the Unwanted Immigration from Suriname." *International Migration Institute* working paper 47 (October). Oxford: University of Oxford.

Van Daele, Jasmien. 2008. "The International Labour Organization (ILO) in Past and Present Research." *International Review of Social History* 53(3): 485–511.

———. 2010. "Writing ILO Histories: A State of the Art." In *Essays on the International Labour Organization and Its Impact on the World During the Twentieth Century,* edited by Jasmien Van Daele, Magaly Rodríguez García, Geert Van Goethem, and Marcel van der Linden. Bern: Peter Lang.

Van de Kaa, D.J. 1987. *Europe's Second Demographic Transition.* Washington, D.C.: Population Reference Bureau.

———. 2004. "Is the Second Demographic Transition a Useful Research Concept? Questions and Answer." In *Yearbook of Population Research,* 4–10. Vienna: Institute of Demography.

Van Kleeck, M. 1913. *Artificial Flower Makers.* New York: Survey Associates.

van Nederveen Meerkerk, Elise, Silke Neunsinger, and Dirk Hoerder. Forthcoming. *Towards a Global History of Domestic and Care Workers.*

Van Onselen, Charles. 1976. *Chibaro: African Mine Labour in Southern Rhodesia, 1900–1933.* London: Pluto Press.

Vansina, Jan. 2005. "Ambaca Society and the Slave Trade c. 1760–1845." *Journal of African History* 46(1): 1–27.

Vause, Sophie, and Sorana Toma. Forthcoming. "Is Feminization Really on the Rise? The Case of International Migration flows from DR Congo and Senegal." *Population.*

Vink, Markus. 2003. " 'The World's Oldest Trade': Dutch Slavery and Slave Trade in the Indian Ocean in the Seventeenth Century." *Journal of World History* 14(2): 131–77.

Virden, Jenel. 1996. *Good-bye, Piccadilly: British War Brides in America.* Urbana: University of Illinois Press.

Voyages. 2012. *Voyages: The Trans-Atlantic Slave Trade Database.* Acessed June 1, 2012. http://www.slavevoyages.org.

Walsh, Lorena S. 2001. "The Chesapeake Slave Trade: Regional Patterns, African Origins, and Some Implications." *The William and Mary Quarterly,* 3rd ser., 58(1): 139–70.

Walton, Marcia. 2011. "Internal Migration in Cambodia: A Case Study of Push-Pull Factors of Migration into Phnom Penh." School of Natural and Built Environment, University of South Australia, Adelaide. Accessed September 19, 2014. http://www.tasa.org.au/uploads/2011/05/Walton-marcia.pdf.

Wang, Hong-zen, and Shu-ming Chang. 2002. "The Commodification of International Marriages: Cross-border Marriage Business in Taiwan and Vietnam." *International Migration* 40(6): 93–116.

Wang, Wendy. 2012. "The Rise of Intermarriage." Washington, D.C.: Pew Research Center. http://www.pewsocialtrends.org/2012/02/16/the-rise-of-intermarriage.

Watkins, Susan Cotts. 1993. "If All We Knew About Women Was What We Read in Demography, What Would We Know?" *Demography* 30(4): 551–77.

Watkins, Susan Cotts, and Angela D. Danzi. 1995. "Women's Gossip and Social Change: Childbirth and Fertility Control among Italian and Jewish Women in the United States, 1920–1940." *Gender and Society* 9(4): 469–90.

Weinberg, Sidney Stahl. 1988. *The World of Our Mothers: The Lives of Jewish Immigrant Women.* Chapel Hill: University of North Carolina Press.

Werner, Cynthia. 2014. "Networks, Gender, Culture and the Migration Decision-Making Process: A Case Study of the Kazakh Diaspora in Western Mongolia." The Mongolian Kazakh Diaspora. Accessed September 19, 2014. http://www.macalester.edu/academics/geography/mongolia/mongolian_kazakhs.html.

Willcox, Walter F. 1896. "The Distribution of the Sexes in the United States in 1890." *American Journal of Sociology* 1(6): 725–37.

Willcox, Walter F., and Imre Ferenczi, eds. 1929. *International Migrations.* National Bureau of Economic Research no. 14. New York: Arno Press.

Williams, Eric E. 1964. *Capitalism and Slavery.* London: Andre Deutsch.

Williamson, Jeffrey G. 1996. "Globalization, Convergence and History." *Journal of Economic History* 56(2): 277–306.

Willis, James J. 2005. "Transportation Versus Imprisonment in Eighteenth-and Nineteenth-Century Britain: Penal Power, Liberty, and the State." *Law & Society Review* 39(1): 171–210.

Wolgin, Philip E., and Irene Bloemraad. 2010. "Our Gratitude to Our Soldiers: Military Spouses, Family Re-Unification, and Postwar Immigration Reform." *Journal of Interdisciplinary History* 41(1): 27–60.

Wood, Arthur Evans. 1955. *Hamtramck, Then and Now: A Sociological Study of a Polish-American Community.* New York: Bookman Associates.

Woodworth, C. K. 2007. "Ocean and Steppe: Early Modern World Empires." *Journal of Early Modern History* 11(6): 501–18.

Worsnop, Judith. 1990. "A Reevaluation of 'The Problem of Surplus Women' in 19th Century England: The Case of the 1851 Census." *Women's Studies International Forum* 13(1/2): 21–31.

Wright, Donald. 1999. *The World and a Very Small Place in Africa: a History of Globalization in Niumi, the Gambia*. New York: M. E. Sharpe.

Wright, John. 2007. *The Trans Saharan Slave Trade*. London: Routledge.

Wyman, Mark. 1993. *Round–Trip to America: The Immigrants Return To Europe, 1880–1930*. Ithaca, N.Y.: Cornell University Press.

Yans-McLaughlin, Virginia. 1977. *Family and Community: Italian Immigrants in Buffalo: 1880–1930*. Ithaca, N.Y.: Cornell University Press.

Yeates, Nicola. 2004. "A Dialogue with 'Global Care Chain' Analysis: Nurse Migration in the Irish Context." *Feminist Review* 77(2004): 79–95.

Yinger, Nancy V. 2006. *Feminization of Migration*. Washington, D.C.: Population Reference Bureau.

Yuh, Ji-Yeon. 2004. *Beyond the Shadow of CampTown: Korean Military Brides in America*. New York: New York University Press.

Zeiger, Susan. 2010. *Entangling Alliances: Foreign War Brides and American Soldiers in the Twentieth Century*. New York: New York University Press.

Zelinsky, Wilbur. 1971. "The Hypothesis of the Mobility Transition." *Geographical Review* 61(2): 219–49.

Zembrzycki, Stacey. 2007. "'There Were Always Men in Our House': Gender and the Childhood Memories of Working-Class Ukrainians in Depression-Era Canada." *Labour / Le Travail* 60(Fall): 77–105.

Zeng, Yi, Tu Ping, Gu Baochang, Xu Yi, Li Bohua, and Li Yongping. 1993. "Causes and Implication of the Recent Increase in the Reported Sex Ratio at Birth in China." *Population and Development Review* 19(2): 283–302.

Zlotnik, Hania. 1987. "The Concept of International Migration as Reflected in Data Collection Systems." *International Migration Review* 21(4): 925–46.

———. 2003. "The Global Dimensions of Female Migration." *Migration Information Source* (March 1, 2003). Accessed September 19, 2014. http://www.migration policy.org/article/global-dimensions-female-migration.

= Index =

Boldface numbers refer to figures and tables.